T0323779

'The concept of psychopathy presents challenges for definition, measurement and full understanding. However, in this highly accessible and well-researched book, the authors have mastered this topic in an engaging and enjoyable way. Drawing direct connections between explanation and intervention provides a truly integrated discussion of this complex but fascinating group of individuals.'

Rachel Taylor, *Senior Lecturer in Psychology,*
University of South Wales

The Basics Series

The Basics is a highly successful series of accessible guidebooks which provide an overview of the fundamental principles of a subject area in a jargon-free and undaunting format.

Intended for students approaching a subject for the first time, the books both introduce the essentials of a subject and provide an ideal springboard for further study. With over 50 titles spanning subjects from artificial intelligence (AI) to women's studies, *The Basics* are an ideal starting point for students seeking to understand a subject area.

Each text comes with recommendations for further study and gradually introduces the complexities and nuances within a subject.

RELIGION IN AMERICA 2E
Michael Pasquier

FINANCE (fourth edition)
Erik Banks

IMITATION
Naomi Van Bergen, Allard R. Feddes, Liesbeth Mann and Bertjan Doosje

SELF AND IDENTITY
Megan E. Birney

PSYCHOPATHY
Sandie Taylor and Lance Workman

For more information about this series, please visit: www.routledge.com/Routledge-The-Basics-Series/book-series/TBS

PSYCHOPATHY

THE BASICS

Psychopathy: The Basics is an accessible text that provides a compact introduction to the major findings and debates concerning this complex personality disorder.

This book provides an overview of the field and covers a wide range of research findings from genetics to psychosocial developmental explanations. It begins with an exploration of the historical conception of the phenomenon of psychopathy and goes on to discuss its social and cultural accounts. It also delves into biologically based explanations, including genetic and evolutionary approaches, along with criminological and entrepreneurial types of psychopathy. Offering a balanced perspective, this book addresses the nature–nurture debate in the field and also discusses widely accepted personality traits of psychopaths. Lastly, it also provides a glossary of key terms and suggestions for further reading.

This book will be an essential read for students of forensic psychology or criminology. It is also an ideal starting point for those interested in the science of psychopathy and personality disorders.

Sandie Taylor is an experienced lecturer and author. Her DPhil in psychology focused on applied memory approaches to facilitate recognition of faces. She has also received an MSc in Criminology and has previously published 4 books (including *Forensic Psychology: The Basics*) and many peer-reviewed articles and book chapters.

Lance Workman is Visiting Professor of Psychology at the University of South Wales. He was formerly Head of Psychology at Bath Spa University. Lance has published widely on psychology, including over 100 articles and 9 books. He was interviews editor for *The Psychologist* for seven years, and he regularly appears in the media.

PSYCHOPATHY

THE BASICS

Sandie Taylor and Lance Workman

Routledge
Taylor & Francis Group

LONDON AND NEW YORK

Designed cover image: © Getty Images

First published 2023
by Routledge
4 Park Square, Milton Park, Abingdon, Oxon OX14 4RN

and by Routledge
605 Third Avenue, New York, NY 10158

Routledge is an imprint of the Taylor & Francis Group, an informa business

British Library Cataloguing-in-Publication Data
A catalogue record for this book is available from the British Library

Library of Congress Cataloging-in-Publication Data
Names: Taylor, Sandie, author. | Workman, Lance, author.
Title: Psychopathy : the basics / Sandie Taylor and Lance Workman.
Description: Abingdon, Oxon ; New York, NY : Routledge, 2023. | Series:
Student reference | Includes bibliographical references. | Summary:
"Psychopathy: The Basics is an accessible text that provides a compact
introduction to the major findings and debates concerning this complex
personality disorder"— Provided by publisher.
Identifiers: LCCN 2022057604 (print) | LCCN 2022057605 (ebook) | ISBN
9781032221021 (hardback) | ISBN 9781032221007 (paperback) | ISBN
9781032221052 (ebook) Subjects: LCSH: Psychopaths. | Antisocial personality
disorders. Classification: LCC RC555 .T39 2023 (print) | LCC RC555 (ebook) | DDC
616.85/82—dc23/eng/20230202
LC record available at https://lccn.loc.gov/2022057604
LC ebook record available at https://lccn.loc.gov/2022057605

ISBN: 9781032221021 (hbk)
ISBN: 9781032221007 (pbk)
ISBN: 9781032221052 (ebk)

DOI: 10.4324/9781032221052

Typeset in Bembo Std
by codeMantra

CONTENTS

WHAT IS PSYCHOPATHY
DEFINITIONS AND HISTORY
OF THE CONCEPTION

What sort of image does the word 'psychopath' conjure up in your mind's eye? Perhaps it's a devious and callous serial killer? Perhaps it's a ruthless businessman who manipulates people and walks over them to achieve his self-centred aims? Could it possibly be a woman, or does this 'not compute'? And what is it that causes psychopathy? Do they inherit this condition (assuming it is a condition) or does it develop from problems during childhood? Also, what is the relationship between the terms psychopath, sociopath and antisocial personality disorder. Can psychopaths be treated or are they destined to remain in this state for life?

These are the sort of questions this book has been written to consider. And, while there are no simple or easy answers, we hope that by the end of it, you have a much greater understanding of how we might address such questions. In order to do this, we need to have a good understanding of the history of thinking about psychopathy and the latest research findings on this topic. We will begin with a definition and description of psychopathy and then explore the concept of psychopathy historically.

DEFINITION AND DESCRIPTION OF PSYCHOPATHY

Psychopathy is defined in the Merriam-Webster Dictionary (accessed 2 Jan. 2022) as a "mental disorder especially when marked by egocentric and antisocial activity, a lack of remorse for one's actions, an absence of empathy for others, and often criminal tendencies". Very often, the traits depicting a psychopath are used as part of the definition, for example, callous, unemotional and

DOI: 10.4324/9781032221052-1

morally depraved. These traits, even though not recognised as an official mental health diagnosis, have been used to describe the psychopath. Kiehl and Buckholtz (2010) broadened the description of a psychopath to include rule breaking, a trait commonly characterising **antisocial personality disorder (ASPD)**. The American Psychiatric Association (APA 2013) published the Diagnostic and Statistical Manual of Mental Disorders (DSM), which is currently in version five (hence DSM-5). They state that psychopathy is a "synonym for antisocial personality disorder". Moreover, they claim that an individual diagnosed with ASPD shows a profile of disregard or violation of other people's rights. O'Donnell and Hetrick (2016) highlighted how psychopathy encompasses personality traits such as impulsivity, emotional and empathic insensitivity, superficial charm and unresponsiveness to punishment.

Psychopathy has been described by many academics, clinicians and researchers over the years. A description, however, that has been referred to consistently belongs to Hervey Cleckley who in 1941 first announced this in his book entitled *The Mask of Sanity*. So ubiquitous is Cleckley's understanding of the psychopath that there are six editions of his book. Cleckley conceived psychopathy as an abnormality that impairs competency, and yet, as Cleckley stated, we are, "confronted with a convincing mask of sanity. All the outward features of this mask are intact…" (1941a, p. 368). Patrick (2019) unpicked the underlying implications of Cleckley's statement. He highlighted how psychopaths present as psychologically normal which only helps them to hide their extreme pathological traits of recklessness and sheer diversity of unrestrained behaviour (see Box 1.1). Cleckley further stated that we can see in psychopaths, "…verbal and facial expressions, tones of voice, and all the other signs…implying conviction and emotion and the normal experiencing of life as we know it ourselves and…assume it to be in others" (1941a, p. 369).

BOX 1.1: SPOT THE PSYCHOPATH

Here are four fictitious cases. Who do you think is likely to be classified as a psychopath?

Case 1: Larry is a high-flying businessman who runs his own company. In pursuit of attaining contracts, he often wines and dines his potential clients. He is currently in a well-respected restaurant entertaining two businessmen, John and David. They had a lovely starter and main meal and are now awaiting their final dessert course. When their desserts arrive, there is something wrong with the order. Larry wanted custard and not ice cream with his pudding. He queries his dessert to the waitress and is quite rude to her. After being rather familiar with her all throughout the evening, even making crass innuendo hinting he would like to sleep with her, his tone suddenly changes. He criticises her competence at being a waitress, accusing her of being stupid and illiterate and claiming how easy it would be for him to have her sacked. He belittles her in front of a packed restaurant and manages to reduce her to tears. Both John and David try to pacify the situation by saying it was a minor mistake that can easily be put right. Larry, however, ignores what they say and continues to verbally abuse the waitress. He claims that he is in the right and that she should be taught a lesson.

Case 2: Mary is out with her friends, Sarah and Hannah, partying. They are all on the dance floor enjoying the music. Mary, in particular, has had a bit too much to drink and is taking up a lot of the dance floor by dancing in an uncoordinated way. She bumps into a number of people but continues to dance around. She eventually steps backwards, and the heel of her shoe spikes the foot of a girl who immediately falls to the floor in agony. Mary is unaware of this and continues dancing. The friends of the girl who fell are deeply annoyed at Mary and accost her. They point out what she had done. Mary immediately goes to the girl and tries as best she can to help lift her from the floor and says she is sorry. She asks the girl if she can buy her a drink.

Case 3: Paul is a university student and is staying in student accommodation, sharing a house with ten others. Each of them has their own bedroom but shares other facilities. Paul gets friendly with one of the female students, Donna, living there. They get on well and find it easy to chat and have a laugh. One night, after having a good long chat over two bottles of wine with Donna, he follows her to her bedroom, puts his foot at the door and forces his way in. She asks him to leave as she is tired and is ready for her bed. He convinces her to allow him to stay for a while just to chat longer. He then forces himself onto her and tells her that she should relax and let him do all the work. He coerces her into sleeping with him. The next morning Paul apologises to Donna suggesting the drink got the better of them both.

Case 4: Sheila is a carer for an elderly man who lives on his own after a recent bereavement. His mobility is not that good, so she does his shopping and cleans the house. The man's daughter is dubious about Sheila, claiming that she is stealing from her father. To prove this, his daughter hides a series of cameras around the house in an effort to catch Sheila stealing. His daughter is in for a big shock. What she sees is Sheila being rough with her father. While washing her father, Sheila is seen touching his genitals and slapping him in the face. When presented with his food, Sheila takes it away and eats it herself in front of him, leaving the poor man to go hungry. When confronted by the man's daughter and showing the footage, Sheila laughs and says that he is on his last legs anyway. She is just helping him to pass away more quickly.

The cases mentioned in Box 1.1 described four individuals. The question was which of the four could be described as psychopaths. It is very clear from cases 1 and 4 that the individuals depicted possessed traits of a psychopath. They were uncaring, hostile and lacked empathy. Case 2 showed empathy and remorse. She was clearly intoxicated and was unaware that she had hurt someone. As for case 3, we are led to believe that he was intoxicated and took advantage of the situation. It is unclear whether he is manipulative and coercive or whether his actions were purely circumstantial. While it is clear that he has an abnormal moral compass, it is difficult to determine whether or not he possesses psychopathic traits. His actions are clearly criminal, but, with regard to psychopathy, this is not a clear-cut case.

As we will see in the next section, psychopathy as a concept and descriptions of the psychopath have been modified over the centuries.

HISTORICAL TIMELINE OF THE CONCEPTION OF PSYCHOPATHY

Classifying individuals according to their behavioural traits is not new. It enables us to make sense of other people's behaviours, and in doing so, it helps us build a knowledge base of the connection between what others do and how we should respond accordingly. This can be seen as a stimulus-response (S-R) association. Hence, when we see people acting in a callous manner for example, we may begin to wonder if they are in some way different to us and find it difficult to access the right response. If someone is acting nasty, is it the correct response to be nasty back? Alternatively, it is easier to find the correct response to someone who is polite. We might begin to classify an individual who habitually acts in a callous manner as psychopathic. This idea of classifying people based on their responses is a very simplistic way of labelling them. Attempt, however, to classify individuals with specific behavioural, emotional and cognitive traits under the umbrella of psychopathy is an ancient human phenomenon (even if the term is relatively new).

According to Thomson (2019), there is a long-documented history of individuals with psychopathic tendencies. Thomson highlights how Theophrastus (371-287 BCE; see Figure 1.1) outlined 30 moral and immoral characters in his book entitled *Characters*. In the 'Shameless Man' section, Theophrastus describes the behaviour of the psychopath.

While psychopaths have been described two millennia ago, more recently individuals with a specific clustering of traits have been singled out as having psychopathy. In 1806, Pinel, a French physician, labelled an individual with such traits as insanity/mania without delirium (*manie sans délire*). The traits Pinel described such as antisocial behaviour and deficits in both emotional and intellectual functioning are considered by clinicians today. Pinel's label was referred to as moral insanity by a physician from England known as Pritchard. The words of Benjamin Rush in 1812 provide a harsher description of the psychopath: "…innate preternatural moral depravity…there is probably an original defective organisation in those parts of the body which are preoccupied by the moral faculties of the mind" (p. 112, cited in Millon, Simonsen, Birket-Smith and Davis 1998).

Figure 1.1 A pictorial representation of Theophrastus

In the 20th century, the emphasis shifted towards clinical descriptions of traits associating criminality with immorality, hedonism, impulsivity and emotional deprivation. Kraepelin (1915) focused on these traits and devised a two-prong classification of obsessive/impulsive (or sexual deviants) from those with personality oddities. In the case of those with personality oddities, there were further sub-divisions such as unstable, impulsive, argumentative and antisocial. Descriptions of psychopaths increasingly relied on applying set personality traits. And as pointed out by Henderson (1939), a Scottish psychiatrist, understanding psychopathy became clouded by descriptions associating the psychopath with disordered behaviour. He argued that disordered behaviour (i.e., criminally oriented) is not synonymous with psychopathy. Instead, Henderson saw the psychopath as an individual experiencing 'moral blindness'. In his book, *Psychopathic States*, Henderson described three types of psychopaths: predominately aggressive, predominately passive or inadequate, and predominately creative. As the label 'predominately aggressive psychopath' suggests, this individual behaves violently towards others and therefore has a dangerous profile. An individual who displays an unstable and neurotic profile that leads to a parasitic lifestyle fitted the predominately passive or inadequate psychopath type. Interestingly, Henderson claimed that the predominately creative psychopath can be 'near genius' in what they do. What all these types have in common is an inability to toe the line and conform to a society's groupthink.

Cleckley (1941a) provided a comprehensive list of traits defining a psychopath. This list included traits referring to the individual's style of behavioural response based on core personality factors such as:

- Being impulsive
- Lacking a sense of guilt
- Being emotionally shallow
- Unable to feel love
- Ability to put on superficial charm and to socially interact

These traits are often associated with many types of personality disorders. Hence, psychopathy can be considered to be a higher ordered category. This implies that psychopathy can be a single dimension of an interpersonal style. One interpersonal style could be social versus withdrawn. It is therefore plausible that some psychopaths will operate at a more social level than others. Other personality disorders such as paranoia or narcissism can also operate in the same way and therefore occupy similar positions on the psychopathy dimension while at the same time preserving their different interpersonal styles. These interpersonal styles of course would define their personality disorder. In this way, psychopathy could be considered as a superordinate construct where other types of personality disorders can be located. This implies that psychopathy can be measured and represented as a scale whereupon other personality typologies can be located at different points. For example, an individual who lacks a sense of guilt and is emotionally shallow would have traits of a psychopath but could also entertain paranoid thoughts eliciting paranoid actions. Such an individual would have an interpersonal

style that is consistent with a paranoid personality – hence a paranoid psychopath. There are many types of personality disorders that
psychopaths can exhibit. Other personality disorders include narcissistic, histrionic and borderline personality disorder (BPD). For
example, as pointed out by Blackburn and Coid (1999), psychopaths
are not unilaterally the same as some exhibit narcissistic and/or
antisocial disorders, while others qualify for a BPD diagnosis. Blackburn and Coid adopted Blackburn's primary-secondary psychopath
distinction. This distinction was, in turn, based on Karpman's (1941)
idiopathic and symptomatic typologies:

- Idiopathic, or true psychopaths, "…experience antisocial behaviour caused by uninhibited instinctual expression that fails to be
  moderated through feelings of guilt or a conscience" (Taylor
  2016, p. 260).
- Symptomatic, or not true psychopaths alternatively, "…experi-
  ence disturbance resulting from psychosis or neurosis causing
  their antisocial behaviour" (Taylor 2016, p. 260).

These categories have been relabelled by Blackburn in 1975 as primary and secondary, respectively. Basically, **primary (or idiopathic)
psychopaths** are devoid of experiencing affective empathy; in
other words, they are incapable of feeling empathy towards others'
pain or discomfort. They are capable of pretending to show empathy given their cognitive (thought induced) empathy often remains
intact. **Secondary (or symptomatic) psychopaths**, alternatively,
present with what Viding (2019) referred to as 'behavioural phenocopy'. This means that despite these individuals showing a similar
behavioural pattern, the underlying causes are different. As we will
see in later chapters, psychopaths have a flawed and disconnected
emotional network. These descriptions of psychopathy throughout
history have relied on forming discrete categories of different types
of psychopaths. In Chapter 2, the different types of classification will
be linked to how it is measured and assessed.

Interestingly, the term **sociopathy** has been used as an alternative
term to psychopathy; however, there is controversy as to whether it is
describing the same cluster of traits signifying a psychopath. The relationship between psychopathy, sociopathy and antisocial personality
disorder (ASPD) is often confusing and begs the question of whether
the same condition is being described – discussed next.

IS THERE A DIFFERENCE BETWEEN ANTISOCIAL PERSONALITY DISORDER, PSYCHOPATHY AND SOCIOPATHY?

Werner, Few and Bucholz (2015) claimed that it is a clinical misnomer to use terms such as psychopathy, sociopathy and ASPD interchangeably. They argued that these differ biologically, psychologically and socially. It is worth exploring here why these terms should not be used interchangeably. To understand psychopathy, sociopathy and ASPD, we need to refer to the Diagnostic and Statistical Manual of Mental Disorders (DSM-5) developed by the American Psychiatric Association (APA) in 2013 (version 5). DSM-5 is considered to be the most reliable and valid source of information regarding the 300 different disorders commonly considered by clinicians. Therefore, it makes perfect sense to review how psychopathy is considered here and references made about sociopathy. Psychopathy, in **DSM-5** (2013), is considered as a subsection of ASPD which is regarded as a "pattern of disregard for, and violation of, the rights of others" (APA, p. 645). Moreover, ASPD is listed under the section on personality disorders, classified under Cluster B (see Chapter 5). In DSM-5, psychopathy, as we have seen, is a sub-section of ASPD which is considered in Cluster B. Here, ASPD is considered to be a superordinate personality type (similar to how psychopathy is a superordinate personality profile discussed earlier). And as before, other personality disorders can be located on the ASPD scale.

There are seven key characteristics of individuals diagnosed with ASPD:

- Lacking remorse
- Being deceitful
- Behaving unlawfully
- Acting impulsively
- Acting irresponsibly
- Showing irritable and aggressive tendencies
- Behaving recklessly and dangerously

According to DSM-5, psychopathy is the same as ASPD but can have an additional provisor of ASPD with psychopathic features if other factors are met such as lacking any fear and anxiety and excessive attention seeking. Hence, to receive a diagnosis of psychopathy, there must be an ASPD diagnosis (when using DSM-5). In a sense, we can think of psychopathy as a sub-division of ASPD (see Figure 1.2). In Figure 1.2, Robert Hare demonstrated the overlap of an offender population with ASPD and psychopaths. Despite the criminal element, Hare highlighted how psychopathy is a sub-part of ASPD.

In the context of a non-offender population, Coid, Yang, Ullrich, Roberts et al. (2009) claimed that 29 per cent of the general population show at least one psychopathic trait; however, only 0.6 per cent of the population will suitably fit the definition of a psychopath. Some experts, however, consider the general population figure to be a little higher than this with rates of around three per cent for men and one per cent for women (Workman and Reader 2021). As regards sociopathy, it too is considered under an ASPD diagnosis.

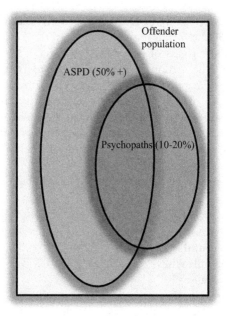

Figure 1.2 Diagram representing the interaction between the dimensions of ASPD, psychopathy and criminality (Adapted from Hare 2005 presentation, 'Without Conscience: Understanding and Treating Psychopaths')

While there is certainly an overlap between ASPD, psychopathy and sociopathy, some clinicians and researchers claim that there are neurobiological and developmental differences (Yildirim and Derksen 2013). There are differences not only between ASPD and psychopathy but also between psychopathy and sociopathy (Mokros, Hare, Neumann, Santtila et al. 2015). As argued by Thomson (2019), DSM-5 dispenses with research showing how ASPD and psychopathy differ. Moreover, DSM-5 fails to address research on sociopathy. Differences between psychopathy and sociopathy are addressed in Box 1.2. As we shall see in Box 1.2, distinguishing sociopathy from psychopathy is still a debate. In this text, we will consider psychopathy as a sub-set of ASPD and omit sociopathy on the grounds of there being continued disagreement over its reliability and validity.

BOX 1.2: IS THERE A DIFFERENCE BETWEEN PSYCHOPATHY AND SOCIOPATHY?

The terms psychopath and sociopath have been confused and used synonymously. Viding (2019) highlighted how the descriptions of sociopaths describe them as being unfeeling towards others and as relentlessly pursuing their goals, even resorting to aggression if needed. They have limited remorse and empathy. They can be aware of the wrongness of their actions but will rationalise their behaviour. Psychopaths, however, do not have any empathy but pretend to care and hide their callous behaviours (Martens 2014). Viding, however, claimed that sociopathy is a vague term devoid of reliable scientific research. Given this, it should not be used. Also, the descriptions of the psychopath and sociopath show behavioural phenocopy. In a non-scientific context, a psychopath is a sociopath but is more dangerous. Not all clinicians, academics and researchers, however, believe that the two are the same. For some, psychopaths and sociopaths exhibit different patterns of behaviours and traits underlying them. Interestingly, Yildirim and Derksen (2013) considered ASPD and sociopathy as clustering at the same point on the emotional responsivity spectrum, whereas psychopathy resides at the opposite end. In the case of ASPD and sociopathy, the problem lies with emotional dysregulation (i.e., an inability to control emotions such as anger and frustration), but for psychopathy, it is more a matter of reduced or no emotional response (i.e., emotional hypo-responsivity). These differences can be explained away by findings from neuroscience and developmental factors. Lykken (2019) made a distinction between psychopaths and sociopaths in terms of their ability to be socialised in accordance with the mainstream societal culture. This, in turn, he argued, was dependent primarily on a 'genetic peculiarity' affecting temperament (hence an underlying neuroscience explanation; see Chapter 4). In the case of the psychopath, parents would find their unruly child difficult to control and socialise. The sociopath, alternatively, can be appropriately socialised provided their parents have been. If their parents have not been appropriately socialised, then this could be due to underlying temperamental inadequacies that can be passed on genetically. Here, we see a nature-on-nurture effect (see Chapter 3). Lykken made a further connection between primary and secondary psychopaths, where primary are psychopaths and secondary are sociopaths. As we will see in Chapter 2, the diagnosis of psychopathy is normally based on Hare's (1980, 2003) Psychopathy Checklist – Revised (PCL-R). It is primarily used on an offender population (whereas the Psychopathic Personality Inventory [PPI] introduced in 1996 is used on non-offender populations). The PCL-R, nevertheless, has been set as the standard for assessing psychopathy but has more recently been criticised as deviating from the original criteria introduced by Cleckley (1941a). Moreover, ASPD and psychopathy as measured by the PCL-R are different constructs (Venables, Hall and Patrick 2014) by virtue of diverse underlying neurobiological factors affecting both cognition and emotion (Seara-Cardosa and Viding 2015). It is important to keep in mind that the descriptions of the psychopath and sociopath overlap considerably. This strongly supports Viding's notion of behavioural phenocopy. Although psychopathy and sociopathy might exist as separate conditions, the evidence for this is limited.

The aim of this chapter, however, is to consider what psychopathy is, and is not, which leads us to another way of conceptualising psychopathy – is it a criminological or personality-derived concept?

PSYCHOPATHY: CRIMINOLOGICAL OR A PERSONALITY DISORDER?

In the historical timeline of the conception of psychopathy, descriptions of what constitutes a psychopath were obscured by the different classifications highlighted. One question that can be asked is whether the underlying traits of the different classifications of psychopaths are the same? If not, then are they truly psychopaths? Moreover, in the previous descriptions of psychopaths, there has been an underlying connection with criminal conduct in the guise of antisocial behaviour. It is important therefore to define what we are actually talking about when we refer to psychopathy. There are four statements to consider:

- Some psychopaths are criminals.
- Some criminals are psychopaths.
- Some psychopaths are not criminals.
- Some criminals are not psychopaths.

These statements imply that psychopaths and criminals are two separate, but overlapping, concepts (see Box 1.3). In Box 1.3, there is a mix of criminals, psychopaths and criminal psychopaths. The traits of a psychopath can be clearly seen in nearly all of the cases described, but not all lead a criminal lifestyle. You might like to consider which of these you would label a psychopath?

Psychopathy is a personality dimension (see Chapter 5) and not a criminological one. There are, however, classifications of psychopathic traits that are driven by criminogenic tendencies such as that described in the ten sub-types of psychopaths by Millon and Davis (1998) (see Box 1.4). Two sub-types are particularly associated with homicide, while the remaining eight sub-types have predisposing traits for antisocial behaviour. The emphasis on Millon and Davis' ten sub-types rests on a criminally based model of what it is to be a psychopath. They paid particular attention to differences in behaviour observed in their sample of psychopaths and the motivations and functions these served for the individuals concerned. It is interesting that their sub-types of the psychopath fit with the robust correlations between psychopathy and ASPD found by Blackburn and Coid (1998) and Hildebrand and de Ruiter (2004). Even more interesting, however, are the positive correlations between psychopathy and other personality disorders, such as narcissistic, borderline and paranoid. These positive correlations help explain the diversity of behavioural styles observed across different psychopaths, which feeds into the sub-types devised by Millon and Davis. While this is an effective classificatory system for an offending psychopathic population, it falls short in accounting for non-criminal psychopaths.

BOX 1.3: CRIMINALS, PSYCHOPATHS AND PSYCHOPATHIC CRIMINALS

Below is a selection of cases where some are criminals, some are psychopaths and some are both.

Case 1: Deyan Deyanov beheaded Jennifer Mills-Westley after stalking and stabbing her in a resort on the island of Tenerife in 2011. He held her head and said, 'God is on earth'. He previously received psychiatric treatment and believed he was the Messiah.

Case 2: Three murders and at least 20 other women were attacked – some were drugged and raped – by Levi Bellfield. He used a hammer to cause head injury and ran over one of his victims because she crossed the road to avoid him (see Box 7.1 for an in-depth profile).

Case 3: Xavier Dupont de Ligonnes shot dead his wife and four children and then severed them into pieces and buried them in the garden. He also killed their two Labradors in the same way. The murders were planned, and he sent letters to friends stating they all had to move to the US because of his job as a secret agent. He was in debt and forged salary slips to get payments from different banks.

Case 4: Joshua Davies, aged 16 years, boasted to friends that he was going to kill his ex-girlfriend for a free breakfast. He tricked her into going to the woods where he smashed her head with a rock.

Case 5: Gerald Stano murdered nine women, but it is suspected that he killed more like 42. He shot, strangled or stabbed his victims. He enticed his victims into his car by supplying marijuana or money. Only when his sexual advances failed did he kill these women. His behaviour towards women was aggressive, and his attitude was misogynistic. He showed no remorse and in fact claimed that one of his victims deserved to be killed as she was a prostitute (see Box 4.5 for an in-depth profile).

Case 6: Tom Skeyhill was a celebrated Australian war hero. He was known as the 'blind soldier poet', blindness being an injury he sustained during the First World War. He met President Theodore Roosevelt who notably said he was proud to share the stage with him. After a medical procedure, his blindness mysteriously disappeared. Lilienfeld and Watts (2021) referred to biographer Jeff Brownrigg, who stated that Skeyhill lied about many aspects of his life, including being blind. He had feigned blindness as a means of getting out of danger. He blamed his slurred speech on his unverifiable injury (when he was in fact drunk) and lied about his battle accounts in Gallipoli.

Case 7: Well-known actor Charlie Chaplin has been accused by people who knew him of behaving in a cruel and mean-spirited manner. He was described as antisocial and a megalomaniac. His children regarded him as a difficult person to interact with.

Case 8: A well-respected neuropsychologist, James Fallon, admits in agreeance with family members, work colleagues and friends, to being callous, self-centred and at times failing to understand why others were upset, and had a 'who cares' attitude (see Box 4.2 for an in-depth profile).

BOX 1.4: THE TEN CRIMINALLY DRIVEN SUB-TYPES OF PSYCHOPATHS

The ten sub-types of psychopaths differ in terms of the behavioural styles used to achieve their goals and motivations. Two sub-types that are particularly associated with criminal behaviour are malevolent and tyrannical psychopaths.

Malevolent psychopaths exhibit extreme hostility and vindictiveness towards others. They tend to have traits such as destructiveness, hatefulness, cruelty, cold-blooded ruthlessness, fearlessness and deficits in experiencing guilt, empathy and remorse but can and choose to justify their actions unethically. Their behavioural style overlaps with paranoid (suspicious, hostile and intense sexual jealousy) and sadistic (cruel, dominating, dogmatic, humiliating, intimidating and hostile) personality types.

Tyrannical psychopaths exhibit traits similar to malevolent psychopaths, but in addition, they are excessively vulgar, intimidating, inhumane and abusive. Sometimes described as the classic psychopaths, these individuals have insecurities and low self-esteem issues. Their traits overlap with sadistic and negativistic (moody, irritable, resentful, sceptical and withdrawn) personality types.

Psychopaths from these two sub-types are often involved in committing murder. Psychopaths in the remaining eight sub-types are less likely to commit murder but are often hostile, violent and aggressive.

Unprincipled psychopaths exhibit traits overlapping with the narcissistic personality type which is why they overestimate their self-worth and self-identity. They are on the periphery of lawbreaking and prone to fraudulent activities. They lack a moral compass, are disloyal, are unscrupulous, take risks, harm others to promote a reputation of being fearless, lack guilt, are malicious and are manipulative.

Disingenuous psychopaths tend to disguise their resentment, moodiness, unreliability and impulsiveness by acting friendly and being sociable. They lack emotional depth and can humiliate their partners while justifying their inappropriate behaviour by blaming others. Their traits overlap with the histrionic personality type (emotionally lacking but exhibiting intense emotion to attain attention).

Covetous psychopaths have a strong belief that they have experienced love and reward deprivation. Envious of others, they seek retribution for their deprivation, limited empathy and guilt and feel they have justified rights over other people. They are prone to stealing and the manipulation of others.

Risk-taking psychopaths exhibit impulsivity, low self-control, restraint and self-reflection. They perform acts to suffice their need for excitement and their fearless disposition and so put themselves in danger. Their traits overlap with antisocial and histrionic personality types.

Explosive psychopaths exhibit unpredictable hostility, rage and assaultive behaviour. They behave this way to release their feelings of being humiliated and frustrated, but they lack the ability to control them. They express hypersensitivity leading them to overreact to benign situations.

Spineless psychopaths, as the term suggests, are very insecure and are cowards. They use aggression to present themselves as being strong and non-anxious. Their traits overlap with avoidant (sensitive to criticism and exhibit anxious behaviour in social situations) and dependent (limited self-confidence and highly dependent on other people) personality types. They present themselves as fearless and dangerous to appear strong which is what motivates their violent actions.

Malignant psychopaths exhibit traits overlapping with the paranoid personality type. They tend to fantasise their retribution towards others instead of performing abusive acts that have failed in the past. They devise plots and become quite deluded about their beliefs of being persecuted.

Abrasive psychopaths exhibit hostility and are argumentative to the extent where they feel they are always right and need to correct others even when they themselves are wrong (little remorse or moral compass). They very much perceive others as objects and are often verbally and physically abusive. They demean others publicly and are antagonistic. Their traits overlap with paranoid and negativistic personality types.

SUMMARY

The definition of psychopathy appears to be straightforward in that a list of personality traits provides us with an understanding of what it is to be a psychopath. When, however, we delve deeper into the psychopathic typology, many different types of psychopaths become apparent. Indeed, if the historical root of psychopathy is considered, researchers, academics and clinicians alike propose a classificatory system that outlines more than one type of psychopath. Cleckley provided a comprehensive understanding of the traits defining the psychopath, and his typology is referred to and still used by clinicians today. Blackburn and Coid used Karpman's (1941) idiopathic and symptomatic typologies and relabelled these as primary psychopathy and secondary psychopathy, respectively. The primary psychopath typifies a true psychopath, while the secondary psychopath shows similar antisocial behaviour caused by a neurotic or psychotic condition. This similarity of antisocial behaviour exhibited by the primary and secondary psychopaths is referred to as behavioural phenocopy. DSM-5 is considered to be the 'bible' of psychiatric and psychological disorders and a reliable source for clinicians and academics. In DSM-5, psychopathy is considered to be at best a sub-type of ASPD. Also, DSM-5 fails to distinguish sociopathy from psychopathy. However, there has been an ongoing debate about whether sociopathy exists in its own right. There appears to be some neuroscientific evidence for it being different from psychopathy; however, this remains unclear. Many claim that the concept of sociopathy muddies the water and should be excluded. This is one reason why we have adopted the approach of psychopathy being a part of ASPD, but also a concept in its own right. When there is any mention of psychopaths, the common perception is that they are criminals – even serial killers. This perception is incorrect because psychopathy is a personality dimension and not a criminal one. It is true that criminals can be psychopaths, but psychopaths are not necessarily criminals. They may have quite a different moral compass to most people but do not always break the law.

FURTHER READING

American Psychiatric Association. (2013). *Diagnostic and statistical manual of mental disorders* (5th edn.). Arlington, VA: American Psychiatric Publishing.

Meloy, J.R. (2002). *The psychopathic mind: Origins, dynamics, and treatment*. Lanham, MD: Rowman & Littlefield.

Thomson, N.D. (2019). *Understanding psychopathy: The biopsychosocial perspective*. London: Routledge.

Viding, E. (2019). *Psychopathy: A very short introduction*. Oxford: Oxford University Press.

IMPLICATIONS OF MEASUREMENT IN SHAPING OUR UNDERSTANDING OF PSYCHOPATHY

As we have seen in Chapter 1, there is a long history of how the conception of psychopathy was developed. Moreover, we saw how the very definition of psychopathy is inextricably linked with how it is classified. In Chapter 1, the conception and definition of psychopathy explored the personality traits signifying what it is to be a psychopath and the different types of psychopaths. In this chapter, we will consider the tools used to measure psychopathy and how this determines our understanding of prognosis severity. In line with more recent debates about psychopathy being a dimension or a spectrum that can be measured as continuous and progressive data points, we will explore whether this is more accurate than a discrete, 'all-or-nothing' phenomenon.

COMMONLY USED ASSESSMENTS

CLECKLEY'S PSYCHOPATHY LIST

1. Individuals who have been classified as having psychopathy exhibit behaviours and cognitions that fit the descriptions of what it is to be a psychopath. What it is to be a psychopath was first described in an empirical sense by Hervey Cleckley (see Chapter 1; Box 2.1). Cleckley used a scientific approach to his clinical and medical observations, and indeed, he meticulously recorded what he observed. All his observations of psychopaths culminated in his work *The Mask of Sanity* in 1941. Cleckley's work enabled him and many other psychiatrists, psychologists and clinicians to

DOI: 10.4324/9781032221052-2

define what psychopathy actually is. The cluster of behavioural and cognitive traits he observed describes an individual who portrays a deficiency of emotional and cognitive development that interferes with ethical and moral integration into their surrounding social world. Cleckley's list consists of 16 basic criteria:

1. Superficial charm and good intelligence
2. Absence of delusions and other signs of irrational thinking
3. Absence of nervousness or psychoneurotic manifestations
4. Unreliability
5. Untruthfulness and insincerity
6. Lack of remorse and shame
7. Inadequately motivated antisocial behaviour
8. Poor judgement and failure to learn by experience
9. Pathological egocentricity and incapacity for love
10. General poverty in major affective reactions
11. Specific loss of insight
12. Unresponsiveness in general interpersonal relations
13. Fantastic and uninviting behaviour with drink and sometimes without
14. Suicide carried out rarely
15. Impersonal, trivial and poorly integrated sex life
16. Failure to follow any life plan

BOX 2.1: UNDERSTANDING AND ASSESSING PSYCHOPATHY – THE WORK OF HERVEY CLECKLEY

Hervey Milton Cleckley was born in 1903 in Augusta, Georgia, the south-east state of America, and died in 1984. He graduated from the University of Georgia Medical School with a medical degree. He became a professor of psychiatry and neurology and later became the chief of psychiatry and neurology. His *magnum opus* published in 1941 was *The Mask of Sanity: An Attempt to Clarify Some Issues About the So-Called Psychopathic Personality*. This textbook became key to understanding how the psychopath operates in society. During the Second World War, Cleckley, in his article for the *Journal of the Medical Association of Georgia*, highlighted how psychopaths appear to be normal but privately engaged in destructive behaviour. He warned the military that new soldier recruits with a psychopathic personality are likely to fail and be disorganised in such a way as to exhaust time and resources. For this reason, he claimed that it is important to vet soldiers closely by checking their past for encounters with the law and excessive alcohol use. Other research that Cleckley was involved with includes the impact of niacin (vitamin B_3) deficiency on mental health. The application of nicotinic acid or niacin, he found, made an effective treatment for specific aberrant mental states and psychiatric disorders such as schizophrenia. In fact, he advocated for the use of megavitamin therapy for schizophrenia. He also practised the controversial 'coma therapy'. Here, a patient was put into a coma using overdoses of insulin or other drugs as a means of controlling psychotic episodes. This was later replaced with electroconvulsive therapy (ECT) which induced the same kind of convulsive fit as coma therapy. ECT, however, was also replaced largely by antipsychotic drugs. Cleckley co-authored the book *The Three Faces of Eve* in 1956 which discussed a case of a woman with multiple personality disorder. It is little known that Cleckley was a psychiatrist for the prosecution of Ted Bundy in 1979. He interviewed Bundy and diagnosed him as a psychopath and claimed he was competent to stand trial or represent himself.

HARE'S PSYCHOPATHY CHECKLISTS

PCL-R

It is not surprising that others such as Robert Hare have followed in the footsteps of Cleckley who is renowned as a key figure in understanding psychopathy (see Box 2.2). Robert Hare devised a checklist of psychopathy symptoms which is very similar to Cleckley's list. Hare might have labelled his list slightly differently, but the sentiment is the same. Hare's Psychopathy Checklist (original) (PCL-22) developed in the 1970s consists of the following items and scored as 'definitely present', 'possibly present' or 'definitely absent':

1. Glibness/superficial charm
2. Previous diagnosis as psychopath (or similar)

3. Egocentricity/grandiose sense of self-worth
4. Proneness to boredom/low frustration tolerance
5. Pathological lying and deception
6. Conning/lack of sincerity
7. Lack of remorse or guilt
8. Lack of affect and emotional depth
9. Callous/lack of empathy
10. Parasitic lifestyle
11. Short-tempered/poor behavioural controls
12. Promiscuous sexual relations
13. Early behaviour problems
14. Lack of realistic, long-term plans
15. Impulsivity
16. Irresponsible behaviour as parent
17. Frequent marital relationships
18. Juvenile delinquency
19. Poor probation or parole risk
20. Failure to accept responsibility for own actions
21. Many types of offence
22. Drug or alcohol abuse not the direct cause of antisocial behaviour

BOX 2.2: UNDERSTANDING AND ASSESSING PSYCHOPATHY – THE WORK OF ROBERT HARE

Robert D Hare was born in Alberta, Canada, on the first day of 1934. Having studied psychology at the University of Alberta, he then spent some time working in the prison system where he became interested in criminal psychopaths. Following a return to university in Canada, his interest in psychopathy began to grow, and over the intervening years, he has, arguably, become the world's leading expert on the nature and assessment of psychopaths. During the 1970s, Hare became dissatisfied with the lack of a consensus on defining or measuring psychopathy. In order to rectify this, in 1980, he released the 'Psychopathy Checklist'. Much of this was based on Cleckley's checklist (see Box 2.1 and main text). Following Cleckley's death in 1984, however, Hare revised his own list which he now called the 'Hare Psychopathy Checklist' (1985). This has subsequently been revised a number of times (see main text). One of his major contributions is the notion that psychopaths are unable to understand much of other people's emotional states. More controversially, he has also written about how he considers psychopathy to be 'hard wired' and related to underlying brain abnormalities, a view for which there is some supporting evidence (see Chapter 4). He dissociates psychopaths from sociopaths with the latter forming a group that respond to growing up under harsh, antisocial circumstances. Some experts prefer the terms primary and secondary psychopaths (terms which Hare later took on board). The label sociopath remains an area of debate. In addition to criminal psychopaths, Hare has also considered those who stay within the law but callously manipulate others. He has suggested that today's dog-eat-dog corporate environment is the perfect training ground for corporate psychopaths. These he labelled 'successful psychopaths' or social predators. He popularised this idea of psychopaths in the workplace in his co-authored book *Snakes in Suits* (Babiak and Hare 2006, revised in 2019) which remains a best seller.

The PCL has undergone revision to the terms used, and two items were excluded as they were considered to be irrelevant. The **Psychopathy Checklist-Revised (PCL-R)** is currently used in forensic settings such as prison. Given the importance of the PCL-R as the standard assessment for psychopathy, we will break down its component factors so that a clearer understanding of how individuals scoring high on the PCL-R can be divided into primary and secondary psychopaths (see Box 2.3). The PCL-R has been administered to individuals with antisocial personality disorder (ASPD), criminal and corporate psychopathy, and controls. As seen in Figure 2.1, the PCL-R identified different constructs due to varying scores for Factors 1 and 2 (Venables, Hall and Patrick 2014).

BOX 2.3: HARE'S PCL-R QUESTIONS

The structure and questions of the PCL-R are similar to the original PCL-22 – so what is different?

Removed

Previous diagnosis as psychopath (or similar)

Drug or alcohol abuse not the direct cause of antisocial behaviour

Questions are more user-friendly in phraseology

Do you...? Did you...? Are you...? Have you...?

Scoring is a three-point scale

0 = item does not apply; 1 = item applies somewhat; 2 = item definitely applies

Change of wording examples

'Many types of offence' is replaced by 'Do you display criminal versatility?'

'Lack of affect and emotional depth' is replaced by 'Do you have shallow affect (superficial emotional responsiveness)?'

'Irresponsible behaviour as a parent' is replaced by 'Are you irresponsible?'

The PCL-R is regarded as a reliable and valid clinical assessment tool for measuring psychopathy. The 20 items assess four correlated first-order factors such as, in this case, interpersonal, affective, impulsive lifestyle and antisocial tendencies. First-order factors are items that cannot be measured directly, but through specific traits, they can be assumed. Hence, in the case of interpersonal factor, the traits measuring this include pathological lying and conning/ manipulative. For the affective factor, traits such as lack of empathy and shallow affect apply. For the impulsive lifestyle, irresponsibility and impulsivity apply. In case of antisocial tendencies, traits such as criminal versatility and early behaviour social deviance apply. These four correlated factors are combined to form the two factors of the PCL-R: Factor 1 Interpersonal/Affective (psychopathic personality traits) and Factor 2 Lifestyle/Antisocial (social deviance).

Each question is given '0', '1' or '2' and totalled. In the US, a score of 30+ is the threshold for diagnosing psychopathy, whereas in German-speaking countries, this is 25. While primary psychopathy is considered to have an underlying genetic basis, secondary psychopathy appears to be environmentally based. Secondary psychopaths have higher trait anxiety but lower psychopathic traits, however. As regards antisocial behaviour, the two variants of psychopathy are comparable. Using the PCL-R, Skeem, Johansson, Andershed, Kerr et al. (2007) found that secondary psychopaths exhibited poorer interpersonal functioning and tended to be more emotionally unstable and withdrawn. Primary psychopaths were higher on assertiveness and dominance but far less anxious than their secondary psychopathic counterparts. Many of those who score high on the PCL-R are already incarcerated in a forensic facility, for having committed crimes.

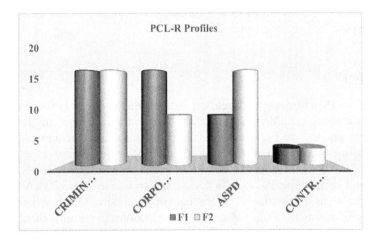

Figure 2.1 Different PCL-R profiles. Note: F1 refers to interpersonal/ affective features and F2 refers to lifestyle/antisocial features. (Adapted from Venables, Hall and Patrick 2014)

The PCL-R, an important assessment for criminal psychopaths, has two variant forms: the Psychopathy Checklist: Youth Version (PCL-YV) and Psychopathy Checklist: Screening Version (PCL-SV) (see Chapters 3 and 5).

PCL-YV

The **Psychopathy Checklist: Youth Version (PCL-YV)** was developed by Forth, Kosson and Hare (2003). It is a test administered by clinicians to 12–18-year-olds as a means to understand the factors contributing towards their development of adult psychopathy and antisocial behaviour (see Chapter 3). In the same vein as the PCL-R, the PCL-YV looks at interpersonal, affective, lifestyle and antisocial aspects. It is administered in the format of a semi-structured interview and the collection of what is known as 'collateral information'. Collateral information refers to important information provided by the individual's known contacts (information that would not be attainable from self-reports). This information is normally used as part of the psychiatric admission process. The PCL-YV provides scores for the four factors, which helps to classify individuals accordingly. The items are very similar to the PCL-R (see Figure 2.2).

PCL-SV

The **Psychopathy Checklist: Screening Version (PCL-SV)** is a rating scale designed by Hart, Cox and Hare (1995) to assess the presence and severity of psychopathic traits linked to a psychopathic personality disorder (see Chapter 5). It is a shorter version of the PCL-R with 12 items that combine overlapping content and exclude specific socially deviant behaviour (see Table 2.1). Also, the items in the PCL-R addressing antisocial behaviour have been redefined in the PCL-SV in such a way that official criminal charges or convictions do not interfere with the overall score. The number of words used on the PCL-SV includes 50 words, which is considerably reduced from the 200 words in the PCL-R. The PCL-SV closely resembles the PCL-R. It is intended for the use of males and females aged 16 years and over. The advantage the PCL-SV has over the PCL-R is its reliability and validity of use in forensic and non-forensic settings. Hence, it can be used in prison and other correctional establishments, forensic and civil psychiatric settings, and within the community. There are two parts to the PCL-SV which are comparable to Factors 1 and 2 of the PCL-R. In Part 1,

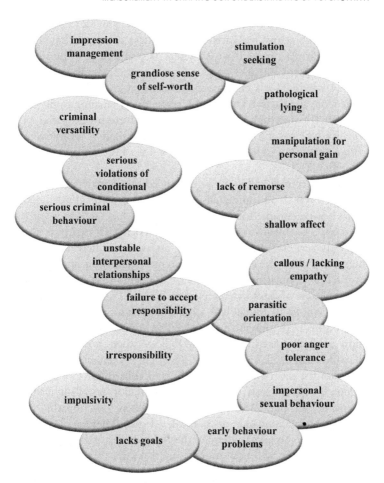

Figure 2.2 Item titles from the PCL-YV (Adapted from Forth, Kosson and Hare 2003)

six of the items reflect the interpersonal/affective traits of Factor 1. For instance, the items reflect an arrogant and deceitful interpersonal style and an individual with poor emotional development. In Part 2, the remaining six items reflect the lifestyle/antisocial traits of Factor 2. Here we see traits relating to an impulsive and irresponsible behavioural style. This also indirectly considers a history of adolescent and adult criminality. The PCL-SV provides a total score and two sub-scores for Parts 1 and 2. These scores are based on a three-point scale from '0' to '2', where '0' = absent, '1' = possibly or partially present and '2' = present. A total score can range between 0 and 24 where 24 is a high score indicative of severe psychopathy. A high score for Parts 1 and 2 is 12, respectively (again ranging from 0 to 12). Scoring high on Part 1 suggests a severe psychopathic personality, whereas in the case of Part 2, a high score is indicative of a pattern of antisocial behaviours suitably describing the psychopathic lifestyle.

The scores on the PCL-SV represent a dimensional measure of the extent to which an individual typifies the prototypical psychopath. It has been recommended that a score of 18+ has a sensitivity of 100 per cent. This means that an individual scoring 18 or more would meet the criteria of a full PCL-R assessment. There is evidence suggesting that the PCL-SV can predict aggression and violence in forensic populations. In 1996, Hill, Rodgers and Bickford found a correlation of 0.69 between scores on the PCL-SV and aggressive behaviour in individuals after release from prison. Moreover, institutionalised individuals involved in antisocial incidents were more likely to score higher on the PCL-SV than those who obeyed the rules. The PCL-R, PCL-YV and PCL-SV enable clinicians to ascertain the severity of psychopathy as a consequence of the score attained. This suggests that psychopathy is not 'an all-or-nothing' phenomenon, but instead is on a scale where psychopathic traits can cluster in abundance or to a lesser degree. There is obviously a cut-off point, however, whereby the individual is assessed as having psychopathy. We will now move away from the three Psychopathy

Table 2.1 The traits of Parts 1 and 2 of the PCL-SV

Part 1 (Factor 1)	Part 2 (Factor 2)
Superficial	Impulsive
Grandiose	Poor behavioural controls
Deceitful	Lacks goals
Lacks remorse	Irresponsible
Lacks empathy	Adolescent antisocial behaviour
Doesn't accept responsibility	Adult antisocial behaviour

Checklist assessments and consider the Levenson Self-Report Psychopathy (LSRP) Scale.

LEVENSON SELF-REPORT PSYCHOPATHY (LSRP) SCALE

The LSRP scale was developed by Levenson, Kiehl and Fitzpatrick in 1995 as a tool to measure the interchangeable traits of psychopathy/sociopathy – hence antisocial personality disorder. There are 26 items in total (see Table 2.2) and two sub-scales:

Table 2.2 Items from the LSRP (Accessed freely from the website titled Psychological Scales)

LSRP items

Success is based on survival of the fittest; I am not concerned about the losers
I find myself in the same kinds of trouble, time after time
For me, what's right is whatever I can get away with
I am often bored
In today's world, I feel justified in doing anything I can get away with to succeed
I find that I am able to pursue one goal for a long time
My main purpose in life is to get as many goodies as I can
I don't plan anything very far in advance
Making a lot of money is my most important goal
I quickly lose interest in tasks I start
I let others worry about higher values; my main concern is with the bottom line
Most of my problems are due to the fact that other people just don't understand me
People who are stupid enough to get ripped off usually deserve it
Before I do anything, I carefully consider the possible consequences
Looking out for myself is my top priority
I have been in a lot of shouting matches with other people
I tell other people what they want to hear so that they will do what I want them to do
When I get frustrated, I often 'let off steam' by blowing my top
I would be upset if my success came at someone else's expense
Love is overrated
I often admire a really clever scam
I make a point of trying not to hurt others in pursuit of my goals
I enjoy manipulating other people's feelings
I feel bad if my words or actions cause someone else to feel emotional pain
Even if I were trying very hard to sell something, I wouldn't lie about it
Cheating is not justified because it is unfair to others

- Primary psychopathy – 16 items measuring psychopathic emotional affect
- Secondary psychopathy – ten items measuring psychopathic lifestyle

The items are scored using a five-point Likert scale:

1	2	3	4	5
Strongly disagree	Disagree	Neither agree nor disagree	Agree	Strongly agree

Scores range from 1 (low) to 5 (high). This means that responses to each statement can be 1, 2, 3, 4 or 5. Depending on the statement, a score of 1 or 5 can be indicative of psychopathy. Hence, strongly agreeing (scoring 5) to the statement 'cheating is not justifiable because it is unfair to others' is not indicative of psychopathy, whereas strongly disagreeing (scoring 1) is. Therefore, generally agreeing with statements that correlate positively with psychopathy allows the tester to assess for this personality disorder. The advantages of using the LSRP are that it is quick to administer, it has cross-cultural validity and it has free access to the public.

Recently, there has been a move away from two to three sub-scales – egocentricity, callousness and antisocial (see Chapter 3). Despite this, the LSRP can still be administered as a means of assessing primary and secondary psychopathic traits.

PSYCHOPATHIC PERSONALITY INVENTORY (PPI)

The PPI was developed by Lilienfeld and Andrews in 1996 based on college student samples. The primary aim was to develop an assessment tool that could assess the full range of psychopathic traits among non-forensic and non-psychiatric individuals (see Chapter 5). The PPI can detect prototypical traits of psychopathy such as superficial charm, dishonesty, manipulativeness, callousness, fearlessness, poor impulse control, guiltlessness, self-centredness and the externalisation of blame. It is a self-report instrument that is theoretically grounded in the literature and assessments concerning psychopathy. The PPI is designed in such a way that it can yield a total score encompassing the global psychopathic traits and yet largely aggregate into eight-factor sub-scales representing the distinct components of psychopathy. As a 187-item self-report assessment, the PPI excludes items indexing antisocial behaviours, thereby making it "a relatively pure measure of the personality-based approach to psychopathy" (Lilienfeld and Andrews 1996, p. 492). By this, Lilienfeld and Andrews meant that the PPI is assessing personality and not criminally based traits. The four-point Likert scale (1 = false, 2 = mostly false, 3 = mostly true, 4 = true) yields a total psychopathy score and a further eight sub-scale scores. The total PPI score provides a reliable score among both undergraduates and forensic samples. The eight sub-scales are as follows:

1. Impulsive nonconformity
2. Blame externalisation
3. Machiavellian ego
4. Carefree non-planfullness
5. Stress immunity
6. Social potency
7. Fearfulness
8. Cold-heartedness

According to Lilienfeld and Fowler (2006), responses to the PPI questions provide, "helpful information regarding respondents' apperceptions of themselves and the world" (p. 111).

YOUTH PSYCHOPATHIC TRAITS INVENTORY (YPI)

The YPI was developed by Andershed, Kerr, Stattin and Lavander in 2002 in response to the need for a more user-friendly assessment for adolescents. The YPI is a 50-item self-report tool used to assess the prototypical constellation of psychopathic traits in youngsters from the age of 12+. Ten core psychopathy traits are derived from ten sub-scales, with each scale housing five items. These ten sub-scales are organised into three factors: interpersonal (or grandiose-manipulative [GM]), affective (or **callous–unemotional [CU]**) and behavioural/lifestyle (or impulsive-irresponsible [II]). There are 20 items for the GM factor, 15 for the CU factor and 15 for the II factor. Items such as dishonest charm, grandiosity, lying and manipulation are housed under the GM factor. In the case of the CU factor, items include unemotional, callousness and remorselessness.

For the II factor, the items include thrill-seeking, impulsivity and irresponsibility. As with the previous assessment tools, the YPI uses a four-point Likert scale that ranges from 1 = Does not apply at all to 4 = Applies very well. According to Andershed et al., the YPI has been found to be a useful tool for identifying non-referred boys and girls presenting with psychopathic-like traits and exhibiting both antisocial and behavioural problems. This is a popular assessment tool and has been translated for use across many different countries, including Portugal, Netherlands, Germany, Italy, Belgium, Sweden and Iran.

IS PSYCHOPATHY A DISCRETE 'ALL-OR-NOTHING' PHENOMENON?

As we have seen, many different assessment tests have been developed for psychopathy. All of these tests have been shown to be reliable and valid assessment tools. Probably, the most recognisable and validated assessments of all are the series of Psychopathy Checklists devised by Hare and his colleagues. The PCL-R, PCL-YV and PCL-SV have proven to be reliable assessment tools for psychopathy – with the PCL-R most commonly administered in forensic and psychiatric settings. All these assessments have two factors that consider psychopathic personality traits and psychopathic lifestyles. These factors are used to differentiate between the two variants of psychopathy – primary and secondary. There are reliable differences in aetiology between primary and secondary psychopaths which the PCL-R effectively measures *via* the two factors. It is interesting, however, how the PPI excludes references to antisocial behaviour indicative of criminality and focuses on the personality element of psychopathy. Psychopathy is after all a concept based around personality rather than a criminality concept *per se*. Hence, the PPI is a reliable assessment for individuals outside of a forensic or psychiatric (often incarcerated for violent and aggressive behaviours) setting. The items contained in all the assessments reviewed here overlap considerably. We might ask why is this the case.

Clearly, we need to have some description and knowledge of the phenomenon we are trying to assess in order to develop a valid assessment tool. But then, we might argue that such a tool is based on a top-down formula of classification and therefore is circular in that we have already classified individuals by virtue of our descriptions of them! This is difficult to get around, but having a reliable assessment tool, such as those we have discussed, does enable us to be more specific about the type of psychopathy an individual has. Importantly, these forms of assessment allow us to classify individuals as being primary or secondary psychopaths, and to ascertain the severity or extent to which a person has psychopathic traits. This is an important point as it does suggest that individuals can vary in their manifestation of psychopathic traits. Hence, you can have some psychopathic tendencies that differ from other individuals with psychopathic inclinations. In Chapter 1, we discussed how psychopathy can be considered as a cluster of symptoms that are exhibited on a sliding scale. And in Chapters 7 and 8, this is borne out when we consider differences in psychopathic severity across criminal and entrepreneurial psychopaths. In the case of entrepreneurial psychopaths, as we will see, their psychopathic traits are attenuated. In addition, they appear to show some insight regarding the negative effects their psychopathic traits could potentially have on them if uncontrolled. The ability to control traits such as impulsivity and antisocial behaviour can help prevent 'brushes with the law'. In contrast, criminal psychopaths find it challenging to control their impulsive and antisocial behaviour which is why they can end up imprisoned. Generally, psychopaths live anonymously within our community. In other words, unless assessed by one of the tests we have discussed in this chapter, it is unlikely that we will realise they have psychopathic tendencies. This is because such individuals are able to mask their psychopathic traits and control them. This might suggest that psychopathy is not 'an all-or-nothing phenomenon'. When we assess individuals for psychopathy using the PCL-R, there are low, medium and high scorers. The score for a psychopathy diagnosis is determined by the threshold point which in the US is 30. To attain this high score, the individual assessed would have had to respond to the items in a manner that highlights the core traits of psychopathy. In other words, psychopathic individuals respond to statements in a predicted way. And this predicted way is in response to statements based on a predetermined understanding, definition, description and classification of what it is to be a psychopath.

Low scorers show some inclinations towards being psychopathic; otherwise, they would score 0. What can we say about individuals who score 20? To attain this score, there would have been many responses with a score of 1 or 2. This implies that such an individual would have psychopathic tendencies. This is evidence that refutes the argument of psychopathy being a discrete 'all-or-nothing phenomenon'. As is the case with understanding human behaviour, nothing is as simple as 'yes' or 'no'. Instead, what we see in the case of psychopathy is a dimension or a spectrum that can be measured as continuous and progressive data points.

SUMMARY

Different assessment tools for the diagnosis of psychopathy date back a long way when we consider the descriptions laid down by Cleckley and clinicians before him. Cleckley led the way with his 16 basic criteria of psychopathy which he derived from his clinical work experience and documented in his famous book *The Mask of Sanity* in 1941. It is from the initial groundwork that the likes of Hare developed the Psychopathy Checklist (PCL) beginning with the original version of PCL-22 which contained 22 items. This was revised to include 20 items and became known as the Psychopathy Checklist-Revised (PCL-R). The PCL-R has been used successfully in forensic settings, and its two factors have been used to distinguish between primary and secondary psychopathy. The higher the score on the PCL-R, the more severe the psychopathy. In the US, the psychopathy threshold is 30, unlike the 25 cut-off point in German-speaking countries. The PCL-R has two variant formats used for different situations. The PCL-YV is the youth version that has been administered by clinicians to 12–18-year-olds. It also looks at fundamental aspects of psychopathy such as interpersonal, affective, lifestyle and antisocial behaviour. The PCL-YV assesses four factors. In the case of the PCL-SV, this screening version is used to assess for the presence of psychopathic traits. The 12 items are reduced from the 20 items in the PCL-R because statements relating to specific forms of socially deviant behaviour are excluded. The PCL-SV has the advantage of being a reliable tool for testing those in non-forensic settings. There are two factors resembling those of the PCL-R. There are other types of assessments for psychopathy. The Levenson Self-Report Psychopathy Scale (LSRP) looks at antisocial personality disorder and considers psychopathy and sociopathy as interchangeable terms. There are 16 items measuring psychopathic emotional affect and ten items measuring psychopathic lifestyle. The former relates to primary psychopathy, and the latter relates to secondary psychopathy. The Psychopathic Personality Inventory (PPI) has been administered to college student samples and is designed to assess all psychopathic traits in both non-forensic and non-psychiatric individuals. This is a 187-item self-report and is used to assess psychopathy as a personality disorder thereby excluding references to antisocial behaviour. The Youth Psychopathic Traits Inventory (YPI), as the name suggests, is used in the assessment of adolescents from the age of 12. There are three factors: grandiose-manipulative (GM), callous-unemotional (CU) and impulsive-irresponsible (II). All told there are 50 items. This is a popular assessment tool used across many countries. What these assessment tools have enabled clinicians to understand is that psychopathy is not an all-or-nothing condition but rather is on a scale rising progressively from none or low presence of psychopathic traits to a preponderance of psychopathic traits. Individuals at the end of the scale assessed to possess a high preponderance of psychopathic traits are those who exhibit the most conduct problems and cognitive and emotional deficits.

FURTHER READING

Gacono, C.B. (2016). *The clinical and forensic assessment of psychopathy: A practitioner's guide.* Abingdon: Routledge.

Jonason, P.K. (2023). *Shining light on the dark side of personality: Measurement properties and theoretical advances.* Göttingen, Germany: Hogrefe Publishing.

Smith, J.M., Gacono, C.B. and Cunliffe, T.B. (2021). *Understanding female offenders: Psychopathy, criminal behavior, assessment, and treatment.* Amsterdam: Elsevier Science Publishing Co Inc.

Tully, R. and Bamford, J. (2019). *Case studies in forensic psychology: Clinical assessment and treatment.* Abingdon: Routledge.

EXPLANATIONS
SOCIAL, PSYCHOLOGICAL AND CULTURAL

As we have seen in Chapters 1 and 2, psychopathy is a long-standing concept where trait descriptions have remained constant since Cleckley's book *The Mask of Sanity*. Academics and clinicians have strived over the years to explain why psychopaths behave as they do. And through the use of clinical interviews, psychological and neurobiological tests, and a life profile of social, emotional and developmental experiences, they have achieved a greater understanding of psychopathy. Findings from all the aforementioned areas have been scrutinised to see if there is anything that might single psychopaths out from the rest of society. In this chapter, we will explore psychosocial and cultural explanations of psychopathy. These explanations can be considered as being nurture-driven, but as we will see in Chapter 4, both nurture and nature (biological) constraints operate interactively. This can be overwhelming to consider conceptually, which is why in this chapter we will focus our attention on nurture explanations. One approach to understanding how nurture influences the development of a child is to separate the contributing factions within society through the eyes of Urie Bronfenbrenner's Developmental Ecosystem Model, devised in 1979. Bronfenbrenner's quote in 1977 sets the context of his model clearly:

> Understanding of human development demands going beyond the direct observation of behaviour on the part of one or two persons in the same place...multi-person systems of interaction not limited to a single setting must take into account aspects of the environment beyond the immediate situation containing the subject.

(p. 514)

DOI: 10.4324/9781032221052-3

DEVELOPMENTAL ECOSYSTEM MODEL

Bronfenbrenner's Developmental Ecosystem Model envelops the notion of both informal (i.e., care-giver, family, friends) and formal (i.e., school, clubs, media, legal institutions) socialising agents impacting on the way the child learns to become a good citizen within society. This learning occurs through the process of **socialisation**. Socialisation encapsulates what it is to be a good citizen. This involves the learning and adoption of society's morals, values, rules and acceptable behaviour. This consensus within society is a positive one that enables people the freedom to live how they want as long as these morals, values, rules and expected behaviour are upheld. Those who contravene society's consensus, in other words, break the 'social laws', are deemed as people living on the fringe of tolerance. And if they seriously contravene these 'social laws', then they will experience the wrath of society, such as punishment, enforced by the various branches of the legal system. Bronfenbrenner's model has been likened to an onion with concentric layers. In the centre, he placed the child who is born equipped with limited biological competencies. The child is encompassed by layer upon layer of firstly informal and then progressively more formal socialising agents. In Figure 3.1, this relationship is depicted by the child connected closely to the microsystem (i.e., care-giver, family, care system), then the exosystem (i.e., family friends, welfare services, neighbours) followed by the overarching macrosystem (i.e., attitudes of society and culture). It is worth noting here that in the past, the mother was considered to be the person who looked after the child. With changes to family structure, the preferable term used today is care-giver as the person caring for the child might not necessarily be the birth mother. We will use care-giver but will use the term mother when referring to specific studies.

Bronfenbrenner considered the child as being devoid of knowledge concerning what behaviour is appropriate and inappropriate. Hence, to be an exemplar citizen, morals, values, rules and acceptable behaviour become engrained through the process of socialisation. Thus, all the informal and formal socialising agents do their job of ensuring the child is socialised appropriately. Sometimes, this goes wrong. Inappropriate socialisation can lead an individual in the wrong direction, creating an intergenerational transmission of

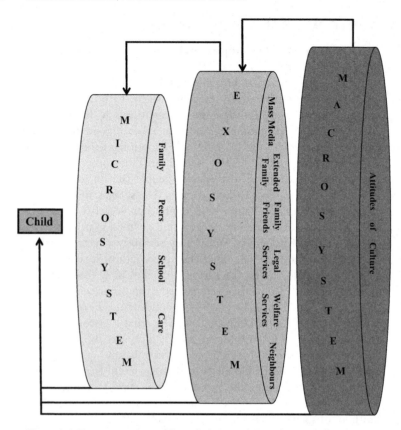

Figure 3.1 Representation of Bronfenbrenner's Developmental Ecosystem
Model (Modified from Taylor (2016). *Crime and Criminality:
A Multidisciplinary Approach*)

inappropriate, deviant or criminal behaviour (and arguably psychopathic behaviour). It is, however, possible that the individual
concerned has a specific biological make-up which promotes the
development of psychopathy. This behaviour then becomes initiated on contact with environmental adversity – a trigger such as
rejecting parents or abuse. It has been shown, for instance, that
childhood adversity is robustly associated with difficulties in social
cognition. Of relevance to psychopathy is the fact that social cognition is important for the ability to recognise and consider the

emotions of others as well as their intentions. This is known as theory of mind (ToM). Psychopaths, as we have seen, have deficits in emotional understanding and are very much concerned with their own feelings and needs. Put simply, they are egotists. The literature has emphasised the importance of traumatic experiences in childhood involving emotional neglect and abuse, sexual abuse, and physical neglect and abuse. There is an abundance of support for this, particularly the effects of harsh and punitive parenting on the development of personality disorders such as borderline personality disorder. However, according to research by Rokita, Dauvermann and Donohoe (2018), the type of adversity most robustly associated with problems of social cognition is physical neglect. This links well with attachment theory (see section on Attachment Theory), because if the child's physical needs are provided for, then it is highly likely that a strong bond is made between the care-giver and the child. The formation of a strong bond is likely to provide the child with security, which, in turn, gives the child a good base from which to explore the social world without fear.

For some individuals, however, the psychopathic behaviour has no known environmental triggers, but occurs due to a biological predisposition (see Chapter 4). As we have seen in Chapter 1, primary psychopaths are more likely to have a biological predisposition driving them to exhibit the classic traits of psychopathy. We also learned that environmental adversity is more likely to be the trigger for individuals classified as secondary psychopaths. It is not as straightforward as that, however. For some primary psychopaths, classic traits defining them can be shaped and subdued by specific early childhood experiences (see Box 4.2). Earliest experiences occur with the interactions and bonds forged with the care-giver, which Bronfenbrenner considers in his microsystem.

THE MICROSYSTEM

There are many childhood factors that can be considered under the microsystem. An emotional bond between the child and care-giver has been researched using attachment theory introduced by John Bowlby and attachment styles by Mary Ainsworth. The impact of family interactions and the dynamics of family life on juvenile delinquency have been researched by Michael Rutter and Henri

Giller under five adverse family factors. David Farrington considered some of these factors in relation to delinquency in boys from the age of ten – known as the Cambridge Study. The influence of peers and psychopathy will be considered here also. We will begin with attachment theory.

Attachment Theory

The microsystem is the first layer of social influence enveloping the child. This influence occurs almost immediately after birth. In fact, Widström, Brimdyr, Svensson, Cadwell et al. (2019) argued that a bond between care-giver and baby can be developed through skin contact once the umbilical cord is severed. After birth is a sensitive period for bonding to take place and is facilitated by the mother secreting the 'love hormone' oxytocin (see Chapter 4). This calms the mother, increases her body heat and induces a maternal closeness with the newborn, which, in turn, induces a feeling of warmth and security when in contact with her skin. The science of skin-to-skin contact supports the development of positive bonding. Additionally, it has been shown that skin-to-skin contact increases the breast-feeding period post-partum. A Dutch study, where mothers were asked to provide one hour of skin-to-skin contact daily for five weeks post-partum (on top of the care-as-usual), showed that this physical bonding increased the breastfeeding duration by months in comparison with those receiving care-as-usual (Cooijmans, Beijers, Brett and de Weerth 2021). Cooijmans, Beijers and de Weerth (2022) found that mothers who provided skin-to-skin contact and care-as-usual one hour daily for five weeks post-partum had babies who cried less and slept longer.

If the mother fails to make a bond at this stage, there is no major harm done, but if bonding continues to fail, then this sign of rejection could be problematic for the future development of the infant. This is a case of the care-giver being the natural mother as there are hormonal influences involved here. Bonds or attachments, however, can be made between infants and care-givers *per se*. Bowlby considered this bond to be an **affectional bond** that is a long-enduring tie. This attachment to the care-giver is considered as an irreplaceable tie. Given that human babies need support and care from the care-giver to survive, the formation of an attachment is imperative. This attachment, however, provides more than sufficing primary drives such as thirst, hunger and comfort, it provides an "emotional tie entwined with dependency" (Taylor and Workman 2018, p. 95). Bowlby claimed that the mother provides a secure base for the infant to return to, someone the infant wants to be near; separation from the mother causes distress in the infant; feeling safe and being protected are provided by an emotional attachment that has an impact on future long-term relationships. When this attachment goes awry or fails to develop, then the individual is adversely affected during childhood and adulthood (see Box 3.1).

Bowlby argued that the need for attachment to the care-giver is hardwired through an evolved neurological system enabling human contact – **intraorganismic organisation**. This is interesting as it provides a link between nature and nurture. For example, the infant wants to connect with the care-giver, but if the care-giver doesn't provide the opportunity to do so (a form of rejection), then nurture (the care-giver interaction) impacts on the infant's ability to form positive emotional relationships. There is evidence to suggest that this type of 'cold' parental environment can initiate a negative social-cognitive perception of the world and can lead to antisocial behaviour in the developing child (Palmer and Hollin 2000). How an attachment forms can interact with the infant's intraorganismic organisation and the development of working models. Working models are formed by the way in which the infant interprets the care-giver's actions in response to signs of distress. If the infant's cries are ignored, for instance, then the working model adopted is one of an uncaring and rejecting care-giver. This will have repercussions for trust issues in future relationships. Is this what happened in the 44 thieves study by Bowlby? (see Box 3.1).

BOX 3.1: BOWLBY'S THIEVES

Bowlby pioneered the notion of maternal deprivation and argued that the early interactions between infant and mother impact on how he/she later understands the world. If the working model formed is one of the insecure attachments with the mother, then this will be generalised to later relationships and attachments. An insecure attachment bond can have negative consequences on emotional, social and cognitive development. To test this hypothesis, Bowlby (1944) interviewed 88 children, 44 of whom were known adolescent juvenile delinquents registered on a child protection programme in London. As a consequence of their stealing, they lived in a clinic. The other 44 children acted as a control group because they had no prior criminal record. Interviewing the parents of both groups of children uprooted information about their child's upbringing such as whether there had been any separation during the early years and for how long. Bowlby found that for the group of children referred to as the 'juvenile thieves', separation (for more than six months in the first two years of life) and maternal deprivation were as high as 32 per cent. These children, he argued, had developed 'affectionless psychopathy' as a consequence of living in the clinic. Affectionless psychopathy did not feature among the control group. His conclusion was that disruption of the early attachment process, such as insecure attachment while in care, can set the stage for later criminality.

Attachment issues during the early years appear to play an important role in the development of psychopathy. Bowlby's contention is that problems with attachment have utility when it comes to understanding why some children become involved in crime. Conradi, Bortien, Cavus and Verschuere (2015) considered how rejection and abandonment play a role in causing interpersonal deficits exhibited by psychopaths. They draw attention to there being two broad facets of the PCL-R: affective–interpersonal facet and behavioural-lifestyle facet (see Chapter 2). As we have seen in Chapter 2, lacking empathy but exhibiting superficial charm and grandiosity is associated with the affective–interpersonal facet. Traits such as impulsivity, irresponsibility and antisocial behaviour are associated with the behavioural-lifestyle facet.

Benning, Patrick, Bloningen, Hicks et al. (2005) claimed that the affective–interpersonal facet correlates negatively with fear and anxiety. They found that behavioural-lifestyle facet correlates positively with depression and anxiety. Interestingly, Fowles and Dindo (2006) explained this by suggesting that both facets lead to the same behaviours expressed by psychopaths in adulthood. They suggest, however, that an environmental risk factor, such as experiencing harsh parental treatment, may impact on both these facets. Poythress and Skeem (2006) took this further by claiming that an inborn deficit might be responsible for the traits of the affective-interpersonal facet. In contrast, they suggest that traits of the behavioural-lifestyle facet might be shaped through nurture-based factors such as parental neglect and abuse. Furthermore, Viding, Blair, Moffitt and Plomin (2005) found that children (twins) who behaved antisocially and scored high on callous-unemotionality were genetically influenced. For those who scored low, they suggest less of a genetic contribution but with the contribution of a shared environment. Blair, Mitchell and Blair (2005) claimed that difficulties of attachment with the care-giver are unlikely to result in psychopathy. They claimed it is the other way around, in that the child has an emotional disturbance which interferes with forging attachment bonds and the socialisation process. For Farrington, however, experiencing harsh parental discipline will impact negatively on the emotional and antisocial elements of psychopathy. If a child experiences punishment and no rewards for good behaviour, then an antisocial model can only be expected. According to Schimmenti (2020), from an attachment-based approach, the child's experiences of neglect, abuse and loss might be a contributory factor leading to psychopathy (see Box 3.2).

BOX 3.2: BAD CHILDHOOD, BAD LIVES

There has been interest in the type of experiences infamous serial killers endured during their childhood. Of particular interest is the relationship and attachment bond with the care-giver. The following cases of serial killers highlight the attachment problems they experienced in childhood. Toates and Coschug-Toates (2022) argued that many of these serial killers experienced a toxic attachment in childhood.

David Berkowitz shot dead five women and one man after stalking them during the night. Known as the 'Son of Sam', he operated in New York City between 1976 and 1977. He was diagnosed as psychotic but what was his childhood background like? Berkowitz was born out of wedlock and adopted soon after as a result of rejection by the biological father. He was told that his mother had died, and he felt responsible for her death. Eventually, he found out that this was not true, and his mother was alive. He felt that she had rejected and abandoned him. This was repeated when his adoptive mother died, and he was left alone often wandering the streets. He had difficulty forging social relationships and felt angry at being abandoned.

Steve Wright strangled five sex workers in the town of Ipswich in England in 2006. While actually having sexual intercourse, Wright would strangle his victims. He was abandoned by his mother and sisters who left him at the age of eight with his father.

Peter Kürten inflicted violent acts on his victims only until he reached orgasm. In other words, when he climaxed during the strangulation of his victims, for instance, he would spare them from death. But for many victims, he would climax too late for them to be spared. Kürten experienced severe physical abuse from his alcoholic father who would also sexually and physically assault other female members of the family. He witnessed all these assaults.

Dennis Nilsen killed 15 young men who stayed with him at different times – they never left. He would resort to killing them as soon as he felt threatened by abandonment. His father left the family very early on in his life and his mother was remote and unresponsive to Nilsen's attachment needs. Instead, his grandfather provided affection which was a double-edged sword as he also groomed and sexually abused the young Nilsen. His grandfather died but Nilsen was encouraged to look into his coffin to suggest the man was merely sleeping. This traumatised Nilsen and confused him about life and death (something that was reflected in the way he kept corpses and arranged them at the dinner table and in bed).

Ted Bundy confessed to killing 30 women resembling his girlfriend who had abandoned him. Bundy was an illegitimate son who was birthed in a home for unwed mothers. She left Bundy there for three months and later collected him. She became known as his sister while his grandparents assumed the role of mother and father. His 'sister' took him away from his 'parents' whom he had bonded with. He lived with his 'sister' and her husband but was unaware that she was his real mother. Eventually finding out that his sister was his mother and that he was illegitimate affected him psychologically giving him an inferiority complex.

When a child experiences a hostile home environment devoid of affection, the survival response is to negate the positive effects of an attachment bond. Schimmenti claimed that this enables the child to screen out memories of attachment trauma, which inadvertently can induce the development of psychopathic traits. Fonagy (2010) identified early attachment trauma as being the major factor preventing the formation of a secure attachment. This type of trauma causes disruptions to the attachment bond (Toof, Wong and Devlin 2020). The two types of attachment trauma defined by Kobak, Cassidy and Ziv (2004) of relevance here are:

- Physical and/or emotional abuse by the care-giver
- Attachment injuries resulting from neglect and abandonment

Warren and South (2006) found a correlation between attachment trauma, such as the above, in childhood and psychopathy. Moreover, in a similar vein to Bowlby's 44 thieves, those in foster care show a higher connection with criminality in adulthood (Yang, McCuish and Corrado 2020). Foster care, according to Papagathonikou (2020), can sometimes be associated with abuse and maltreatment, both of which are risk factors for offending.

Children who come from families where there is no affection and are often left to fend for themselves are unlikely to form a secure attachment. Attachment style has been researched extensively, but it was Ainsworth who categorised different attachment types.

Attachment Style

Ainsworth (1967) developed the PDD model – an acronym for protest, despair and detachment. Using an experimental set-up that became known as the 'strange situation', Ainsworth was able to observe the behavioural interactions between the mother (as used by Ainsworth) and infant (see Box 3.3).

BOX 3.3: STRANGE SITUATION

The mother and infant enter a room that has a one-way mirror allowing the observer to watch the activity taking place without being seen. The room is festooned with toys for the infant to play with. The observer watches to see the nature of verbal and behavioural inter-actions between the infant and the mother. Important behaviours include the infant looking at the mother and initiating communication and checking to see where the mother is. Once a baseline of interaction between the infant and the mother is established, the mother leaves the room and the infant's reaction to this is recorded. Soon after the mother vacates the room, a stranger enters and sits down. The reactions of the infant are recorded. The mother returns while the stranger is in the room who then leaves so that the infant and the mother are once again alone. From all the observations recorded, Ainsworth was able to identify three clear categories: **insecure avoid-ant** (mother ignores the infant's cries, hence the infant expects to be rebuffed and thus ignores the mother), **securely attached** (mother responds to the infant's needs and always provides comfort and security) and **insecure anxious-resistant** (mother provides unreliable and inconsistent care, hence the infant resists contact).

An infant who forms a good attachment bond with the care-giver is referred to as being securely attached (or B-dyad), and Ainsworth found that 65 per cent of infants fell into this category. Most of these infants were observed playing with the care-giver, showing distress on her departure and approaching her when she returned. They were wary of the stranger who was treated very differently. The two insecure attachments showed very different interactions. Insecure avoidant attachments (or A-dyad) were indifferent and ignored the care-giver (see Figure 3.2). No distress was shown when the care-giver left the room, and there was no contact seeking on re-entry. The stranger was treated in the same way as the care-giver; 25 per cent of infants fell into this category.

In the case of insecure anxious-resistant attachments, infants were wary of the care-giver but showed no distress when left alone in the room. Anger was expressed on the return of the care-giver, and although contact was sought, when it was provided infants rebuffed any interaction; ten per cent of infants were found to be in this category. These category behaviours have been observed in older toddlers and in the responses made to the Attachment Q Sort

(AQS), a card sorting task, used by care-givers to describe their child (Bretherton 2005). An intergenerational effect has also been found by Main (1985) where the care-giver's category of attachment is the same as their child. Hence, "Attachment behaviour is held to characterise human beings from the cradle to the grave" (Bowlby 1969, p. 129). There is a clear relationship between the development of deviant behaviour and being one of the 35 per cent of individuals who fall into these two insecure types of attachment style (A and C; Del Giudice and Belsky 2011; Workman, Taylor and Barkow 2022). A proportion of these will develop psychopathic traits in later life. The question of why a third of infants become prone to developing along these lines will be addressed in Chapter 4. From Main's research, a further category was introduced called **insecure disorganised/disoriented** (or D–dyad) infants (see Box 3.4).

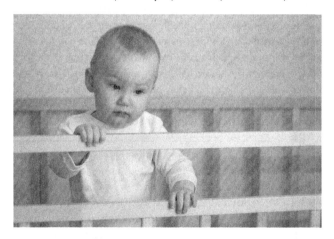

Figure 3.2 Infant learns to be ignored

BOX 3.4: THE D-DYAD

Infants in the D-dyad category have experienced traumatic and unresolved attachments. And it is these infants, Main argued, who are more likely to have experienced neglect and abuse. Such experiences have led to a working model of a care-giver who is unpredictable and unresponsive to their needs. According to Soloman and

George (1999), these infants are fearful of their care-giver and show approach-avoidance behaviours. Although a hotly debated topic, a disorganised attachment has been linked with a specific gene. Interestingly, however, this gene has been considered to interact with environmental factors such as the nurturance received. The gene referred to is the DRD4 gene, which is the normal structure of the gene (a 4-repeat allele). This gene contributes towards infant attachment to the care-giver. In the case of D-dyad infants, a different structure of the gene is found – DRD4–7R (a 7-repeat allele). We all inherit two alleles (i.e., DRD4 + DRD4); however, inheriting at least one 7-repeat allele occurs in 71 per cent in D-dyad infants versus 29 per cent in non-D-infants (Lakatos, Toth, Nemoda, Ney et al. 2000). Lakatos, Nemoda, Birkas, Ronai et al. (2003) found that infants with the DRD4–7R structure of the gene were wary of strangers, often exhibiting difficult and problem behaviours. But is this too simplistic? For Bakermans-Kranenburg and van Ijzendoorn (2006), nurturance plays a large role in attenuating any effects of the DRD4–7R allele. Those who had sensitive and responsive care-givers showed fewer problematic behaviours. Those who had insensitive and unresponsive care-givers showed extensive problematic behaviours and a disorganised pattern of attachment.

Research has recently revisited the connection between psychopathy and insecure attachment. Alzeer, Michailidou, Munot and Kyranides (2019) studied 211 adults aged between 18 and 40 years. Adopting the Relationship Scale Questionnaire and the Parent Adult-Child Relationship Questionnaire, they were able to assess the role of attachment. Additionally, they assessed psychopathic traits using the Levenson Self-Report Psychopathy Scale (see Chapter 2). Alzeer et al. found that those who scored high on psychopathy also experienced dismissive and fearful attachments in childhood, which was the opposite for those whose scores were low for psychopathy. This, they argue, demonstrates the predictive utility of insecure attachment and the future development of psychopathic traits. In 2021, Kyranides, Kokkinou, Imran and Cetin found that the attachment type was the most significant factor contributing to callous–unemotional (CU) traits in an adult population. Avoidant and anxious attachment styles have also been examined in the context of the 'dark tetrad' personality traits – that of narcissism, Machiavellianism, sadism and psychopathy (see Chapter 5). Nickisch, Palazova and Ziegler (2020) found an association between psychopathy, sadism and Machiavellianism and insecure avoidant and insecure anxious-resistant attachment styles. Narcissism, however, correlated negatively with insecure anxious-resistant attachment. Nickisch et al. concluded that narcissism diverges from the other dark tetrad traits in relation to the insecure attachment styles. Attachment and parenting will be further considered under the five adverse key family factors discussed next.

Five Adverse Family Factors

Rutter and Giller (1983) highlighted five family factors that can have adverse effects on a child's development:

1. Parental criminality
2. Intra-familial discord
3. Disciplinary inconsistencies between parents
4. Large family size
5. Low socioeconomic status

(Although the two latter points are important, our attention will focus on the first three points).

Parental Criminality

As children learn what is acceptable behaviour and what is morally correct initially from their parents, it makes sense that parents with criminal values and attitudes will pass these on to their children through inappropriate socialisation. Fagan and Tyler (2005) introduced the term legal socialisation to explain how children are socialised by the family (and others) into assimilating the prosocial values and behaviours of their culture. These prosocial values and behaviours become adopted by the child. Moreover, many of these prosocial values and behaviours are morally influenced. For example, helping a lost infant to a place of safety is not only showing prosocial behaviour but behaviour that reflects a moral duty. If the wrong set of values and behaviours are instilled by criminal parents, then we can expect the child to perceive antisocial behaviour and the justifications for it as the norm. A clear relationship between parental criminal values and behaviours and aggression in their children has been found in many studies (see Box 3.5).

BOX 3.5: BAD APPLES DON'T FALL FAR FROM THE TREE?

A child or teenager adopting a criminal lifestyle and behaving aggressively towards others increases if the parents are criminals. According to Thomson (2019), antisocial parents contribute towards the child developing psychopathy. Parents who are imprisoned can cause a host of problems for their children such as neglect, social isolation and psychosocial developmental impediments. These combined can increase the likelihood of criminality. Bamvita, Larm, Checknita, Vitaro et al. (2017) found that boys whose father had committed many violent crimes showed increased antisocial and psychopathic traits. A study looking at the impact criminal parents have on their children showed that the more frequently parents indulged in criminal activity, the more likely their offspring will act aggressively in early childhood (Tzoumakis, Dean, Green, Zheng et al. 2017). Junger, Greene, Schipper, Hesper et al. (2013) looked at the prevalence of crime (through arrest data) in the Netherlands across three generations. This involved looking at siblings, parents and grandparents of families in Dutch cities. A clear trend showed a link between both parental and grandparental arrests. Arrests were found to be concentrated within families such that 7.8 per cent of the family cohorts accounted for 52.3 per cent of the crime suspects. Hence, familial arrests are a major risk factor for offspring criminality. The longitudinal Cambridge Study in Delinquent Development began between 1961 and 1962 with 411 boys aged from eight to nine years (West and Farrington 1973, 1977). All the boys lived in working-class inner-city areas of South London. The study focused on whether any of these boys showed delinquent and/or criminal behaviour and what was influencing this. The important childhood risk factors for offending among the eight-to-ten-year-olds included family criminality, poor parenting (i.e., ineffective discipline and supervision), risk-taking and other troublesome behaviours. Farrington, Coid, Harnett, Jolliffe et al. (2006) reviewed the data when the participants were in their 40s and found that for those whose antisocial behaviour began at the age of 21, these childhood risk factors were absent. Interestingly, Farrington, Coid, Harnett, Jolliffe et al. (2006) reported that 40 per cent of these males in 1993 were convicted up to the age of 40, which was the case for their fathers (28 per cent), mothers (13 per cent), brothers (43 per cent), sisters (12 per cent) and their wives (nine per cent); 63 per cent of the males who had convicted fathers were themselves convicted. This translated to 30 per cent of the remaining males in the study. This supports the intergenerational transmission of criminality where offspring follow in the footsteps of previous generations. A case of bad apples don't fall far from the tree?

Intra-familial Discord

Intra-familial discord can be exhibited in many different ways. One of the most common ways this can occur is through family arguments and disagreements – sometimes resulting in physical, emotional and sexual abuse, rejection and neglect towards the children (see Box 3.6). This familial disturbance can have a profound effect on the child's psychosocial development and can cause intense fear and insecurity (Taylor and Workman 2018; see Figure 3.3). This can vary from emotional to cognitive development, which, in turn, can impact on the child's ability to forge attachments with the parents. As we have seen earlier, this will influence the capacity to develop close loving bonds in adult relationships. And as Bowlby claimed, such children are vulnerable to the development of affectionless psychopathy. Taylor and Workman (2018) suggested that children who experience neglect and rejection are also deprived of guidance concerning what is acceptable behaviour. This, they argue, can lead to misbehaviour and antisocial tendencies. As we have seen, familial criminality can influence child members of the family to follow suit by adopting the same values and models of behaviour. Intra-familial discord can also lead a child into antisocial behaviour due to inappropriate socialisation. According to Taylor and Workman, children who are poorly socialised, and left to their own devises, will think it is okay to be disrespectful towards others and to behave antisocially. This can often lead to contravention of the law and to beliefs that are in direct conflict with society's morals and values.

BOX 3.6: ARGUMENTS AND DISAGREEMENT IN FAMILIES CAN HARM CHILD DEVELOPMENT

There are four types of child abuse or mistreatment: emotional (such as verbal hostility and rejection), physical, sexual and neglect. Children, however, who are not directly in the line of intra-familial discord but witness such events, still experience maltreatment. Additionally, when children witness intimate partner violence, and other types of violence occurring in the family, there is an increased incidence of children externalising their behaviours. For example, children can show violent behaviours towards their peers or act in antisocial ways. Furthermore, the development of personality disorders is known to be positively associated with maternal verbal abuse. Sigfusdottir and Silver (2009) concluded from their study of Icelandic adolescents that intra-familial discord can cause anger and depression which, in turn, increases the probability of engaging in delinquency. Metcalf, Dickerson, Milojevich and Quas (2021) examined the effects of maltreatment on children in the context of developing traits of primary and secondary psychopathy (see Chapter 1). Children who had experienced proactive (without provocation) and reactive (with provocation) aggression were more likely to have traits of secondary psychopathy. They were also more likely to be highly anxious and to have experienced trauma. Those identified with traits of primary psychopathy, alternatively, had low anxiety and trauma. Interestingly, both groups reported the same level of low affective (emotional) empathy. Metcalf et al. claimed that by examining the maltreatment history of children, it is possible to identify high-risk groups for psychopathic traits before any antisocial acts have been committed. Trauma experienced in childhood (Baglivio, Wolff, DeLisi and Jackowski 2020) and familial discord (Sijtsema and Lindenberg 2018) have been found to contribute towards the development of psychopathic traits. Clearly, early family disharmony can have a big influence on socioemotional development.

Figure 3.3 Parents arguing can affect the child's socioemotional development

Disciplinary Inconsistencies Between Parents

In 1983, Maccoby and Martin argued that there are two dimensions of parental interaction – affection and control – which can be combined into four disciplinary styles:

- Low affection and low control – rejecting and undemanding/ permissive (neglecting)
- Low affection and high control – rejecting and demanding/ restrictive (authoritarian)
- High affection and high control – accepting/warmth and demanding/restrictive (authoritative)
- High affection and low control – accepting/warmth and undemanding/permissive (indulgent)

Authoritative parental interactions provide the most effective socialisation style for instilling a good moral compass. The other types of interaction provide poor socialisation. From a longitudinal study by Weiss, Dodge, Bates and Pettit (1992), authoritarian styles of socialisation, where the child is shouted at, cause non-compliance and resentment. They argued that harsh disciplinary styles are often associated with aggressive behaviour towards other children at kindergarten. Weiss et al. claimed that such behaviour is due to negative disciplinary styles. How inconsistent, intense and frequently these negative disciplinary styles are used also play a role. Interestingly, they found inconsistent and erratic disciplinary practices to be more culpable for delinquency than the different interactive styles *per se*. Inconsistent and harsh punishment increases the likelihood of children becoming aggressive and hostile (Patterson 2002). In other words, when parents adopt unpredictable punishment regimes, the children respond poorly and are more likely to act aggressively than prosocial. Children who have been subjected to 'spanking', which is often adopted in the authoritarian punishment approach, are more likely to behave antisocially. Spanking only delivers the opposite message to the desired outcome. This is because the child endeavours to avoid being spanked rather than understanding the underlying reasons for being punished in the first place. This approach to punishment, arguably, provides a model of violence for the child to emulate. It is interesting that some researchers argue that antisocial behaviour in children with defiant disorders (see Chapter 6) can be controlled by spanking when it is used appropriately and when non-physical forms of punishment have failed. Children who experience no punishment – a permissive approach – fail to learn behavioural boundaries and tend to misbehave at the onset which then continues into adolescence. Being rejected has the worst outcomes in terms of knowing behavioural boundaries. These children are more likely to pursue a career of antisocial behaviour that often leads to contact with the criminal justice system.

It is well established that inconsistent and harsh punishment can be a contributory factor towards juvenile and adolescent delinquent and antisocial behaviour, but is there evidence that it increases the likelihood of psychopathic tendencies? Molinuevo, Pardo, González and Torrubia (2014) examined the self-reported memories of childhood from 75 institutionalised juvenile male offenders. They completed the Alabama Parenting Questionnaire and the Psychopathy Checklist: Youth Version (see Chapter 2). Their results provided a profile of ineffective parenting. This included inconsistent discipline and ineffective supervision that were associated with higher scores of psychopathy. Two of the four factors associated with these parenting styles were lifestyle and antisocial. A study by Deng, Wang,

Shou, Lai et al. (2020) examined the effects of a negative parenting style versus a positive or mixed parenting style on a sample of 361 Chinese children aged between nine and 13 years. Of the children with a higher level of psychopathic traits, the majority had experienced negative parenting. Despite being different to Western culture, similar parenting styles were identified in China. Glenn (2019) reviewed the early life predictors concerning the development of psychopathic traits such as being callous and unemotional and concluded there is a person-environment interaction. Glen argues that some children are more sensitive to the environment (regardless of it being a positive or negative experience) which is why the person-environment interaction model is referred to as differential susceptibility (Belsky 2005; see Chapter 5). This implies that some children are particularly sensitive to an adverse home life that puts them at risk of a poor outcome. For example, in Box 3.4 we discussed the D-dyad and its link with the DRD4–7R allele. Here, the child has a predisposition towards being wary of strangers and an increased likelihood of exhibiting problem behaviours. According to Nikitopoulos, Zohsel, Blomeyer, Buchmann et al. (2014), infants with this 7-repeat allele are more likely to be sensitive to specific forms of parenting. If the parenting is positive, then the outcome of developing psychopathic traits is lower. If, however, parenting takes on a negative form, this coupled with the 7-repeat allele increases the likelihood for psychopathy.

Negative parenting styles such as harsh and over-controlling interactions with the child are a good predictor of higher levels of callous and unemotional traits (Wagner, Mills-Koonce, Willoughby and Cox 2019). This also induced punishment insensitivity, lowered fear response and a lack of conscience in the child. Particularly when this type of negative parenting was directed at the infant by the care-giver during the first six months, the outcome was a deficit in empathic-prosocial behaviours. Some researchers argue that a harsh and controlling parent is more harmful than an insensitive and unresponsive one because it provides inconsistency and negativity in the guise of harsh and punitive behaviour (Willoughby, Mills-Koonce, Propper and Waschbusch 2013). In Box 3.7, examples of negative parenting and the impact this has on child development are examined by psychotherapist Harper West.

BOX 3.7: PSYCHOTHERAPIST, HARPER WEST, EXAMINES

Harper West (2021) described a fictionalised case based on many therapy sessions with families and their children with behavioural problems. West observed how families and familial dyads interact together. West gave the following account of a daughter and her parents in the waiting room:

> Give me your backpack', 'No, here, take your water bottle', 'Stand up straight', 'Sit over here, not over there', 'Don't be scared', and 'Now be sure to talk to Ms. West about everything we talked about'...they [the parents] had described that their 7-year-old daughter was argumentative, refused to use the toilet...

West claimed that parents who are over-controlling and verbally harsh can make their children feel the need to attain a sense of autonomy by refusing to do things (see Figure 3.4) – in this case refusing to toilet train. Moreover, West claimed it is easy to spot such parents as they are often overly verbose to their children and tend to talk at them. This talking at them often entails criticism and corrections to the child's behaviour. This kind of negative interaction is also known as intrusive parenting. West also regarded parents practising such methods as being out of touch with age-related and age-expected behaviours. The example West provided is a parent who punishes harshly, shames or rejects a four-year-old child for spilling milk. Shaming can cause self-blaming, other blaming or blame avoidance. Other blaming is of particular interest as the individual fails to accept accountability and in so doing might adopt many negative behaviours such as bullying, controlling others and antisocial acts. According to West, the following responses associated with other blaming typify psychopathic traits: rejecting authority and discipline, lacking remorse and empathy, inability to accept blame and responsibility and to apologise, self-centred, hostile, aggressive, reckless, intimidating, manipulative, deceitful, superficially charming, having a superiority complex and using gas lighting as a means to destabilise someone.

Interestingly, according to DSM-5, these traits are associated with antisocial personality disorder, conduct disorder, narcissistic personality disorder, histrionic personality disorder and oppositional defiant disorder.

Figure 3.4 Defiant daughter reacting to a controlling mother

Influence of Peers

We have seen the important role played by care-givers and other family members in the socialisation process. However, in 1995 Judith Rich Harris argued that too much emphasis is attributed to the family in the importance they have in socialising their children. She advocated instead for a **Group Socialisation Theory** (GST; Workman et al. 2022). GST provides another avenue for the socialisation of children. It highlights the important and often overlooked approach of children socialising each other. Children make friendships with other children and often form small groups. These provide a positive interpersonal relationship based on the notion of reciprocal interactions. When children play together, their social interactions help them to acquire new social skills and to practice these skills in order to develop them further. Harris stated:

> Children are born with certain characteristics. Their genes predispose them to develop a certain kind of personality. But the environment can

> change them. Not 'nurture' – not the environment their parents pro-
> vide – but the outside-the-home environment, the environment they
> share with their peers.
>
> (1998, p. 147)

In effect, Harris claimed that the internal working model formed
with the care-giver is only applicable to this attachment relationship.
It has no generalisable utility. Hence, children form many different
internal working models for their multitude of relationships with
peers and close friends. In order to be part of the group or have a
set of close friends, children need to avoid modelling on their parents' behaviour and instead behave like their peers. This will prevent
them from being ostracised by their peers. Children, however, need
to ascertain what kind of people they are. They need to work out
which social category or group they want to aspire to, and they do
this through making social comparisons with other children. Once
this has been established, they then acquire the norms, attitudes,
values and behaviours of the peer group they wish to join. Harris
argued there is a majority–rules rule that dictates how the members
of the group will behave. If this is not adhered to, then the members
of that group will either put pressure to conform or will force the
new member to leave. Children do not always get the social category
right and might persevere with a number of peers before hitting the
jackpot. Harter (2006) highlighted the importance of making social
comparisons for the development of self-concept and self-esteem.
Negative appraisals from peers can cause problems for self-esteem,
so it is important to fit in and follow the rules of the group. GST
also predicts that the adopted peer-group behaviours can enter the
home, but the reverse cannot occur. Not all children fit in with their
peers. Some become rejected by their peers. An interesting question
pertains to the fate of rejected children. Do these children become
victims of bullying, or do they do the bullying? (see Box 6.4).

Clearly, our peers have an impact on how we thrive socially and
emotionally as children and adolescents. With our peers, we form
attachment bonds and share the same norms, value system and attitudes. Groups of peers also develop a commitment to the group
and participate in the same types of activities. These groups can of
course be positive or negative, but what they have in common is a
glue that binds members together. Hirschi (1969) encapsulated this

in his Social Bond Theory (SBT). This has been used to explain why some individuals adhere to delinquent peers. In a similar vein to GST, SBT predicts that children and adolescents are more likely to develop stronger bonds with their peers than their parents and, as a consequence, will gravitate towards the behaviour exhibited by these friends. If such friends happen to be delinquent, then the behaviour exhibited will reflect this delinquency. SBT states that an attachment to peers or a group occurs first. Once the attachment is established, there is a commitment to what the peers or group represent which might entail getting involved in the activities they do, such as performing antisocial acts. Finally, each member becomes immersed in the group's value system. This value system reflects either that of the wider society or a sub-group of society, as would be the case of a delinquent group. Moreover, members of a group will perceive each other as being part of the in-group and those members of other groups as the out-group. In-group/out-group perceptions often lead to prejudices and can be the underlying cause of hatred and the dehumanisation of those who are different. This may be seen in many quarters of life, but within the context of antisocial behaviour, different delinquent groups can often be seen fighting with one another.

It has been questioned whether gang members, in particular the leaders, are more likely to have psychopathic traits than non-gang members. Given that similar types of people join a delinquent group or a gang, it raises the question of whether they are antisocially inclined at the onset. Sanchez-Jankowski (1991) conducted research on gangs and was able to identify gang members by virtue of their psychopathic traits such as impulsive behaviour, callous, liars, unreliable, and lacking both morals and empathy. These types of individuals decide to join gangs which reflect their psychopathic traits such that they are with like-minded people who share the same social, cognitive and emotional deficits. Furthermore, they are likely to be socially rejected – the rejected peers (most possibly the 'aggressive sort'). These traits remain constant throughout the lifespan (Hemphälä, Kosson, Westerman and Hodgins 2015; see Chapter 6), but are less fully developed in childhood (McCuish and Lussier 2018). Antecedents of psychopathic traits, however, can be observed in children as early as three years of age (Fanti and Kimonis 2017), so it is no surprise that children as young as five have been documented as joining a gang (Augustyn, Ward and Krohn 2017). Most gang members, however, are older than this, reaching adolescence and joining between 12 and 15 years when peers are most influential. In 1999, Hare stated that:

> Gangs have always provided greater opportunities for young psychopaths. Their impulsive, selfish, callous, egocentric, and aggressive tendencies easily blend in with – and may even set the tone for – many of the gang's activities.
>
> (p. 176).

Joining a gang can offer a new identity based on an alternative socialisation that favours antisocial behaviour. This alternative socialisation or indoctrination to the gang tends to attract individuals who already have the propensity for psychopathy (see Box 3.6). We will consider the importance of socialisation for the perpetuation of cultural attitudes under Bronfenbrenner's macrosystem. For some individuals, however, subcultural attitudes that are in conflict with mainstream culture become instated. As we have seen, these subcultural attitudes often influence the behaviour of individuals who are at risk of developing an antisocial mentality.

THE MACROSYSTEM

Cultural Attitudes

According to Bronfenbrenner, the macrosystem encapsulates the attitudes of a country's mainstream culture. Countries across the world have their own mainstream culture that is reflected in their society. In any society, there is a dominant mainstream culture that most of us for the most part aspire to. Despite different countries having their own cultural attitudes, it is remarkable just how similar the underlying principles governing and driving these mindsets are. The important principles of moral values and behaviours are ubiquitous globally. It seems that although we have our differences of cultural attitudes, when it comes to humanity and what constitutes moral behaviour, we have more in common than most people realise. It comes as no surprise therefore that psychopaths have similar traits regardless of the culture they are born into. Moreover, amoral behaviour is considered to be one of the main characteristics that psychopaths exhibit (Koenigs, Kruepke, Zeier and Newman 2012). It is important to realise that cultural attitudes are often shaped by parental socialisation. As we discussed earlier, social cognition can be disrupted by adversity during childhood and can also lead to personality disorders. One aspect of poor social cognition is poor theory of mind and understanding of others' emotional states. This deficit with understanding and, more to the point, with feeling emotions interferes with the development of moral perception, moral decision-making and moral conceptual understanding (Levy 2007). Costa, Azevedo, Relva and Simões (2022) investigated the relationship between moral sensitivity and psychopathic traits. Through the administration of a series of self-report psychopathy inventories, they analysed the results from 520 university students aged between 17 and 49 years. Their findings showed a negative association between moral sensitivity and psychopathy. Moral sensitivity is important to how we interpret situations and take into account the moral implications of our actions on others. This links with how we employ our social cognitive skills (such as ToM and empathy). Moral sensitivity, according to Costa et al., can act as a protective factor against the development of psychopathy. Given that parents are important in socialising us to adopt the mores and values of our society, children who are neglected, rejected or abused are less likely to attain this effectively. As we saw earlier under Bronfenbrenner's microsystem, there is a robust association between ineffective parenting and developing psychopathic traits.

Cultural attitudes and socialisation have also been considered by sociologists using the concepts of subcultures, contra-cultures and youth cultures as alternatives to the mainstream culture. Subcultures, contra-cultures and youth cultures are important to our understanding of how individuals affiliate with an antisocial mindset. The question we could ask is, are individuals attracted to these sub-sets of cultures within our societies because they, by their very nature, engage in antisocial behaviour? Alternatively, have such individuals been rejected by their peers and society but accepted by these sub-sets of cultures? There has been a history

BOX 3.8: IMPACT OF DIVIDED CULTURAL ATTITUDES

Individuals who are antisocial have slipped through the net of socialisation. This accounts for their failure to conform to their society's respective mainstream cultural attitudes. In the case of youth cultures, the representative attitudes are removed from the past generation such that the new generation behave differently and have alternative norms and lifestyle. Contra-cultures tend to be in conflict with the dominant mainstream attitudes. Matza (1964, 1969) claimed that there are three forms that youth cultures take: Bohemian, Radical and Delinquents. Of relevance here is the delinquent youth cultures. It is interesting how Matza makes a link with delinquent gangs in areas where there is deviancy, such as family members in prison or the socialisation of criminal ideals. This was discussed earlier in the context of the microsystem (e.g., criminal parents and rejected peers). There have been numerous reports of knife and gun crime in the UK, in particular gang murders and innocent bystanders. Often, such killings are committed by two peers, but many are committed by gang members. This fits with the cycle of violence where youngsters are socialised into a subculture of violence. They, in effect, adopt the very same attitudes and behaviours of their parents. In relation to psychopaths, similar attitudes are endorsed. These attitudes further encompass notions of toughness, aggression and excitement. These attitudes are corroborated by scores attained on the Five Factor Model of Personality (FFM; Lynam 2002; see Chapter 5). Psychopaths also perceive their behaviour as justified and often deny responsibility for any injury to others as a consequence of their actions. They believe that their victim is at fault and will condemn others who condemn them for their behaviour. Interestingly, psychopaths will also argue that their peers (and/or gang members) take precedence over their victims. Carson and Ray (2019) found that children who exhibit callous-unemotional traits, antisocial, non-empathic and manipulative behaviour tend to join gangs. In the final analysis, Ray (2018) suggested that antisocial gang members reinforce psychopathic behaviour by the nature of their social interactions.

of research by sociologists into subcultures, contra-cultures and youth cultures (see Box 3.8).

Gender Identity

Cultural attitudes have a daily impact on our behaviour. In fact, these are so ingrained from one generation to the next through socialisation that attitudes specifying gender traits, for example, are considered as set in stone. These traits encapsulating our gender are an example of how social categorisation operates within our culture, and we become aware of them early on in our development. This awareness of our gender, that is, what it is to be male or female, is a consequence of the socialisation process. In many cultures, the attitudes pertaining to gender see men and women as having different traits. These gender traits provide an understanding of gender identity. Societies tend, however, to exaggerate these gender traits into gender stereotypes (some of which incidentally do have a biological basis). Hence, when we consider the typical descriptions of men and women held by society, we find interesting differences. These differences, in some cases, arise out of biologically driven characteristics that have been reinforced through socialisation (Eagly 1995; Eagly and Wood 1999). Some differences, however, are driven by social and political ideologies. For example, using Ruble's (1983) adjectives for males and females, we find the following descriptors (see Table 3.1).

Table 3.1 Adjectives used to describe the male and female gender

Male adjectives	Female adjectives
Dominant	Considerate
Aggressive	Emotional
Competitive	Cries easily
Active	Aware of people's feelings
Ambitious	Gentle
Leadership	Kind
Independent	Needs approval
Self-confident	Tactful
Persistent	Devotes self to others
Not easily influenced	Understanding
Operates well under pressure	Excitable in a crisis

Ruble, Martin and Berenbaum (2006) highlighted how similar gender-role behaviour is across cultures where males are still considered as dominant, independent and competitive, while females are passive, non-aggressive and a provider of emotional support to others. According to Nielsen, Stefanick, Peragine, Neilands et al. (2021a, 2021b), however, gender being perceived as a masculinity-femininity spectrum precludes individuals who do not fit into these traditional gender dichotomies. This has clearly become somewhat of a heated debate in recent years as our understanding of gender has evolved. Research exploring gender issues in psychopaths has not received much attention except for the number of male and female psychopaths incarcerated. So, what can we say about the impact of gender socialisation on individuals with psychopathic traits? This will be the focus of our attention in the quest to understand whether psychopaths respond differentially to gender socialisation than non-psychopaths.

Traits of the Psychopath in Relation to Gender

The three-factor model (see Chapter 5) divides psychopathic traits into the:

- Interpersonal factor (e.g., manipulative and superficial charm)
- Affective factor (e.g., lack remorse and empathy)
- Behavioural factor (impulsive and lack realistic goals)

According to Jackson, Rogers, Neumann and Lambert (2002), this model is more successful at capturing psychopathic traits in women. Differences between psychopathic men and women were found concerning reactions to stress and shame and risky behaviour such as driving (Lee and Salekin 2010). Despite this, there has been little research examining gender differences in psychopaths for interpersonal, affective and behavioural factors. Interestingly, Lehmann and Ittel (2012) found that women who scored high on psychopathy were more aggressive than those with low levels of psychopathic traits. Also, their aggression was channelled differently to their male counterparts. They were more likely to internalise their aggression against themselves through self-harming behaviour. Psychopathic male aggression was externalised and was more goal-directed and proactive (Cima and Raine 2009). There is evidence, therefore, for differences in the nature of aggression across male and female psychopaths. Physical abuse in childhood links with male psychopathy but not female psychopathy. Sexual abuse in childhood, however, links with female psychopathy but not so for their male counterparts (Weizmann-Henelius, Grönroos, Putkonen, Eronen et al. 2010). According to Miller, Watts and Jones (2011), abuse was found to play a more significant role in the development of female psychopaths. A thesis by Therese Wennberg at Örebro University in 2012 found that there are differences between male and female psychopaths, especially on the behavioural factor. Female psychopaths were more impulsive but exhibited fewer external aggressive behaviours than their male counterparts. As with previous findings, both male and female psychopaths had been victims of abuse in childhood,

---

BOX 3.9: FEMALE PSYCHOPATHS ARE DIFFERENT

Psychopaths all share core traits such as lacking empathy, guilt and remorse. Female psychopaths tend to behave differently from their male counterparts, which is partly explained by differences in their socialisation of gender. Females are regarded as the more sensitive, emotional, empathic and caring of the genders because they give birth, lactate and spend more time caring for offspring than males. Males are perceived as more dominant, in control and aggressive. Female psychopaths have been found to differ from their male counterparts in seven ways:

1. They involve and manipulate others into doing their own 'dirty work'.
2. They operate by trying to destroy the character and reputation of others.
3. They are attracted to caring professions and organisations.
4. They are more likely to be violent to someone they know like a family member.
5. They seek victim status as a way to manipulate and attain sympathy. Hence, they appear to be vulnerable rather than powerful like their male counterparts. Tactics such as telling lies of being stalked help boost their self-esteem and attain admiration.

6. They can easily fake genuine emotions such as crying. Females tend to score higher on emotional intelligence than their male counterparts.
7. They tend to be promiscuous and form many short-term relationships. Promiscuity is a strategy for attaining admiration and controlling/manipulating others. This admiration can make them feel superior.

Many female psychopaths experienced sexual abuse, rejection and neglect, which feeds into their need to be important and wanted. Hence, their behaviours are geared towards filling a void and healing emotional wounds.

but the nature of abuse differed: for males, this was physical, and for females, this was psychological (e.g., sexual and verbal abuse, neglect). Researchers have also identified ways in which female psychopaths behave differently from male psychopaths (see Box 3.9).

Considering the adjectives listed by Ruble in Table 3.1, we can see from Box 3.9 how male and female psychopaths still gravitate towards gender norms but do so in manipulative ways. It is interesting how the aggressive response in male psychopaths is externalised through violent behaviour. In the case of female psychopaths, despite being more aggressive than non-psychopathic females, their aggression is internalised through self-harming behaviour. Females are described by Ruble as emotional, cry easily and excitable in a crisis. These descriptions fit with female psychopaths channelling their aggression towards themselves and by damaging the reputations of others. We know, however, that female psychopaths can be violent and can even kill people. While male psychopaths tend to be violent and kill strangers, female psychopaths have a tendency to show violence towards people they know (e.g., people in their care and family members). It is uncommon for females to show violence towards people, but it is interesting how female psychopaths can be violent to those under their care. In common with non-psychopathic women, these women are attracted to caring professions and organisations. Female psychopaths have difficulty sustaining long-term relationships and tend to be promiscuous. Females score higher than males on emotional intelligence; in other words, they are superior at recognising emotions in others and feeling empathy. Female psychopaths are very good at 'hood-winking' others into believing they are upset or upset for others (good at imitating emotions but not actually feeling them). This, in part, fits with the superior ability of non-psychopathic females to be in tune with the feelings of others. Males are more likely to use physical aggression, which might, in part, be due to their physical prowess, unlike females who often damage the reputation of their foes. Female psychopaths operate in the same way by character assassination. In line with females being more vulnerable than their male counterparts, female psychopaths often manipulate others to get what they want by pretending to be victims. Not only can telling a good yarn about being stalked by the opposite sex provide them with sympathy from others but it is also a good strategy for self-adulation. It appears that female psychopaths operate within the sphere of female gender characteristics over and above the core traits indicative of psychopathy.

SUMMARY

Bronfenbrenner's Developmental Ecosystem Model provides a social structure surrounding the developing child that consists of both informal and formal socialising agents. These agents combine to instil society's morals, attitudes, values and acceptable behaviours on the developing child so that he/she becomes a good citizen. The first and most impressionable of the early stages of socialisation come from the microsystem. The microsystem includes the child's care-givers, family unit and peers. There is robust evidence to suggest that attachment in infancy leaves a big impact on the child. When parents fail to form a bond with their child, Bowlby found that the child can feel rejected which can lead to acting antisocially. The type of attachment formed can be divided into one secure and three insecure types. All three insecure attachment styles can cause problems for the infant and can lead to antisocial behaviour. There is evidence that dismissive and fearful attachments in childhood can lead to the development of psychopathic traits. Parents who are criminally inclined tend to espouse criminal attitudes and socialise their children accordingly. The extent to which parents of such children contravene the law appears to influence how aggressive these children become. This supports the notion of intergenerational transmission of criminal and aggressive behaviour. Intra-familial discord can interfere with a child's ability to forge a secure attachment which, according to Bowlby, can lead to affectionless psychopathy. Moreover, where there is intra-familial discord, the chance of experiencing neglect and rejection increases, which in turn can prevent appropriate guidance on how to behave. Parental violence can also provide the wrong model of how to behave and lead children to imitate this form of antisocial behaviour. More specifically, it has been shown that trauma and familial discord can contribute to the development of psychopathic traits. Parental disciplinary interactions with their children can vary in the level of affection and control shown such that an authoritarian style, where there is low affection (rejecting) but high control (demanding and restrictive), is a combination that is likely to cause resentment, non-compliance and aggressive behaviour. Spanking can also result in aggressive behaviour, as children fail to learn the moral implications of their behaviour and instead will try to avoid being spanked. There is evidence, however, that inconsistent and harsh punishment is a greater underlying cause of delinquency than any of the punishment styles. Peers are noted as having more of an impact on children's behaviour than their parents. Group Socialisation Theory predicts that children's behaviour is influenced by how peers behave, simply because they want to belong to that group. The problem arises when peers gravitate towards individuals who are delinquent or antisocial. Often, aggressive rejected peers gravitate to like-minded peers and behave antisocially. Some will adopt the socialisation of a delinquent gang and become part of a subculture endorsing violence, aggression and antisocial behaviour. Subcultural attitudes can be the antithesis of mainstream cultural attitudes. Bronfenbrenner addressed the influence of cultural attitudes in the macrosystem. These attitudes influence our behaviour which is ingrained through socialisation, but if, for instance, inept or criminally oriented socialisation occurs, then the values, norms, morals and behaviours will counter mainstream cultural attitudes. Delinquent gangs oppose mainstream cultural attitudes, and many of these gang members exhibit psychopathic traits. Gender socialisation is another example of how cultural attitudes influence behaviour. Male and female psychopaths are more aggressive than their non-psychopathic counterparts, but their traits appear to be extensions of their gender stereotypes.

FURTHER READING

Bernstein, A. (2012). *Emotional vampires: Dealing with people who drain you dry, revised and expanded* (2nd edn.). New York: McGraw-Hill.

Black, W. (2015). *Psychopathic cultures and toxic empires.* Scotland: Frontline Noir.

Daynes, K. and Fellowes, J. (2012). *Is there a psycho in your life?: Britain's leading forensic psychologist explains how to spot them – and how to deal with them.* London: Coronet.

Vaknin, S. (2018). *Narcissistic and psychopathic parents and their children.* Rhinebeck, NY: Narcissus Publications.

EXPLANATIONS
BIOLOGICAL

When we consider the biological bases of psychopathy, it is important to realise that there are two quite different questions we can ask and that these require very different types of answers. First, we might ask what are the biological factors that are associated with the development of psychopathy? Such factors include a person's genes, hormones, and neural development and functioning. We can think of these as 'here-and-now' causal questions. That is, they examine what is going on in the body and brain right now and what went on during development that might have led to this state. These are sometimes known as **proximate** questions. The second type of biological question asks what is it that maintains this condition or state within a population? That is, might there be evolved factors that provided an advantage to the ancestors of current psychopathic individuals which thereby led to the maintenance of this condition. This is an evolutionary question, which some evolutionists label a functional or **ultimate** question. If you find this distinction confusing, then don't worry you will have a good grasp of this difference by the end of the chapter. For now, a simple way of thinking about the difference is that proximate questions deal with 'how' and ultimate ones deal with 'why'. Before considering proximate biological questions, we begin by examining the ultimate evolutionary questions – what is it about psychopathy which maintains it in our species?

DOI: 10.4324/9781032221052-4

ULTIMATE BIOLOGICAL EXPLANATIONS: THE EVOLUTIONARY ROOTS OF PSYCHOPATHY

Evolutionary psychology is based on the premise that human nature evolved to its current state during a period of rapid hominin evolution known as the *Pleistocene* epoch between 11,700 and 2.5 million years ago. This means that our current abilities and proclivities were forged out of the recurrent adaptive challenges of the ancient past (Barkow, Cosmides and Tooby 1992; Buss 2019; Reader and Workman 2023; Workman and Reader 2021). This might sound like we can portray our current behaviour as a series of well-honed adaptations. There is, however, an important caveat we need to factor in, that is, the notion of the **mismatch hypothesis** (Barkow 1989; Workman and Taylor 2021). The mismatch hypothesis suggests that, because our social and physical environment has changed more rapidly than evolutionary change, many of our tendencies to respond are not suited to the challenges we now face. Because we spent over 99 per cent of our evolutionary history dealing with the challenges presented by the African savannah, we now have internal states, including fears and opportunities, better suited to that environment than to dealing with the obstacles of modern life. During the *Pleistocene*, an individual would most likely have known everyone in their (relatively small) tribe; they would not have had to work 9–5 and deal with a demanding line manager or negotiate the trials and tribulations of a large town or city. They would not have had to commute or master technology, school and college life, and consider fashion, roads, fast food, smartphones, the internet and bank accounts, to name but a few. Of course, there are many benefits to all of these features of modern life. They are after all designed to aid comfort, convenience and pleasure. But each has its drawbacks such as a greatly increased likelihood of obesity, serious road traffic accidents and novel stresses such as trying to live up to apparently perfect role models or being trolled. According to two of the original proponents of evolutionary psychology, Leda Cosmides and John Tooby (1992), we are living in a computer age with a Stone Age Brain.

How, you may ask, might this approach help us to understand psychopathy? As we saw in previous chapters, individuals diagnosed with this unfortunate condition frequently cause harm, grief and distress to other people. Moreover, those psychopaths who engage in criminal behaviour are also a major financial and social burden to society. Due to this, many experts perceive psychopathy as maladapted thinking and behaviour. Evolutionists, however, look at things somewhat differently. Evolutionary psychologists, in particular, have suggested that, rather than considering psychopathy as a failing, under certain circumstances, it might be considered an alternative competitive adaptive strategy. It's worth pausing to consider what this statement means. You are probably aware that natural selection depends on passing on copies of your genes. This means of course that adaptive responses do not necessarily lead to socially valued outcomes (Ribeiro da Silva, Rijo and Salekin 2015). Hence, evolution has nothing to say about the morality of behaviour in members of our species. It is simply concerned with which strategies aid gene replication (see Box 4.1). With this in mind, it is interesting to note that a number of studies suggest psychopaths, as a group, have high reproductive success (Babiak and Hare 2006; Rowe 1995). This may well be because, lacking a moral compass, in the case of men at least, they are more likely to impregnate with impunity (Rowe 1995). Furthermore, for both sexes, as freeriders, they regularly gain resources unfairly and without reciprocation. This means that, while their behaviour is considered immoral in all societies, under the right conditions it may be a successful adaptation. This raises the question, what conditions? In a nutshell, psychopathic thinking and behaviour can be adaptive under very harsh conditions. (Or, according to the mismatch hypothesis, it may well have been during the ancient past before the establishment of legal systems and police forces.) It might also make adaptive sense when nearly everybody else is generally somewhat altruistic (see Figure 4.1). In order to comprehend evolutionary explanations of psychopathy, we need to explore two important evolutionary concepts: **Life History Theory (LHT)** and **Frequency-Dependent Selection (FDS)**.

Figure 4.1 The African savannah (where 99 per cent of hominin evolution occurred), with all of its challenges and opportunities, differs greatly from modern human environments

BOX 4.1: PATHOLOGY OR ADAPTATION? THE NEW SCIENCE OF EVOLUTIONARY PSYCHOPATHOLOGY

One important question that evolutionary psychologists like to pose is whether an 'abnormal' state of mind or behavioural response is a case of pathology, or a case of an adaptation better suited to our ancient past? While many phobias can be seen as adaptations – spiders and snakes are often poisonous so it makes sense to be susceptible to phobic avoidance responses, others such as schizophrenia, where individuals may hear voices and hold bizarre false beliefs, are more likely to be cases of pathology. Researchers interested in the new field of evolutionary psychopathology have considered whether a whole range of mental states and behavioural responses should be regarded as adaptations or as pathology (Glenn, Kurzban and Raine 2011; Nesse 2019). To complicate matters further, some traits (characteristics) might also be a by-product of selection. An example of this is the fact that a huge proportion of humans suffer from backache due to the evolution of bipedal (walking on two legs rather than four) locomotion. On balance, bipedal locomotion has arisen through natural selection because it frees the hands for tool use and gesture, but in comparison to quadrupedal locomotion, it leaves us prone to back pain. Some disorders are debatable. Post-partum depression is a case in point with some experts perceiving this state as a by-product or even as a pathological state, while others perceive it as an adaptation that might elicit additional support from family members (Hagen 1999). One current area of debate is psychopathy. Although a contentious theory, some experts hold the view that this is an alternate strategy to normal human reciprocation responses (labelled by some a cheater-hawk strategy, see main text, Book, Visser, Volk, Holden et al. 2019). This raises a question for evolutionary psychopathologists – how do we know whether a particular 'abnormal' behaviour pattern reflects an adaptation, a by-product of an adaptation or a pathological state? One way of providing evidence that a particular strategy is an adaptation is to determine whether it generally boosts 'inclusive fitness'. Inclusive fitness refers to the proportion of copies of an individual's genes which are passed on to future generations. This can occur either directly by producing offspring or indirectly by providing aid to other relatives such as nephews and nieces. While there is little evidence that people with psychopathic traits aid relatives, there is good evidence that they do well in terms of gaining access to mates and hence in the production of offspring (Babiak and Hare 2006; Rowe 1995). This has been taken as evidence by evolutionists that psychopathy may well be a type of adaptation.

LIFE HISTORY THEORY

Life history theory considers the trade-off that organisms (including humans) make in order to pass on their genes given the challenges of the environment. This, importantly, includes the social environment. One vital trade-off is how much time and effort to allocate to individual development before reproducing. If an organism reproduces as early as possible, this is described as having a 'fast life history', whereas reproducing later is known as a 'slow life history'. Under favourable conditions, including warm parental attention, people tend to develop a slow life-history strategy, forming trusting and enduring relationships and breeding in maturity. When, however, conditions are harsh, such as where parents invest little time and effort in their children and where they show very little affection, the offspring become less likely to be trusting as adults, breed early, have a series of short-term relationships and tend to be exploitative and hostile (Chisholm 1996). In other words, they are more likely to develop a fast life history, and for some, this includes antisocial behaviour. Evolutionary psychologists relate this to attachment theory. You may recall from Chapter 3 that, based on her strange situation experiments, Mary Ainsworth suggested infants form one of three types of attachment styles:

- Type A (Insecure avoidant): The infant is less distressed when the mother leaves the room and is as easily comforted by a stranger as by the mother (25 per cent).
- Type B (Secure): The infant cries when the mother leaves the room but is quite rapidly comforted on her return (65 per cent).
- Type C (Insecure resistant): The infant remains clinging to the mother, shows great anxiety when she leaves the room and is not easily comforted when she returns (ten per cent).

As we saw in Chapter 3, the development of deviant behaviour is more likely if you happen to fall into type A or C (with around 35 per cent of individuals falling into one of these two insecure types of attachment style; Chisholm 1996; Del Giudice and Belsky 2011; Workman, Taylor and Barkow 2022). A proportion of these are likely to demonstrate psychopathic traits later on in life. Developmentalists generally perceive such individuals as acting in a dysfunctional way. This raises the question of why should 35 per cent of infants become prone to developing along insecure lines? This seems a remarkably high proportion of the human population. When evolutionists see such high figures, they tend to think this must be an adaptation.

Psychosocial Acceleration Theory

One of the first researchers to make use of life history theory to help explore deviant behaviour within an evolutionary framework is Jay Belsky. Along with his co-researchers Laurence Steinberg and Patricia Draper, Belsky developed the **psychosocial acceleration theory**. The psychosocial acceleration theory proposes that those falling into attachment categories A and C are using adaptive strategies (Belsky 2005; Belsky, Steinberg and Draper 1991). In particular, it suggests that both boys and girls brought up under harsh unsupportive conditions (particularly where the father is absent) reach sexual maturity earlier and go on to produce offspring at a significantly earlier age (Tither and Ellis 2008; Workman and Reader 2021). This is particularly the case for the 25 per cent who fall into the insecure–avoidance group. (According to Belsky, in contrast, the ten per cent in the insecure–resistant group tend not to reproduce themselves and are more likely to shift their investment to other younger relatives.) Although the notion of developing sexual maturity earlier following a harsh upbringing is controversial, it does have some empirical support. In 2010, Belsky and his co-workers uncovered evidence that both boys and girls in this category complete puberty earlier than those in the other two categories (Belsky, Houts and Fearon 2010). Hence, there is evidence that, under such circumstances, they are more likely to gravitate towards a 'fast life history' strategy.

Once again, we might ask why should such a large proportion of people become likely to develop a fast life history? In order to understand why this makes sense to evolutionary psychologists, we need to think beyond our current circumstances and lifestyle. The argument here is that, during the ancient past, many parents may have been unable to provide the levels of support we expect today (in fact, many children would have lost one or both parents prior to reaching adulthood). Hence, when provided with cues that the future is likely to be harsh and uncertain, a fast life history including breeding early may have been a successful strategy for our ancestors. Also, importantly, under such circumstances, it may have paid them to be less trusting of others.

Cheater-hawk Lifestyle

Based on the work of Belsky and his co-workers, subsequent evolutionists made use of life history theory to suggest that a sub-set of those individuals who are both raised under harsh conditions and inherit a particular combination of genes are more likely to develop what has become known as a 'cheater–hawk' lifestyle. (A cheater–hawk lifestyle refers to those who are both exploitive [cheater] and aggressive [hawk]; see Book and Quinsey 2004; Book, Visser, Volk, Holden et al. 2019). A cheater–hawk lifestyle can, of course, also be described as psychopathy. Note that above, we stated they are 'more likely' to gravitate to such behaviour. Many will grow up to enter into stable romantic relationships; it's more a matter of a substantially increased likelihood of developing such traits. This is where the genetic component comes into play. We will discuss genetic evidence for psychopathy later on, but for now, life history theory suggests that the genes some individuals inherit, when combined with a harsh upbringing, can lead some down the 'cheater–hawk' fast life-history path of psychopathy (Coyne and Thomas 2008; Glenn and Raine 2014).

Clearly, this ultimate (evolutionary) explanation of why some gravitate towards cheater–hawk, psychopathic behaviour raises questions concerning the proximate (causal) mechanisms. Put simply, something physiologically must be happening to the bodies of young people based on their early experience that causes them to go through puberty more rapidly. We will explore this later on in the chapter. Before this, we need to consider the second important concept evolutionists have brought to the debates concerning the existence of psychopathy in our species.

FREQUENCY-DEPENDENT SELECTION

It is often assumed that evolution leads organisms to develop optimal solutions to life's challenges. In a sense, this is true since those members of a population who are best able to develop strategies to overcome social and environmental challenges will thereby pass more copies of their genes on to future generations than those less able. And since genes are the 'currency of evolution', we can expect to see genes for optimal responses arising. Since the middle of the 20th century, however, evolutionists have realised that the optimal solution might change depending on the strategies others in a population adopt (Maynard Smith 1982). Importantly, when the vast majority of individuals are doing the same thing, it might pay you to do something very different. If this all sounds a bit esoteric, then here's a simple example. Many insect species exist as different morphs (Rowell and Cannis 1972). That is, they can have two or more colour varieties; this is especially true for butterflies. When one morph becomes very common, they are more frequently eaten by predators than other, less common, morphs simply because the predators are used to searching for the more common form and are more likely to overlook the less common ones. This means that adopting a less common form gives you a selective advantage. Technically, this is known as frequency-dependent selection. So, it can pay to be very different. And this can also be the case for behaviour patterns. If everybody is a 'dove', it might pay you to be a 'hawk'. This brings us back to evolutionary theory and the existence of psychopathy. In 1995, American evolutionary psychologist Linda Mealey suggested that at least some psychopaths are maintained in the population because they are behaving as hawks in a world inhabited, broadly speaking, by doves (Mealey 1995, 2005). That is, most of us are reasonably nice. Most of us engage in mild acts of altruism from making a hot drink for our partners to giving directions to a stranger to loaning a friend in need some cash. We do these things partly because we know that were the situation reversed our 'kith and kin' would do likewise. We also do these things because of our natural empathy for others. Because, however, the vast majority of us do these things all of the time, we leave ourselves open to 'non-reciprocators' (cheats) who simply don't play by the rules. Unencumbered by normal empathic responses or the commitment to reciprocate, psychopaths are often able to exploit our social norms and gain unfair advantages with impunity. This strategy only works provided their numbers in a population remain low. Once they become common, the whole human system of reciprocation breaks down. In the light of this, it is worth remembering that population estimates of psychopathy are between one and three per cent (see Chapter 7). As a thought experiment, imagine that the proportion of psychopathic individuals rose to around 20 per cent of the population. How might this affect our social behaviour? Given this means we are likely to encounter exploitative individuals on an almost daily basis, then we would need to maintain a state of vigilance and suspicion. In fact, at this level, the constant small (and sometimes very large) acts of reciprocation that we engage in regularly would most likely cease. Social life would be very different. Due to this breakdown of trust, the population, in general, would no longer be open to exploitation, and psychopathy would become a victim of its own success. This, in turn, would lead to a reduction in success for psychopaths, and they would leave fewer offspring.

Hence, over generations, the proportion of the population would fall. At some point, however, this strategy will become sufficiently rare for it to become effective again leading to a rise in numbers. Hence, according to experts such as Mealey, frequency-dependent selection allows for the maintenance of psychopaths in the population, but in relatively small numbers. While Mealey's hypothesis remains controversial, there is some indirect supportive evidence. There is, for example, evidence that psychopathy is partly heritable. Plomin and co-workers found that the risk of developing the condition shows a five-fold increase for first-degree male relatives of psychopaths (Plomin, DeFries, Knopik and Neiderhiser 2016; see below). Additionally, psychopathic men are more promiscuous than other men (Rowe 1995), often resort to sexually coercive behaviour (Buss 2019; Lalumière, Harris, Quinsey and Rice 2005) and have a higher success rate in poaching others' mates (Jonason, Li and Buss 2010).

This brief synopsis of Mealey's use of frequency-dependent selection to help explain the existence of psychopathic individuals might appear to run counter to the life history account as outlined earlier. In reality, however, her model is not one of genetic determinism but rather suggests that this environmentally contingent propensity may be opened up for some individuals who are reared under harsh conditions. Hence, those committing to life history theory are not in conflict with those who follow Mealey's frequency-dependent selection argument.

PROXIMATE BIOLOGICAL EXPLANATIONS – GENETIC, NEUROLOGICAL AND HORMONAL

Armed with a knowledge of these ultimate explanations for the continued existence of psychopathy, we can now begin to examine the proximate biological roots of this condition. We can broadly divide these into three areas:

- Genetic factors
- Neurobiological factors
- Hormonal factors

It's important to realise that it is somewhat artificial to split these areas into three factors since they are clearly related. Genes, for example, have a major influence in the development of the brain and the hormones we each manufacture. It does, however, make them easier to digest by taking each in order. We begin with genetic factors.

GENETIC FACTORS

The extent to which individual differences between people are related to genetic differences is an age-old question. It is also one that tends to polarise opinion. You may well have a view on the importance of 'nature versus nurture' in explaining human behaviour and internal states. In the case of psychopathy, however, such debates transcend mere academic intrigue. If there is a genetic foundation to such behaviour, then understanding how inherited factors interact with upbringing in the development of the condition may help us to improve interventions. (Note that this is also the case for neurological and hormonal factors.) In fact, while we are still a long way from a full understanding of this relationship, during the last decade a great deal of advancement has been made with regard to genetic vulnerabilities to psychopathy. But how do researchers gather evidence to support (or refute) the notion that genes are involved in the development of psychopathy? There are two main ways of tackling this question: behavioural genetics, which attempts to determine the extent to which variation in a trait (variance) is due to genetic or environmental factors, and molecular genetics, which attempts to identify the specific genes involved in a trait (Glenn and Raine 2014). We will consider each in turn.

Behavioural Genetics

Behavioural genetics is concerned with the concept of heritability. It draws on both psychology and evolutionary biology to investigate the effects of genes and the environment on individual differences in features such as personality and intelligence. It is also, controversially, involved in understanding the contribution of genes to psychological 'disorders' such as schizophrenia, alcoholism and autism (see Figure 4.2). In recent years, behavioural geneticists have turned their attention to psychopathy. Twin studies have been of particular interest here. It is well known that identical or 'monozygotic' (MZ) twins, sharing all of their genes, are more alike than fraternal or dizygotic (DZ) pairs who share only half of their genes by common descent (see Figure 4.2, Boxes 4.2 and 4.3). This is true of personality factors such as extraversion or agreeableness and intelligence as measured by IQ tests. One important method used by behavioural geneticists is to compare the correlation between MZ twins with the correlation between DZ twins on a particular trait (Plomin 2018; Plomin, DeFries, Knopik and Neiderhiser 2016). The rationale here is that, because MZ twins share 100 per cent of their genes, while DZ twins share 50 per cent of theirs, if genes play a prominent role in the trait, we anticipate uncovering a significantly higher correlation between the former pairs than between the latter ones. Note that the degree to which the scores of a pair of twins correlate is known as the concordance rate (see Box 4.4). Hence, a 100 per cent concordance rate would only occur when each pair of twins has identical scores on a given measure. In real life, this almost never occurs. This is normally measured on a scale of 0.0 to 1.0 (the latter being equivalent to the elusive rate of 100 per cent). In terms of intelligence, which has a high rate of heritability, the concordance for MZ twins is around 0.75 (Plomin 2018).

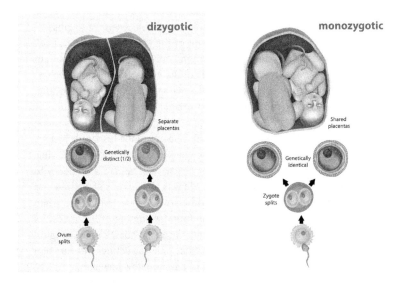

Figure 4.2 The differences between monozygotic (right) and dizygotic (left) twins. Note that not only do monozygotic twins share all of their genes due to arising from only one fertilised egg but they also share a single placenta. This means that the intrauterine environment is also virtually identical, while the dizygotic twins have separate placentas meaning their environment is slightly different even when in the womb.

BOX 4.2: JAMES FALLON – THE PROSOCIAL PSYCHOPATH?

James Fallon is a North American biologist who came to prominence for two different but related reasons (Taylor 2016). During the late 20th and early 21st centuries, Fallon became well known for his neuropsychological studies of psychopathic serial killers. Through the use of various scanning techniques, he was able to identify areas of the brain such as the amygdala and the orbitofrontal cortex which differ in psychopaths when compared to non-psychopathic controls (see main text). In 2005, at the age of 58, he compiled a series of PET scans of the brains of members of his own family including himself. In examining the scans, to his great surprise, he found his own scan fitted in perfectly with the psychopathic serial killer group! Moreover, he later discovered that he shared a variant of a specific gene which has been implicated in the development of aggressive behaviour. This is a specific variant of the MAOA or 'warrior gene'. Note that MAOA stands for the monoamine oxidase A gene variant and is believed to affect the levels of the neurotransmitters, such as serotonin and dopamine, that influence mood (Godar, Fite, McFarlin and Bortolato 2016). As you can imagine, these findings came as quite a shock to Fallon. But being a scientist, he began to examine his own feelings and behaviour. He also examined his family history. Looking back over his own life, he quickly came to realise that, while he had not committed violent or illegal acts, he had a tendency to be callous towards other people. He was also quite self-centred and did not always understand why others were upset. Moreover, when looking into his family history, he found a number of his ancestors had been involved in murders. This raises the question, if biological factors such as genes and abnormal brain structure and function are involved in the development of psychopathy, how come, Fallon, despite his tendency towards callousness, became a well-respected neuroscientist with a stable family life? That stable family life may well be a clue to understanding his behaviour. In addition to having a stable family himself, he also had well-adjusted parents who were loving and supportive during his childhood. James Fallon's case illustrates the importance of childhood experiences and how they mitigate against biological factors in determining the paths we take in life. In Fallon's view, he has grown up to be a 'prosocial psychopath'. All of this is documented in his autobiography *The Psychopath Inside: A Neuroscientist's Personal Journey into the Dark Side of the Brain* (Fallon 2013).

BOX 4.3: ARIEL AND ALICE – HOW DIFFERENT CAN TWINS BE?

In his book *Without Conscience,* Robert Hare describes a set of twin girls, Ariel and Alice, who differed more than a little as they grew up (Hare 1999). Their parents, Helen and Steve, took pride in sweet-natured Ariel's achievements as she graduated from law school and went on to become a successful solicitor. In contrast, Alice became a drug addict who regularly disappeared only to phone home asking for money. Even as children, while they were both attractive, they differed in behaviour and mood as night differs from day. While Ariel, although not immune to teenage angst, was honest and trustworthy, Alice was aggressive and was even suspected of killing the household's pet kitten. As Ariel progressed in her career, Alice eventually spent time in prison for theft and prostitution. In despair, Helen and Steve could not understand how their twins could have turned out so differentially. They looked so similar and had more-or-less identical upbringings. So how could a set of twin girls take such different paths? Part of the answer lies in the fact that, despite their similar looks, they were actually non-identical (dizygotic) twins. This means that they shared only 50 per cent of their genes by common descent. They were, in effect, sisters from two separate fertilised eggs who happened to share a womb (see Figure 4.2). Hare uses this case to illustrate the extent to which genetic differences can make a huge difference in behaviour between people even from the same family. Despite having almost identical upbringing and sharing the same womb, Ariel made a success of her life, while Alice showed clear signs of psychopathic traits.

BOX 4.4: HERITABILITY OF CHARACTERISTICS AND CONCORDANCE RATES IN TWINS

The estimation of the extent to which a characteristic is passed down from parents to offspring genetically is called its heritability. The Canadian evolutionary psychologists Martin Daly and Margo Wilson defined heritability as "the proportion of the observed phenotypic variance that can be attributed to correlated variance in genotypes" (Daly and Wilson 1983, cited in Workman and Reader 2021, p. 42). In other words, heritability is an estimation of the extent to which a characteristic (phenotype) is due to genetic (genotype) rather than environmental factors. While the concept of heritability has been very useful for farmers to help them breed in ways that will improve their stock, some social scientists have reservations about applying it to human characteristics. If, for example, twin studies suggest a high level of heritability of a psychological condition, then this might be taken to suggest that there is little we can do to ameliorate it. As we have emphasised throughout this chapter, however, both evolutionary psychologists and behavioural geneticists are at pains to emphasise the interactive nature of genes and the environment. Figure 4.3 demonstrates the differences between concordance rates in mono and dizygotic twins (measured from 0.0 to 1.0). Note that for reading disability, the data suggest a high level of heritability, whereas for alcoholism, there is a relatively low level of heritability, especially for women.

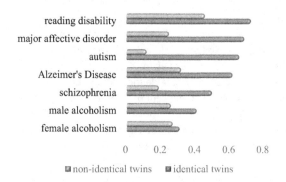

Figure 4.3 Concordance rates for twins on seven different psychological traits. Note white bars represent dizygotic (non-identical) twins and black bars represent monozygotic (identical) twins. (Based on Plomin, DeFries, McClearn and McGuffin 2001)

So much for the brief simple statistics lesson, the question is what do the studies show? Longitudinal twin studies demonstrate that genetic factors have a significant influence on the development of psychopathy, and in particular on the levels of callousness (Viding and McCrory 2018). Despite this, such studies have also shown these genetic risks can be counteracted by protective environmental factors such as where mothers and other family members have provided positive feedback. The downside to this is that harsh parenting increases the probability of such genetic propensities leading to psychopathic traits (Viding, Jones, Paul, Moffitt et al. 2008). Moreover, as we highlighted earlier, the risk of developing psychopathic traits is increased five-fold for first-degree male relatives of psychopaths (Plomin, DeFries, Knopik and Neiderhiser 2016). In summary, in examining a number of studies of personality traits by behavioural geneticists, experts Andrea Glenn and Adrian Raine suggested that genes contribute around 50 per cent of the variance in the development of psychopathy with the environment accounting for the remaining 50 per cent (Glenn and Raine 2014). While this all suggests genes play an important role in psychopathy, at this point it is important to highlight two caveats. First, there are no genes that 'code for' psychopathy. This is because, as in all genetic effects on behaviour, genes work in a probabilistic manner rather than a deterministic one (Viding 2019). Inheriting the genes only increases the chances of developing psychopathy, with the environment (especially the home environment), as we saw earlier on (see Chapter 3), also playing an important contributory role. Second, psychopathy is clearly a **polygenic** condition; that is, multiple genes are involved. Some individuals may have only some of these genes, and others may have more of them.

We will be on safer ground here when we discover which genes are associated with the condition. This leads us to the field of molecular genetics.

Molecular Genetics

Molecular genetics concerns the structure and function of specific identified genes. While this specialist area can be traced right back to the discovery of the structure of DNA by Watson and Crick in the middle of the last century, it is only during the current century that it has made strides in elucidating the relationship between genes and behavioural disorders. With regard to psychopathy, there are two ways in which genes related to this disorder have been investigated – **candidate gene studies** and **genome-wide association studies** (Glenn and Raine 2014; Viding 2019). A candidate gene consists of a single gene that is believed to be implicated in the development of a condition. Each position on a chromosome that alternate genes (alleles) can occupy is called a **locus**. For some loci, only one form of a gene can occur, whereas others can have one of a number of alternate alleles. In this case, the condition is described as **polymorphic**. (Note that polymorphic refers to the existence of more than one possible gene at a specific locus, whereas polygenic refers to a number of separate genes being responsible for a characteristic.) Hence, candidate gene studies determine which alleles of a particular gene are associated with a particular condition. So far, only a small number of candidate studies have considered psychopathy, but they indicate that genes that influence the activity of two hormones/ neurotransmitters, namely, serotonin and oxytocin, can increase the risk of developing psychopathy (Glenn and Raine 2014; Viding 2019). You may well have heard of both of these neurotransmitters as in recent years they have entered the public domain through the media. Broadly speaking, serotonin is an important hormone and neurotransmitter that is involved in feelings of happiness and general well-being, whereas oxytocin is very much the chemical that underlies attachment. People in love have elevated levels of oxytocin and most of us produce this when we look at young babies. In fact, because oxytocin increases when we demonstrate (reciprocated) affection and empathy, it is often referred to as the 'love hormone'. If those who demonstrate psychopathic traits such as callousness do have genes that can lead to abnormal production of serotonin and oxytocin, then this finding makes logical sense and might be seen as a step forward in our understanding of the biological roots of the disorder. As usual, however, when it comes to the biological underpinnings of a behavioural state, these findings are not straightforward. Because candidate gene studies generally only consider single genes, and since most behavioural disorders are polygenic, single genes typically have small effects. In the case of the studies that examined the genes coding for alterations in serotonin and oxytocin production, such genes only account for a small proportion of the variance in the characteristic. It may well be that we need to discover a large number of genes, each of which has a very small effect on behaviour. This is the notion of genes having additive effects on the development of disorders such as psychopathy. Additive effects are where each additional allele contributes to the disorder (Glenn and Raine 2014). This means that the chance of developing a characteristic/disorder increases with each specific gene. In contrast, nonadditive effects mean that alleles configure in a unique way to influence the development of a personality characteristic.

Although candidate studies have helped us to understand the relationship between genes and behaviour, they are limited since, as we have seen, individual genes have only a very small effect on the development of a trait (or technically on the variance of a trait). Genome-wide association studies (GWAS), however, have proved to be a more powerful technique. This is because GWAS involves a rapid scan of the entire genome to establish genetic variations that are associated with specific characteristics (Plomin 2018). Also, because they typically involve very large numbers of participants, they are far more powerful than candidate gene studies. They work by identifying polymorphisms that are more common in groups with specific characteristics/disorders such as schizophrenia or autism. The first GWAS study was performed by Professor of developmental psychopathology Essi Viding and her co-researchers in 2010. It involved children who exhibited psychopathic traits such as callousness and uncovered a common gene in the sample that is involved in brain development. Once again, however, this study only accounted for a small proportion of the variance (less than one per cent; Viding, Hanscombe, Curtis, Davis et al. 2010; Viding, Price, Jaffee, Trzaskowski et al. 2013). Future studies will need to be undertaken with larger samples if more genes are to be identified.

In summary, we can state that candidate gene and genome-wide association studies are beginning to help us understand the genetic underpinnings of psychopathy, but so far, they have only just begun to scratch the surface (Viding 2019). Clearly, while there is substantial evidence that genes account for around 50 per cent of the variance in the development of psychopathy, identifying the specific genes and how they interact with the environment is an ongoing project. For some people, the odds from both genes and life experiences seem to be stacked against them (see Box 4.5).

BOX 4.5: GERALD STANO – DID THE COMBINED EFFECTS OF NATURE AND NURTURE LEAD TO THE DEVELOPMENT OF A SERIAL KILLER?

In 1998, at the age of 46, Gerald Stano was executed at Florida State prison for the murder of nine women. It is almost certain, however, that the actual number of women he killed was around 42 (Flowers 1993; Toates and Coschug-Toates 2022). His methods of killing varied from shooting and stabbing to strangulation. How might we explain this repeatedly cruel and callous homicidal behaviour? This may well be a good example of having a lethal combination of a neglectful upbringing and inherited factors. Stano was born (as Paul Zeininger) in New York in 1951, the fifth child of an alcoholic sex worker mother. At six and a half months, he was given up for adoption. His adoptive mother, Norma Stano (whose name he took), described him as having been neglected both physically and emotionally (Toates and Coschug-Toates 2022). By five years of age, he was already displaying serious antisocial behaviour including regularly biting other children. When asked to describe a happy event from his childhood, Stano recalled enjoying strangling a chicken. As a teenager, Stano experimented with alcohol and drugs, regularly stealing to support these habits. He began his murderous behaviour around the age of 18 or 19, and by the time he married at the age of 24, he had already killed several women. This was generally achieved by enticing them into his car using money or marijuana. According to Toates and Coschug-Toates (2022), his killings often followed failed attempts to induce such women to have sex with him. Stano's marriage did not last long as his wife left him following abusive behaviour including one occasion when he attempted to strangle her. His negative experiences with women (including his own mother) appear to have played a part in his increasingly misogynistic and aggressive behaviour towards women. This was, in part, associated with discovering that his biological mother had been a prostitute. According to Flowers, when asked if he had killed a certain woman, he replied: "She was a whore. I gave her just what she deserved. Damn right I killed her" (Flower 1993, p. 67). While little is known about his biological mother (and less still about his father who had nothing to do with Stano), it is known that all of her children were eventually removed for adoption and that she engaged in criminal activity. You may recall from earlier on in the chapter, when we considered life history theory, that individuals who are raised by uncaring parents are more likely to grow up to be callous and exploitative. In the case of Gerald Stano, it seems likely that the dice were loaded against him both from the nature and the nurture sides of his development.

NEUROBIOLOGICAL FINDINGS

During the 21st century, great strides have been made in the field of neuroscience. One reason for this is the rapid technological advancements in neuroimaging techniques. Whereas 20th-century biological psychologists used to speculate about what is actually going on in the human brain *via* indirect evidence, in recent years they have been able to see areas involved in processing specific input and output. While the neurobiological study of psychopathy, as with genetics, has been somewhat of a latecomer to the party, during the last 15 years, imaging techniques have led to two main hypotheses to account for psychopathy. These are the **paralimbic cortex** and the **integrated emotion system** hypotheses. They are both the products of very specialised research; here, we provide a brief synopsis of each. Those wishing to develop a more specialist understanding are guided to a review by Blair, Meffert, Hwang and White (2018).

The paralimbic hypothesis proposes that a group of specialised interconnected areas of the cerebral cortex known collectively as the paralimbic cortex, which are normally involved in emotional processing and self-control, are disrupted in psychopathy (Blair, Mefert, Hwang and White 2018; Kiehl 2006). The paralimbic system is positioned next to, and connected with, the limbic system that deals with processing primary emotions. Hence, it is believed to play an important role in modifying emotional responses and self-control. The paralimbic cortex includes, for example, parts of the temporal and frontal cortex and parts of the amygdala (confusingly parts of the amygdala are also within the limbic system). The paralimbic hypothesis suggests that abnormalities in cortical areas within this are related to psychopathy and antisocial behaviour.

Evidence to support this model is based on MRI scanning studies (see Figure 4.4) that have uncovered anomalies in the structures of the amygdala and the ventromedial frontal cortex. Moreover, reductions in the temporal cortex have been uncovered both for youths and adults classified as psychopathic (Blair, Mefert, Hwang and White 2018).

The integrated emotion system hypothesis is somewhat different from, and arguably more complex than, the paralimbic cortex hypothesis. Whereas the latter emphasises problems with the paralimbic cortex, the former concentrates on various 'dimensions of functioning' (Blair, Mefert, Hwang and White 2018). These dimensions include empathy, inappropriate response to threat and response control. In order to get to grips with the integrated emotion system hypothesis, it is important to outline the difference between two forms of empathy – cognitive and affective (see Chapter 6). Cognitive empathy involves forming internal representations of the thoughts and intentions of others. In contrast, affective

Figure 4.4 MRI (magnetic resonance imaging) scanner seen through the window of the control room. This imaging technique uses a strong magnetic field and radio waves to create detailed computer-generated images of internal organs including the brain. Note that the clinicians are able to see in fine detail the structure of the brain. Some studies indicate that those with psychopathy (and/or antisocial personality disorder) have been observed to have abnormalities in brain areas such as the limbic and paralimbic systems.

(emotional) empathy runs deeper in as much as it involves feeling the emotions of another, observed person. This is achieved by picking up on emotional cues given off by the other person, a process that involves a number of brain areas, but for which the amygdala plays a prominent role. (Note that other areas are also involved such as the hippocampus which works in conjunction with the amygdala and is important in processing emotional memories.) According to the integrated emotion system hypothesis, due to impairments in the amygdala, the affective empathy component does not function correctly in psychopaths. This impairment is quite specific to certain emotional states. They have, for example, normal recognition of facial expressions of disgust and anger, but show impairments in the recognition of sadness, fear and happiness (Marsh and Blair 2008). This might help us to understand why people who are psychopathic often behave in such a callous, uncaring manner with regard to emotional responses. Moreover, due to this inability to process emotional responses appropriately, they may also be prone to perceiving acute threat when this is not actually the intention of the other person. Hence, this helps to explain their inappropriate response to threat and response control.

Another part of the integrated emotion system hypothesis suggests that the amygdala is crucial for various forms of reinforcement-based learning. As we develop, most of us find positive social feedback as a form of reinforcement-based learning in that, for example, praise and a smiling parent or peer are positively reinforcing. For the vast majority of children, distress cues, such as expressions of sadness and fear in others, rapidly become perceived as aversive. By the same measure, happy expressions come to be regarded as rewarding. Work on fMRI (the form of MRI which demonstrates moment-by-moment brain activity rather than just structure) has shown that the amygdala is heavily involved in processing cues indicating all of these emotions. Yet for individuals with psychopathic traits, there is reduced activity in the amygdala when presented with, for example, fearful expressions. Hence, according to the integrated emotion system hypothesis, individuals who become psychopathic are those for whom the amygdala (and other brain regions) did not develop correctly (Blair, Mefert, Hwang and White 2018). In a sense, they do not develop the hardware or the software that allows them to share another's emotional states.

Observations Following Acquired Brain Injury

Findings from both the paralimbic cortex and the integrated emotion system hypotheses raise, the eternal question, how did such
neurological deficits arise? Having read this far you will not be
surprised to learn that most theorists consider this to be due to
the double whammy of an inappropriate parenting style and an
unfortunate combination of genes. (Note that in either case, there
is always a great temptation to 'blame the parents'.) Interestingly,
in addition to the above findings from neurobiology, a great deal
of insight has been gained from studies of non-psychopathic individuals whose behaviour has changed, sometimes quite rapidly and
dramatically. Here, we enter the realm of acquired brain injury. Adri-
ane Raine and his co-researchers have spent many years gathering
together studies of individuals who have incurred damage to specific areas of the brain and whose behaviour has then begun to
overlap with that of psychopaths (see, for example, Yang and Raine,
2018). Based on the work of Mendez (2010), Glenn and Raine
(2014) described a case where, over a four-year period, a previously law-abiding 60-year-old man started to molest children. They
also describe a case of a woman in her 50s who, over an 18-month
period, became increasingly callous, mood variable and dishonest
(including engaging in shoplifting). In both of these cases, it was
eventually determined that there had been progressive frontotemporal dementia, that is, a condition following damage to areas of the
frontal and temporal cortex, which includes changes in cognition
and personality (see Figure 4.5).

In both of the cases of frontotemporal dementia described by
Glenn and Raine, the patients shifted substantially from well-
balanced and reasonable responses to thoughtless and uncaring
behaviour. From these and other similar case studies, neuropsychol-
ogists have suggested that those with psychopathic traits are likely
to have deficits in the same brain regions. Hence, in addition to
the areas identified by MRI scans, acquired brain injury through
dementia also suggests that parts of the frontal and temporal cortex
may be disrupted in psychopathy.

As we can see, there is growing evidence that psychopathic
individuals have abnormal structure and function in various brain
areas including the amygdala and various areas of the frontal and

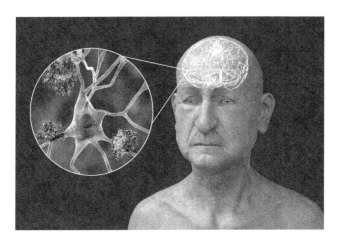

Figure 4.5 Diagram to illustrate frontotemporal dementia (also known as Pick's disease). In this condition, there is progressive damage due to the build-up of amyloid plaques (as illustrated in the expanded circle) which destroy neuronal networks. Incidentally, this is the form of dementia that the film star Bruce Willis has recently been diagnosed with.

temporal cortex. There is also evidence for the involvement of genes in the disorder. One way of connecting genes to brain functioning is *via* hormonal release and action. That is, genes are largely responsible for the production of hormones, and their release is largely controlled by (and affect) specific brain regions. (Note that in both cases, the environment also has an important input into the system.)

HORMONAL FACTORS

Hormones are chemical messengers released by the endocrine glands into the bloodstream, which then travel to and affect the response of target organs (see Figure 4.6). One of the main target organs is the brain. Hence, many hormones are known to influence our internal state and behaviour. Two hormones that have been implicated in psychopathy are testosterone and cortisol (Glenn and Raine 2014; Viding and Kimonis 2018). Although it is somewhat of a simplification, in some sense we can think of these two chemical messengers as acting in opposite ways. Increases in testosterone are associated with dominance and success in competition for men. In contrast, cortisol is known to increase in men who have lost in sporting competition with other men (Jimenez, Aguilar and Alvero-Cruz 2012). (Interestingly, it is worth noting that this pattern of increased testosterone following a sporting win and increased cortisol following a loss is also observed in women, albeit to a lesser extent.) Hence, while testosterone, which is released by the testicles and the adrenal glands, is associated with aggression and dominance, cortisol (also released by the adrenal glands) is involved in fear and withdrawal responses. For this reason, cortisol is often referred to as

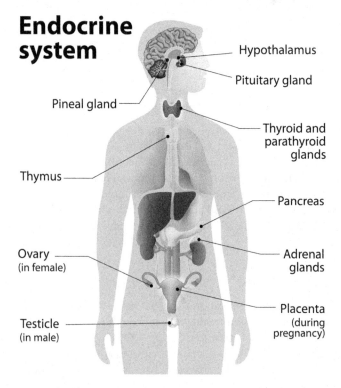

Figure 4.6 The human endocrine system illustrating all of the endocrine glands for both men and women

the 'stress hormone'. It does this by stimulating areas of the brain including the amygdala and parts of the prefrontal cortex to prepare the body for 'flight-or-fight'. Likewise, testosterone release also modifies the activity of the amygdala and the prefrontal cortex. In this case, however, high levels are associated with confidence and competitiveness. Because of this relationship, biological psychologists have hypothesised that people with psychopathic traits might have abnormally high levels of testosterone and abnormally low levels of cortisol (Glenn and Raine 2014). Broadly speaking, this hypothesis has some empirical support (Viding and Kimonis 2018). Of course, the term 'broadly speaking' suggests that, as in many biologically based explanations, there are caveats in this explanation.

While some studies have found a clear relationship between low levels of circulating cortisol and CU (callous-unemotional) aspects of psychopathy, others have failed to replicate this finding (Viding and Kimonis 2018). Similarly, while some suggest a relationship between elevated levels of testosterone and psychopathic traits, this is not true of all studies in this area (Glenn and Raine 2014). One solution to such mixed findings is to suggest that we need to consider the balance of cortisol and testosterone together. In fact, given that each has an effect on the amygdala, it may well be that it is the ratio of these two hormones which is unbalanced in people with psychopathic traits rather than looking at absolute levels (Glenn and Raine 2014; Terburg, Morgan and Van Honk 2009). To complicate matters further, there is some evidence that elevated levels of another sex hormone, which is a precursor to androgen, dehydroepiandrosterone (DHEA), are also implicated in psychopathy. Johnson, Dismukes, Viacco, Briesman et al. (2014) found that juveniles who demonstrate psychopathic traits had abnormal ratios of cortisol and DHEA (see also Kamin and Kertes 2017).

Hence, while there is evidence that abnormal hormonal balances are implicated in male psychopathy, the precise nature of this relationship is an area that requires further research. Moreover, as with biological explanations of behaviour in general, it is often difficult to disentangle cause and effect. Do abnormal ratios of various hormones such as cortisol, testosterone and DHEA lead to psychopathic behaviour or does psychopathic behaviour lead to abnormal levels of these chemicals? One way to study this is to examine changes in behaviour following alterations in hormone levels in non-psychopathic individuals. While it would be unethical to manipulate hormone levels for experimental purposes, it is known that athletes who make use of synthetic androgens to enhance performance also experience a lowered threshold for aggressive response (Chegeni, Pallesen and Sagoe 2021). Furthermore, girls who were exposed to prenatally high levels of androgens show increased levels of rough-and-tumble play compared with other girls (Verona and Vitale 2018). (Note this does not, of course, mean that they are any more likely to develop psychopathic traits in later life.) In fact, biopsychologists in general contend that one reason males are more physically aggressive than females is due, in part, to their substantially higher levels of circulating testosterone (Giammanco, Tabacchi, Giammanco, Di Majo et al. 2005).

As we pointed out earlier, it is somewhat artificial to partition out genes, hormones and neurobiological factors when attempting to understand the biological foundations of psychopathy. As we have seen, hormones have direct effects on parts of the brain, while genes are involved both in the development of the brain and in the production of hormones. We have discussed them separately in order to make them more digestible. It is important to realise, however, that a comprehensive explanation of the biological bases of psychopathy will inevitably involve a synthesis of all of these factors. Moreover, proximate biological explanations are only a part of the story. A fuller explanation will no doubt involve the integration of evolutionary, developmental and social factors.

SUMMARY

There are two separate but related approaches to understanding the biological bases of psychopathy. First, we can consider the ultimate evolutionary factors which maintain the condition within our species. Second, we can consider the proximate biological causes such as genetic, hormonal and neurological factors. Evolutionary psychologists view psychopathy as an adaptation that, under the appropriate conditions, may have helped our ancestors to pass their genes on successfully. This is supported by the finding that men with psychopathic traits are frequently successful in impregnating women. Life history theory has been developed by evolutionists to explain why people (and other species) shift their reproductive strategies to suit their environment. Under harsh rearing conditions, individuals may adopt a 'fast life history', reproducing at an early age and investing less in each individual offspring. Some experts have suggested this is the strategy adopted by psychopathic individuals. Frequency-dependent selection suggests that, when everybody else adopts a strategy, it may pay a minority of individuals to adopt an entirely different one. This has been applied to psychopathy. In this case, the suggestion is that, while the vast majority of humans gravitate towards reciprocal altruism, this allows for the evolution of freeriders (such as psychopaths) who reap the benefit without paying the cost. There is clear evidence that genes are involved in the development of psychopathy. Through their studies of twins, behavioural geneticists have estimated that psychopathy has a heritability of around 50 per cent. Molecular geneticists have attempted to identify which genes are implicated in the development of the condition. Both candidate gene studies and genome-wide association studies have been used to help identify such genes. Thus far, the genes identified have only accounted for a relatively small amount of variation in the condition. Neurobiological studies that have made use of MRI (and fMRI) scanning techniques suggest there are problems associated with both the function and the structure of various brain areas including the amygdala and specific areas of the cerebral cortex. Such studies suggest that psychopathic individuals may have an intact cognitive empathy processing system but an impaired affective (emotional) empathy processing system. Those with specific acquired brain injury, who may then develop abnormal moral behaviour, support the notion that psychopathy involves neurological problems. Abnormal levels of circulating hormones have been implicated in the development of psychopathy. In particular, there is evidence that the balance between testosterone (the 'hormone of dominance' in men) and cortisol (the 'stress hormone') is different in people with the condition. Abnormal levels of the precursor to testosterone, dehydroepiandrosterone (DHEA), have also been implicated in the development of psychopathy.

FURTHER READING

Glenn, A.L. and Raine, A. (2014). *Psychopathy: An introduction to biological findings and their implications*. New York: New York University Press.

Plomin, R. (2018). *Blueprint: How DNA makes us who we are*. London: Allen Lane/Penguin Books.

Reader, W. and Workman, L. (2023). *Evolutionary psychology: The basics*. Abingdon: Routledge.

Taylor, S. (2015). *Crime and criminality: A multidisciplinary approach*. Abingdon: Routledge.

EXPLANATIONS
PERSONALITY–PSYCHOPATHY INTERACTION

We often conceive of the psychopath as a 'psycho', 'criminal' or 'serial killer', but is this a fair description of who they are? As we have seen in Chapter 1, psychopathy lies not on a criminological but rather a personality dimension. The traits typifying psychopathy are more extreme than those describing antisocial personality disorder (ASPD). This is one reason why psychopathy is considered a sub-set of ASPD. In order to understand how the personality of psychopaths differs from individuals with ASPD, other personality disorders and the general population, it is important to be familiar with the different theoretical approaches to personality. It is through understanding personality and how it is assessed (see Chapter 2) that we can appreciate the extent to which the personality of psychopaths deviates from non-psychopaths. There have been many approaches to understanding personality over the years, but an influential division has been the person-situation debate. In the case of the person aspect of the debate, an individual's behaviour can be perceived as being a consequence of personality traits that are consistent across diverse situations. Alternatively, those supporting the importance of the situation would argue that our behaviour is not entirely governed by our traits. Situationists advocate that different situations will have inherent characteristics which moderate our behaviour accordingly. Using foul-mouthed language might be something accepted among like-minded friends at the local pub, but at one's grandmother's birthday party in a care home, this use of language would be toned down. Hence, the characteristics of the situation act to dictate what is appropriate behaviour, regardless of one's traits. In this chapter, we will explore the concept of personality by using the

DOI: 10.4324/9781032221052-5

person–situation division as a guideline. In order to understand the relationship between personality and psychopathy, we first need to have an understanding of how the concept of personality has been developed by psychologists interested in individual differences. First, however, we will address the status of psychopathy in DSM-5.

STATUS OF PSYCHOPATHY IN DSM-5

As stated in Chapter 1, psychopathy is placed as an extension of ASPD (DSM-5 2013). According to the American Psychological Association, psychopaths have extreme traits to those seen in individuals diagnosed with ASPD, traits such as a disregard for and violation of other people's rights. There is considerable overlap between ASPD and psychopathy traits such as the seven key characteristics discussed in Chapter 1. To be considered as having psychopathy, DSM-5 has added the provisor of additional features such as a lack of fear and anxiety, as well as the need for extreme attention seeking. If a clinician follows DSM-5 when making a diagnosis of psychopathy, the individual concerned is first identified as having ASPD. This implies that psychopathy is a sub-division of ASPD. DSM-5 classifies ASPD as a personality disorder under Cluster B. ASPD is a **superordinate personality type** where other personality disorders can be located. This means that an individual with ASPD can also show a cluster of narcissistic traits for example. An individual diagnosed with ASPD could exhibit narcissistic traits, therefore classifying them as an individual who has a narcissistic antisocial personality disposition. Narcissism is not the only personality disorder that can be considered as part of this superordinate personality type. Other personality disorders such as borderline and histrionic can also be part of ASPD. As discussed in Chapter 1, there are researchers, academics and clinicians who perceive psychopathy as being distinct from ASPD. As we have seen, Yildirim and Derksen (2013) demonstrated how the neurobiological and developmental characteristics differ across ASPD, psychopathy and sociopathy. This is a contentious area, and some argue that sociopathy does not exist (see Chapter 1). When considering DSM-5 and the views of other eminent experts on psychopathy such as Robert Hare, it becomes apparent that there is robust support for the overlap between ASPD and psychopathy. Mainstream personality theories have enlightened our understanding of psychopathy and ASPD. We will explore these in the context of the **person–situation debate**.

PERSON-SITUATION DEBATE

Furr and Funder (2021) revisited the debate of whether a person's traits or the situations they find themselves in will have more of an impact on their behaviour. They argued, however, that we should be focusing on a person–situation interaction instead of a person–situation competition approach to understanding why we behave as we do. For many years, there have been two perspectives. One perspective is that our personality traits determine how we behave regardless of the different types of situations we might find ourselves in. The other perspective downplays the importance of personality traits *per se* and instead advocates that the situations we might find ourselves in have, in their own right, characteristics influencing how we behave. Therefore, the traits we possess do not induce us to behave consistently across different situations. If we accept the view that situations strongly influence personality, then aspects of the situation predict how we behave. This view depreciates the argument that personality traits are inflexible and resistant to the situational forces influencing our behaviour. For example, if you are normally a shy person when interacting face-to-face with a group of strangers, giving a talk where you are far removed from your audience might be less of an ordeal. The situational dynamics are different because there is no face-to-face interaction, and you might be distanced further by being on a platform behind a lectern. Hence, the issue of being shy is outweighed by the characteristics of the situation. At the heart of the person–situation debate is the issue of consistency, and whether this consistency is proof of the existence of our personality being trait driven. Consistency can be construed in two ways. First, stability refers to a person expressing the same trait characteristics over time. Second, the expression of traits across different situations remains somewhat similar. Trait theorists would argue that you cannot map a specific trait to a specific situation but rather the trait maps on to a class of behaviours expressed across many situations. According to Epstein (1983):

> ...strong evidence for the existence of broad, cross-situational dispositions or traits...there is enough cross-situational stability in behaviour to allow one meaningfully to refer to personality attributes without having to specify the situations in which they occur. Such a conclusion does not deny that situational factors...influence...behaviour.

(p. 112)

This does not, however, address the extent to how consistently or differently people vary across various situations – simply because the limiting factor to researching this is the number of situations explored and their diversity.

Nevertheless, trait approaches to understanding personality have prevailed over the years. As we have seen in Chapters 1 and 2, Cleckley (1941a) described the psychopath using a trait approach, and Karpman as early as 1941 even introduced traits for the two distinct variants of psychopathy – primary and secondary. Hence, the use of traits to describe psychopathic behavioural expression is not new. The five trait approaches that have made a contribution towards our understanding of personality *per se* but also to how psychopaths deviate from the norm are:

- Hierarchical model of personality (Hans Eysenck)
- The five-factor model, FFM (Robert McCrae and Paul Costa)
- The three-factor model (David Cooke and Christine Michie)
- The dark triad of personality (Delroy Paulhus and Kevin Williams)
- The dark tetrad of personality (Erin Buckels, Daniel Jones and Delroy Paulhus)

We will consider these trait approaches followed by the situational approach of Walter Mischel.

TRAIT APPROACHES

Hans Eysenck: Hierarchical Model of Personality

Eysenck (1970) developed a hierarchical model of personality (see Figure 5.1) by observing how people behaved in set situations such as talking to friends in a bar. He observed specific responses such as being the main speaker among the group of friends. If the individual's response was consistent throughout the evening, then this would provide evidence of how the person typically behaves in this situation. This he referred to as habitual responses. A profile of the individual's behaviour across other situations demonstrated that such a person who likes to talk in social situations is likely also to be sociable and amenable to interacting with other people. Hence, they are likely to have the trait of sociability. Sociability, therefore,

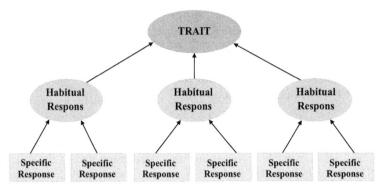

Figure 5.1 Hierarchical structure of Eysenck's model of personality

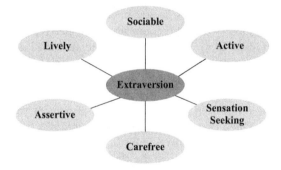

Figure 5.2 Trait examples of extraversion

describes an individual who is inclined to seek the companionship of others and engage in a friendly, pleasant social exchange.

In the case of extraversion, there are a number of traits that co-occur including sociability (see Figure 5.2). According to John, Naumann and Soto (2008), "Extraversion implies an energetic approach toward the social and material world and includes traits such as sociability, activity, assertiveness, and positive emotionality" (p. 120).

Using factor analysis (a statistical procedure that identifies linkage across different traits), Eysenck was able to establish which traits are highly correlated together. Moreover, these highly correlated traits were consistent across different individuals. These correlated traits enabled Eysenck to establish a **super trait** (i.e., factor) or a personality type. Eysenck identified three super traits:

1. **Extraversion–Introversion**
2. **Neuroticism–Emotional stability**
3. **Psychoticism–Self-control**

In the example of sociability, it would be gauged along a continuum of extraversion to introversion. An individual who is extremely sociable and talkative would score towards the extraversion end of the scale. An individual who enjoys his or her own company is likely to score towards the introvert end of the continuum. Individuals scoring high on the super trait of neuroticism possess traits indicative of emotional instability by exhibiting disproportionately high levels of anxiety, irrationalism, depression, low self-esteem, moodiness or fear for instance. In contrast, those who are emotionally stable are well balanced and less emotionally labile. Such individuals are described as stable. Of relevance to our discussion of psychopathy is the third super trait, psychoticism, introduced by Eysenck in 1952 to account for individuals seemingly without conscience or remorse (see Box 5.1).

Eysenck introduced a measuring tool known as the Eysenck Personality Questionnaire (EPQ). This consisted of a series of statements about how one behaves and reacts under specific conditions. These statements arose under the three super traits, such that if a person answered 'yes' to statements considered to demonstrate high sociability, then a high score towards the extraversion end of the continuum would be obtained. Similarly, statements indicative of high neuroticism and psychoticism would have been answered positively. Hence, Eysenck concluded that individuals' scores indicated a predisposition towards reacting and behaving in specific ways. These propensities were more likely to occur under adverse circumstances. These three super traits have cross-cultural validity.

BOX 5.1: PSYCHOPATHS TYPIFY THE THIRD SUPER TRAIT

Eysenck introduced a third super trait to describe individuals who exhibited a set of highly correlated traits suggestive of a personality that was significantly negative and devoid of a conscience. This super trait was called psychoticism. Traits associated with psychoticism include aggressive, impulsive, cold, egocentric, impersonal, tough-minded, un-empathic, creative and antisocial. Interestingly, Eysenck found that individuals who scored high on psychoticism tended to reside in prison. Being particularly cruel, insensitive, inhumane and hostile towards others differentiated these individuals from those scoring high on neuroticism. Eysenck referred to such individuals as psychopaths and considered their behaviour exhibited the most psychopathology. Boeree (1998) concurred that those scoring higher than average on the psychoticism super trait tended to be reckless, exhibit inappropriate emotional responses and have an outright disregard for common sense. Interestingly, Heath and Martin (1990) claimed that psychoticism "is conceptualized as a continuum of liability to psychosis (principally schizophrenia and bipolar affective disorder) with 'psychopathy' (i.e., antisocial behavior) defined as 'a halfway stage towards psychosis'" (p. 111). Moreover, psychoticism is significantly associated with scales of hostility, tough-mindedness, immaturity, refutability of cultural norms and attitudes in opposition to authority. Hence, the higher the score on the psychoticism scale, the more likely that the individual is a psychopath and overlaps with the criminal world. There have been numerous studies supporting Eysenck's contention that the higher the psychoticism, the less likely the individual will hold pro-authority attitudes. For example, Rigby and Slee (1987) found that children who score high on psychoticism held anti-authority values. Children who bullied other children were higher in psychoticism (Slee and Rigby 1993). Romero, Luengo and Sobral (2001) found that delinquent children scored higher than average on psychoticism. Psychoticism also correlates highly with conduct problems and antisocial personality disorder (ASPD). Eysenck posited that individuals high on extraversion could also be at risk of exhibiting impulsive and antisocial behaviour as a consequence of having low levels of arousal and the need for excitement. The contribution of extraversion to delinquent, psychopathic and antisocial behaviour has had mixed reviews. Some studies find a relationship, whereas other studies do not. The contribution of psychoticism to psychopathy, however, has much support. Eysenck also stated that psychopaths can be creative as a consequence of having traits such as egocentrism and tough-mindedness. These traits enable such individuals to focus solely on the pursuit of their desired choice of career or achievement. Not every researcher in the area agrees with this contention, however.

Robert McCrae and Paul Costa: The Five-Factor Model

The **five–factor model (FFM)** of McCrae and Costa (1987) is popularly known as the 'Big Five', simply because there are five discrete factors: openness, conscientiousness, extraversion, agreeableness and neuroticism. The first letter of each factor spells out the word OCEAN. These factors were derived using factor analysis where participants' responses from two personality questionnaires were imputed and analysed for mutually exclusive clusters of traits. Five such clusters were formed, and from this, the Big Five came to life.

These factors are on a continuum where individuals can score anywhere between:

- Openness to experience – Closedness to experience
- Conscientiousness – Unconscientiousness
- Extraversion – Introversion
- Agreeableness – Antagonism
- Neuroticism – Emotional stability

Openness depicts characteristics such as insight and imagination (Power and Pluess 2015). Individuals who score high on openness have traits that drive creativity and tendencies towards being curious, eager to learn, adventurous and wanting to engage in new experiences. At the other extreme of this factor, people who score low tend to be set in their ways and resist engaging with new ideas, new experiences and theoretical concepts. **Conscientiousness**, according to Power and Pluess, involves traits of thoughtfulness, impulse control and goal-directed behaviours. Those who score high on this factor tend to be mindful of others and how their behaviours impact on those around them. They are organised and demonstrate good planning skills with an eye for detail and accomplishing immediate tasks and deadlines successfully. Alternatively, those who are low scorers fail to accomplish tasks successfully, dislike structure and working to schedules, are thoughtless towards others and fail to take care of things and return belongings. As discussed earlier, extraversion is characterised by traits of sociability, excitability, assertiveness and emotional expressiveness. High scorers enjoy the limelight and crave being with other people, being the centre of attention and talking to others. Being surrounded by other people helps to energise them. The downside is they sometimes speak before thinking. Introverts, however, enjoy their own company, find it difficult to initiate conversation and often avoid socialising and being in the limelight. **Agreeableness** encompasses traits such as kindness, trust, altruism and prosocial behaviours. High scorers tend to be cooperators who have genuine concern and empathy for others. They will help those in need and enjoy making others happy. The opposite is true of low scorers who show limited interest in other people and their problems, and instead of caring about how people feel, they will insult, belittle and manipulate people to serve their own purposes. In the case of **neuroticism**, those who score high on this factor demonstrate emotional instability. This means they tend to experience high levels of stress and show generalised anxiety that makes them worry and get upset very easily often over nothing. They exhibit extreme shifts of mood and demonstrate an inability to recover from stressful events. Alternatively, low scorers are emotionally stable and cope well with stressful events, often showing a relaxed composure.

David Buss argued that these personality factors have biological origins and are important for shaping our social landscape. Twin studies, however, have found both a nature and nurture component to the five factors (Jang, Livesley and Vernon 1996). Although these factors tend to be stable over time, research findings suggest that both agreeableness and conscientiousness increase as people age. Miller, Pilkonis and Morse (2004) acknowledged the usefulness of the FFM for examining the presentation of personality traits in problem personalities such as psychopathy. It was, however, Widiger and Lynam (1998) who transliterated traits of the PCL-R (see Chapter 2) to the neuroticism, extraversion and openness factors of the FFM known as the NEO-PI (Costa and McCrae 1992). They concluded that the traits inherent in the PCL-R map on to one or more facets of the NEO-PI. Facets in this context, for example, refer to the traits anxiety, depression and anger proneness that comprise the factor of neuroticism. Widiger and Lynam found results describing the typical psychopath where scores for agreeableness and conscientiousness were low. There were mixed findings for the traits of the neuroticism and extraversion factors. Their findings are supported by numerous studies showing how low scores on agreeableness and conscientiousness encapsulate the typical traits of psychopaths (Miller, Lynam, Widiger and Leukefeld

2001). Moreover, some researchers such as Miller, Lynam, Widiger and Leukefeld (2001) claimed that these results summarise the core personality of the psychopath and provide a good marker for the identification of such individuals.

Ghaderi, Amirsardari and Agashteh (2019) demonstrated that psychopathy in male prisoners can be predicted by low scores on agreeableness and conscientiousness (see Figure 5.3).

Interestingly, however, low scores on agreeableness were the only factor predicting psychopathy in female prisoners (see Figure 5.4). Hence, in the case of agreeableness, the low scores on this factor would see both male and female imprisoned psychopaths as exhibiting traits of callousness and manipulation. In the case of conscientiousness, where the psychopathic male prisoners scored significantly low, their female counterparts did not. As a rule, research on female psychopaths has received limited attention in comparison to their male counterparts. This means that there is little research done to explain why there were differences between the male and female imprisoned psychopaths. Even so, Ghaderi et al. suggested that the reason for these differences can be traced back to Costa and McCrae (1992) showing a general gender difference in scores across all five factors of the FFM. According to Costa and McCrae, females tend to have a higher level of conscientiousness than males. This it would seem, astonishingly, is also a characteristic of female psychopaths. Ghaderi et al. conducted their research in Iran and speculated that some of the differences they found between male and female psychopaths could be a characteristic of cultural differences. For example, they stated that, "…the reason behind

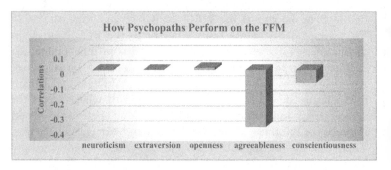

Figure 5.3 Correlations of the five factors for male psychopaths in prison

women's imprisonment in our society is the irresponsibility of their husbands and not their own. Thus, if husbands act responsible, it is less likely that their spouses are imprisoned…most responsibilities are assumed by men" (p. 6).

The PCL-R Factors 1 and 2 have been used to differentiate between primary and secondary psychopaths. These factors have been explored in relation to the FFM and the Psychopathic Personality Inventory (PPI; see Chapter 2 and Box 5.2). The two-factor model of primary and secondary psychopathy continues to be widely accepted (Sellbom and Drislane 2021). The emotional detachment seen in primary psychopaths prevents them from experiencing deeper affect and forming meaningful relationships. While Takamatsu and Takai (2019) described primary psychopaths in this way, they highlighted the impulsiveness, emotional disturbance and antisocial lifestyles of secondary psychopaths. We can often differentiate the primary and secondary psychopaths among delinquent and criminal pairings (see Box 5.3).

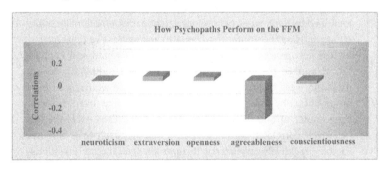

Figure 5.4 Correlations of the five factors for female psychopaths in prison

BOX 5.2: FACTORS 1 AND 2, AND THE FFM FOR PRIMARY AND SECONDARY PSYCHOPATHS

Primary psychopaths are characterised as callous, charming, narcissistic and manipulative, and typically, they show no emotional and anxious expression. This is in contrast with secondary psychopaths who tend to express emotion and anxiety. They are also impulsive, aggressive and narcissistic. The PCL-R can differentiate between these two types of psychopaths *via* Factors 1 and 2 (Hare 2003). Factor 1 is associated with low levels of anxiety (Marcus, Fulton and Edens 2013) unlike Factor 2. Whereas primary psychopaths tend to be of positive mood and show low levels of anxiety and inhibition, secondary psychopaths are the opposite in that they are anxious and hostile and express anger using aggression. But is there a relationship between the two types of psychopaths and the FFM? Interestingly, Ross, Lutz and Bailley (2004) demonstrated that Factor 1 produced a negative correlation with agreeableness (excluding tendermindedness) and Factor 2 produced a negative correlation with agreeableness (excluding modesty) and conscientiousness. Others have found that Factor 1 produced a negative correlation with neuroticism and Factor 2 produced a positive correlation with neuroticism. Also, Factor 1 produced a positive correlation with extraversion and openness and Factor 2 produced a negative correlation with extraversion. Hicks, Vaidyanathan and Patrick (2010) identified two sub-types of criminal psychopaths: emotionally stable (characterising the primary psychopath) and aggressive (characterising the secondary psychopath). Falkenbach, Reinhard and Zappala (2021) applied the NEO-PI-R to a non-criminal sample of individuals who were divided into two cohorts – those who scored high on psychopathy using the Psychopathic Personality Inventory (PPI; see Chapter 2) and the remaining participants. Factor 1 of the PPI negatively correlated with neuroticism and agreeableness, whereas Factor 2 negatively correlated with agreeableness and conscientiousness. A statistical procedure called cluster analysis pooled traits that occurred together. Falkenbach et al. found two distinct cluster patterns: primary and secondary. In the case of the primary cluster, individuals exhibited low neuroticism and agreeableness, slightly increased levels of conscientiousness and openness, but high levels of psychopathy, extraversion and narcissism. Individuals in the secondary cluster were high on neuroticism and aggression but low on agreeableness, conscientiousness, openness and extraversion. Falkenbach et al. made an interesting observation from their findings. They highlighted how some primary psychopaths can be more successful than others as a consequence of having higher levels of

conscientiousness (competence and the motivation to achieve coupled with glibness and planning from Factor 1 of the PPI), openness
and extraversion. There are many psychopaths who are considered
to be successful in different walks of life (see Chapter 8).

BOX 5.3: GWENDOLYN GRAHAM AND CATHERINE MAY WOOD: AN EXAMPLE OF A PRIMARY AND SECONDARY PSYCHOPATHIC COUPLING?

Graham and Wood became known as 'The Lethal Lovers' after falling in love and murdering five elderly women who suffered from
Alzheimer's disease. They met in 1986 while working at a nursing
home and became romantically involved. They wrote letters to each
other, writing "I love you forever and X days". It was later revealed
that the 'X' referred to the number of elderly women they had murdered. Eventually Wood provided an account of the first murder,
claiming that Graham had smothered an elderly woman. Four more
women were murdered using the same *modus operandi* over the next
few months. Graham and Wood broke off their romantic liaison, and
the pair would have evoked no suspicion over the deaths at the home
had Wood's most recent ex-husband not repeated to the police what
he was told about how they were murdered. When interrogated by
the police both Wood and Graham played prisoners' dilemma by
blaming the other for instigating the crimes. Wood claimed to be
merely the lookout, while Graham had masterminded all the crimes.
Graham, however, claimed she was coerced, controlled and manipulated into being the accomplice. According to Lowell Cauffiel (1992)
in his book *Forever and Five Days*, Wood is a manipulative psychopath
who masterminded the murders. Wood was also so convincing that
she manipulated the courts into believing that Graham was the real
perpetrator. In Cauffiel's analysis, he concluded from the evidence
that Wood planned all the murders and manipulated Graham. The
motivation for doing this was to ensure that Graham would remain
romantically involved with her. Graham left her, nevertheless. Wood

took her revenge by reporting Graham to the police as the planner of all the murders. If Cauffiel's analysis of the available evidence is correct, then it would appear that Wood exhibits the traits of a primary psychopath – manipulative, antisocial and vindictive. Graham, however, is not innocent in all this and confessed to her latest girlfriend all the murders. If we take a closer look at Wood's background, it becomes apparent that she came from an abusive home, so she married in 1979 at 17 years of age and had a baby soon after. She ignored her baby daughter and became withdrawn. Her husband suggested she find a job which she did at the Alpine Manor nursing home in Michigan, US. It was there that she met a group of lesbians, one of whom was Graham. The other women regarded Wood as a pathological liar who would manipulate people and intentionally cause conflict among the group and considered her to be the dominant partner in crime. Wood was later diagnosed as a pathological narcissist. She divorced her husband and remarried but divorced her second husband also. Graham also experienced a tragic childhood. She was neglected and was both physically and sexually abused by her father. Graham was later diagnosed as having borderline personality disorder with 'other' psychopathic characteristics. It is very likely that she was a secondary psychopath.

David Cooke and Christine Michie: The Three-Factor Model

The PLC-R has become synonymous with the assessment of psychopathy and is generally administered to individuals who score at least 18 out of 24 on the Psychopathy Checklist: Screening Version (PCL-SV). The PCL-SV is used to confirm the presence of psychopathic traits. Due to there being fewer items (12), it takes less time to administer. In 2001, Cooke and Michie modified the PLC-SV, a two-factor model to a three-factor model of psychopathy (see Figure 5.5). Instead of the full 12 items, they included nine items, and from these nine items, they developed a hierarchical three-factor model using a factor analysis statistical approach. As we saw in Chapter 3, there are three factors:

1.   Interpersonal (arrogant and deceitful style that captures traits such as manipulative, superficial charm, grandiose self-perception)

2. Affective (deficient affective experience leading to traits such as lacking remorse, guilt and empathy and shallow emotion)
3. Behavioural (impulsive and irresponsible style that captures traits such as impulsive, lacking realistic goals and needing stimulation)

Various studies (see Chapter 3) have noted that female psychopaths react differently to these factors than their male counterparts. This might be explained away by the deselection of gender-biased items such as the exclusion of relational aggression and violent perpetration which occurs less frequently among female psychopaths. Hall, Benning and Patrick (2004) conducted a study on 310 incarcerated offenders and found that the first factor related to social dominance, the second factor related to low social closeness and violent offending, while the third factor was associated with reactive aggression and disinhibition. Blais, Elliott and Forth (2014) supported the finding of the third factor being associated with aggression but additionally with criminal behaviour. While the three-factor model has

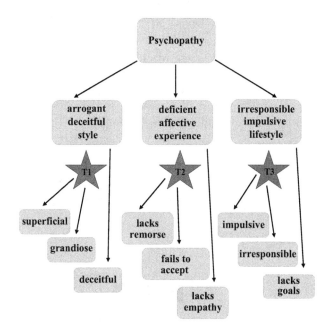

Figure 5.5 Cooke and Michie's three-factor model (Adapted from Cooke and Michie 2001)

received support, it is the dark triad of personality that is currently more often referred to in association with psychopathy.

Delroy Paulhus and Kevin Williams: The Dark Triad of Personality

Paulhus and Williams (2002) introduced the '**dark triad**' (DT) of personality by focusing on three characteristics that typify the behaviour of psychopaths: narcissism, Machiavellianism and psychopathy. Paulhus (2014) argued that these characteristics "should be studied in concert" (p. 421). Narcissism refers to the person's self-perception of superiority, while Machiavellianism describes the need to manipulate others. It is the psychopathy element, however, that consists of the traits we associate with psychopathic behaviour such as being callous and unemotional. The three elements of the dark triad correlate positively with one another, but individuals can score higher on one in comparison to the other two (Paulhus and Williams 2002; see Figure 5.6). For example, a person can score higher on psychopathy than narcissism or Machiavellianism. A person can also be highly manipulative in a callous way (Muris, Merckelbach, Otgaar and Meijer 2017). Paulhus and Williams compared the three dark triad elements with the FFM (see Figure 5.7). It is interesting that narcissism, Machiavellianism and psychopathy correlate negatively with agreeableness and conscientiousness. Furthermore, psychopathy also correlates negatively with neuroticism. Low scores on the factors of agreeableness and conscientiousness consistently define individuals with psychopathy.

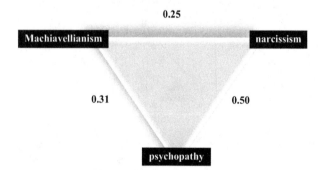

Figure 5.6 Correlations across the three dark triad measures (Adapted from Paulhus and Williams 2002)

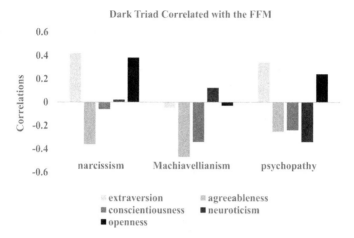

Figure 5.7 Correlations between the dark triad and the FFM (Adapted from Paulhus and Williams 2002)

Having the dark triad tends to positively correlate with being young and male, and being driven by the need for power, achievement and sex. Other traits found include values reflecting self-enhancement, a selfish disposition and underdeveloped defence mechanisms (Kaufman, Yaden, Hyde and Tsukayama 2019). Kaufman et al. found a negative correlation with conscientiousness, agreeableness, empathy, compassion and 'a quiet ego' (in other words, they were the opposite of this by being egotistic). Paulhus and Williams (2002) demonstrated that measures of antisocial behaviour were significantly predicted by the psychopathy element of the dark triad. Both narcissism and Machiavellianism failed to predict such derisive behaviour. There are many cases of psychopaths showing the dark triad and none more so than that of Malcolm Webster (see Box 5.4). Workman and Reader (2021) argued that males who have the dark triad are more likely to exhibit sexual harassment behaviours. Such behaviours might have been adaptive for some, particularly aggressive individuals, in order to pass on their genes in our evolutionary past (Zeigler-Hill, Besser, Morag and Campbell 2016). Despite Malcolm Webster's motivation for murder being the gain of monies, he did physically harass the women in his life and used sexual means to operationalise his *modus operandi*.

BOX 5.4: PSYCHO KILLER QU'EST-CE QUE C'EST?

Malcolm Webster was born in London in 1959. As a child, he struggled to make friends but was happy to be a loner. His father was a detective chief superintendent in charge of the Fraud Squad and was a hard taskmaster and very controlling. His mother was a policewoman but gave up her career once she had children. Webster had a strange upbringing, for one thing, every time his father had to use the bathroom, the rest of the family had to leave the house so that he could do his daily ablutions in an empty house (Lavery 2012). Although a loner, Webster would draw attention to himself by behaving in a bizarre way, such as faking medical conditions and fainting (acts that continued into his adulthood) whenever he was asked to do something he didn't want to do. He was behaving antisocially by the age of seven and was nicknamed 'Pyro' because he was fascinated by fire. He was considered to be a weakling by his peers as he supposedly had epilepsy and asthma – again medical conditions that were faked. He left school unqualified but managed to get a series of jobs. He eventually trained as a nurse and met his girlfriend who became pregnant – he insisted she had an abortion. The girl's father described Webster as someone who always went his own way and had noticed that as soon as he employed him to work in his nursing home, items such as money went missing, so he was sacked. Webster just walked away unbothered at the age of 19. Webster dated another girl who would soon commit suicide and was the first death associated with him. He dated a married woman who eventually returned to her husband. Webster was devastated not because he loved her but because he was rejected. He went to the United Arab Emirates where he was accused of causing the deaths of three children in his care (their deaths could not be proven to be a result of Webster as they do not perform autopsies, so he returned to England with the help of his father). A colleague there said he behaved strangely and was found semi-conscious after injecting insulin into his arm. Once back in England, he worked as a nurse and met and married his first wife whom he would kill in order to attain her life insurance. Webster drugged his wife on many occasions until he faked an accident in the car while she was in a drug-induced sleep. This was pre-planned as a farmer saw a man who fitted the description of Webster parked in the very spot days before the incident. He described the man as doing some kind of reconnaissance of the road. After the accident, Webster set fire to the car leaving his wife inside who burned to death. He delayed in telling the emergency services that there was someone inside until after it had exploded. Webster would use the same *modus operandi* of drugging his second wife. She fortunately escaped his killing plans by being suspicious of his insistence on taking her savings out of her account. So, does Webster have the dark triad? Most definitely. He was charming, manipulative, egotistic, narcissistic, cunning, impulsive and opportunistic. Records show his reckless spending of money and deliberately causing harm to those in his inner circle. He behaved violently and controlling towards his wives. He gaslighted, guilt tripped and bullied them. Typical of a psychopath, he was uncaring, cold and calculating. Even his grieving during his first wife's funeral, Claire Morris, was play-acted – a psychopath mimicking the emotions expected of him. Her brother said, "It causes me great pain to think that she experienced all the joys and angst of first love and yet it was a farce. It was a false love, just a ploy by a psychopath" (Lavery 2012). The evidence for the prosecution amounted proving him to be deceitful and manipulative and a murderer. He is currently serving a life sentence with a minimum of 30 years.

Erin Buckels, Daniel Jones and Delroy Paulhus: The Dark Tetrad of Personality

Whereas the dark triad was developed by Paulhus and Williams (2002) to represent a constellation of three socially unpleasant personality factors, the 'dark tetrad' was developed in 2013 by Buckels, Jones and Paulhus to include an additional factor of 'everyday sadism' (see Figure 5.8). Sadism is generally defined as a state of mind whereby pleasure is derived from inflicting physical and emotional pain on others. Interestingly, however, in the context of everyday sadism, the list includes:

- Pleasure derived from violent video games
- Internet trolling and bullying and cyberstalking
- Overly interested in weaponry

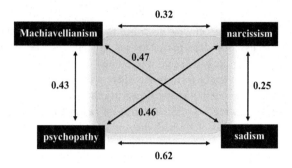

Figure 5.8 Correlations across the four dark tetrad measures (Adapted from Paulhus, Buckels, Trapnell and Jones 2021)

- Revenge
- Endorsement of a toxic leadership style
- Negativity
- Sexual violence
- Behaviour of a sadistic nature

Whether the dark triad should be replaced by the dark tetrad has divided opinion. In an online study by Johnson, Pluffe and Salofske (2019), 615 university students based in Canada completed a series of inventories including the dark triad and an assessment of sadistic tendencies. They found a conceptual overlap between sadism and psychopathy but concluded that sadism as a construct was unique enough to uphold the dark tetrad. Physical sadism was robustly associated with psychopathy due to the common underlying traits of wanting to hurt and dominate others. Findings suggest that sadism is a good measure for predicting delinquency among high school students. Sadism has also been found to play an important role in the proclivity aspect of revenge porn. This means that, although revenge porn can be explained away by the dark triad factors (especially psychopathy), the repetition of the act relates to the dark tetrad factor of sadism (Thomason-Darch 2021). The inclusion of sadism, Thomason-Darch suggests, will help differentiate personality profiles of different types of psychopathic perpetrators, which is useful in developing tailor-made interventions. The general thought about the factor of sadism is that it stands alone as a measure. For Mededović and Petrović (2015), the inclusion of sadism is an asset and helps to expand our understanding of the psychopathic personality.

SITUATIONAL APPROACH

Walter Mischel: Social-Cognitive Perspective

According to Mischel (1968), our behaviour is the product of an interaction between the situation and personality characteristics. This way of thinking about personality led Mischel to develop the **social-cognitive perspective**. This involves the importance of how we think and make judgements about the situations we find ourselves in. Such cognitive processing interacts with our learned behaviours, and it is this interface between the two that is central to the development of our personality. Mischel's model of personality became known as the person–situation debate, which is often referred to as 'trait versus state'. The central question to this debate is whether the trait is more predictive of the behaviour than the situation. He accepted that traits such as intellect show stability across different situations but not all personality traits are as robust and pervasive. These traits are more influenced by the situation and the situational constraints posed. He reviewed a number of studies, all of which used personality scores as a means of predicting how individuals behave. According to his calculations, there was only nine per cent agreement between behaviour across different situations. This implied that 91 per cent of behaviour across different situations failed to be accounted for *via* personality tests. He argued that behaviour is inconsistent across different types of situations but consistent when the situations are similar. We tend to be creatures of habit and behave similarly when we come across situations that have the hallmark of a previously encountered event. Mischel's approach involves an interplay between the specific attributes of a situation and how an individual perceives the situation. He outlined five person variables impacting on how an individual is likely to behave (see Table 5.1).

The question that Mischel addressed was whether our behaviour is consistent across a diversity of situations as trait theorists suggested. He was also interested to know whether we have behaviours that are tailored to specific situations. In a study conducted by

Table 5.1 The five person variables and their definitions

Competencies	*Cognitive, intellectual and social skills*
Cognitive strategies	Perceptions of an event may differ from one person to another and consequently will influence the response
Expectancies	The anticipated results from a series of behaviours are played in one's mind
Subjective values	The possible outcome from different behaviours is given an arbitrary value
Self-regulatory systems	We are bound by rules and given standards that regulate how we behave

Shoda, Mischel and Wright (1994), boys with behavioural problems were observed across five different situations:

1. Positive contact by a peer
2. Teased, provoked or threatened by a peer
3. Praise offered by an adult
4. A warning from an adult
5. Punishment from an adult

The boys' responses to these situations were recorded using the following:

1. Verbal aggression
2. Physical aggression
3. Whining
4. Compliance
5. Prosocial talk

Behavioural observation occurred over a six-week summer camp period. For five hours a day and six days a week, the children's behaviour was observed, which translated to 167 hours per child. Shoda et al. found that the children's behaviour was consistent within set situations but not across differing situations. Hence, a boy who responded using physical aggression towards having been provoked by a peer would respond consistently in this way regardless of whether the provocation occurred in the playground or the classroom. This response, however, did not occur if the punishment was metered out by one of the adults. Furthermore, behaviour was more consistent across similar than dissimilar situations (similarity being defined by shared factors such as peer or adult involvement and positive or negative interactions). The children's interpersonal responses, although consistent with specific situations, showed individual differences. In other words, each child developed his own stable behavioural profile, also known as a behavioural signature. This meant that each child had his own repertoire of situation-behaviour relationships. These findings support there being a robust effect of situational context on these boys' behaviour. This links in with the point raised in Table 5.1 of cognitive strategies, in that we all have a characteristic style of behaving. For Mischel, individuals have stable personalities, but their level of cognitive, intellectual and social competencies will impact on how they perceive situations. Furthermore, as we see in Table 5.1, there are a host of other factors which come into play such as what we expect the outcome of our behaviour to achieve coupled with our sense of obeyance to the rules that regulate what we should and should not do. According to Pervin (2003):

> ...we must recognise what I have called the stasis and flow of human behavior – that people have general patterns of functioning but also are capable of adapting to specific situational demands...our task is... to appreciate and understand the interplay between the two.

> (p. 451)

Does this way of thinking about personality also apply to psychopaths (see Box 5.5)?

BOX 5.5: IS THE PSYCHOPATH ALWAYS THE SAME NO MATTER WHAT?

In a study by Schimmenti, Passanisi, Pace, Manzella et al. (2014), attachment experiences of the most severe psychopaths showed that insecure and disorganised attachment styles are most likely to be observed in such individuals (see Chapter 3). Incidences of neglect, rejection and abuse featured strongly in their childhood backgrounds. Schimmenti et al. concluded that the more severe the adversity experienced, the more insecure the attachment bond. This they further argued contributed towards the development of a psychopathic personality. Schimmenti (2012) claimed that such childhood experiences combine with temperamental traits associated with psychopathy – callousness and unemotionality. It would appear that the more adversity experienced, the more severe the psychopathy. Cumulative environmental factors in early childhood are associated with developing psychopathic tendencies (Sevecke, Franke, Kosson and Krischer 2016). This suggests therefore that not all psychopaths will behave in the same way – in other words, there will be individual differences. It is useful to examine studies that have compared psychopaths from different cultures. Verschuere, van Ghesel Grothe, Waldorp, Watts et al. (2018) compared 7,450 criminal offenders with psychopathic characteristics (as rated using the PCL-R) from the Netherlands and the US. Of the personality traits and behaviours typifying psychopaths, characteristics such as callousness, selfishness and antisocial behaviour featured among the U.S. sample. In the case of those based in the Netherlands, dominant characteristics included being irresponsible and living off the backs of others. Another study of 372 and 474 Finnish and Dutch psychopaths, respectively, also revealed cultural differences in the juvenile psychopathic characteristics exhibited. Boys *per se* scored higher than girls, while boys from the Netherlands had higher psychopathy scores than their Finnish counterparts (Oshukova, Haltiala-Heino, Hillege, de Ruiter et al. 2016). Although there are consistent 'core' psychopathic traits exhibited in individuals cross-culturally, there are also cross-cultural traits that are different such as 'cold heartedness' as shown in Middle East countries like Saudi Arabia and Egypt when compared to the US (Latzman, Megraya, Hecht, Miller et al. 2015). Hence, not only are there individual differences resulting from the differential way in which childhood/environmental experiences interact with temperamental core traits associated with psychopathy, but also there are gender and cultural differences. This implies that there will be differences among psychopaths *per se* in their development of cognitive styles, competencies, expectancies and ways of self-regulation. If this is taken further still, then we can also infer that there will be differences across psychopathic individuals in their responses to similar situations as a consequence of their cognitive styles. This makes perfect sense given that not all psychopaths are criminals and that some psychopaths live successful lives holding down successful careers (see Chapter 8). There are, however, behaviours, emotional and cognitive, and temperamental characteristics of psychopaths that will raise their heads above the parapet to haunt them at times.

As pointed out by Pervin (2003), there are traits associated with psychopathy, but these alone do not account for their behaviour. From Chapter 3, we can see how childhood and environmental factors influenced the behaviour of psychopaths, but this alone was not enough to account for psychopathy. For one thing, not all individuals who have experienced adversity in childhood become psychopaths. This is why Belsky (2005) introduced the person-environment interaction model known as differential susceptibility. This highlights how some children are more sensitive to adverse environmental factors. Why should this be so? The missing link is a biological predisposition (see Chapter 4). This biological predisposition can show itself through temperamental factors like coldness, callousness, emotionlessness and selfishness, all of which are apparent in spades in psychopaths. Biological and social factors interact to create a toxic combination. This, coupled with a cognitive style that lends itself to negative perceptions of people and specific situations, can lead to caustic responses commonly exhibited by psychopaths. Researchers have looked at behavioural consistency across both different and similar situations. They have weighed up the contribution of inherent traits against the extent to which a person's behaviour and attitudes change when the situation changes. The general consensus is that we have traits influencing the direction of our behaviour. For example, being shy makes us less likely to be extrovert in an unfamiliar situation. In the home environment among family members, however, such an individual is likely to be less shy. Hence, the nature of the situation has a big impact on how our traits are externalised.

In the next section, a different approach to understanding the psychopath's personality will be adopted by considering the overlap with the criminal personality proposed by psychiatrist Samuel Yochelson and clinical psychologist Stanton Samenow.

DOES THE PSYCHOPATHIC PERSONALITY CONVERGE WITH THE CRIMINAL PERSONALITY?

Yochelson and Samenow (1976) conducted a longitudinal study spanning 14 years on 30 incarcerated males. From their observations, they were able to develop their criminal personality theory. They were able to classify the different types of thinking errors made regardless of the criminal acts committed. They suggested that there is a set thinking process associated with the criminal personality. The criminal personality, they argued, provides a framework for the cognitive, emotional and behavioural processes driving criminally inclined individuals. This in turn influences the nature of lifestyle followed. Some of the factors associated with criminals include:

- Craving for power and control
- Behaving as predators
- Needing to be considered as unique and the best
- Egocentric and selfish
- Achieving aims by whatever means
- Short-term thinking
- Cognitive distortions
- Blaming others

Yochelson and Samenow also listed a series of crime-related thinking errors relating to the crimes themselves (see Table 5.2).

Table 5.2 A selection of crime-related thinking errors (From Yochelson and Samenow 1976)

Examples of crime-related thinking errors

Loner: leads a secretive life and feels separate from others

Lying: lies to create a false story as a way of keeping control

Closed channel: so self-righteous that they have a closed mind

Victim stance: blame others when things do not go their way

Lack a time perspective: want immediate gratification

Inability to put oneself in someone else's shoes: self-centred

Inability to consider injury to others: perceive themselves as the injured party

Inability to assume obligation: obligations are a hindrance and take away their control

Take ownership: they take what is owned by others as they believe it's their right

No interest in responsible tasks: find responsibility boring

Pretentiousness: overestimate their abilities and believe they are right

When the thinking errors listed by Yochelson and Samenow are considered, it is easy to see a strong overlap with the social behaviour of the psychopath (even non-criminal psychopaths). As pointed out by Hare in 1991 and DSM-5 in 2013, psychopaths have difficulty in regulating their self-control and seek immediate gratification. This influences what they do in the short term with no regard to the future. They often show carelessness, impulsivity and rule breaking as a means to achieving their goals. This is exemplified by the Porteus Maze test where the solution to a series of mazes involves keeping within the lines. One measure taken called the Test Quotient (TQ) correlates with planning and foresight, while the Qualitative Error (Q) correlates with carelessness, impulsivity and rule breaking. Psychopaths score high on Q. Porteus (1959) noted that workers scoring high on Q often had disciplinary problems. Psychopaths also hold attitudes that reflect the criminal personality. They often support attitudes that go against the norm of society and endorse tough-mindedness, aggression and the need for excitement. Psychopaths have a tendency to perceive and believe their actions to be justified. Sykes and Matza (1957) defined five attribution techniques used by psychopaths. First, they deny responsibility for their behaviour and instead will blame an external factor. Second, they deny the injury they caused to others by minimalising the harm done. Third, they deny any wrongdoing to their victim by claiming he/she deserved what happened to them. Fourth, they condemn their condemners. Fifth, they use the loyalty card by arguing that their actions were for their peers over any victims that got in the way. All five attributions closely resemble the criminal personality. Psychopaths have limited emotional empathy and are poor at taking on someone else's perspective. Additionally, as discussed previously, they are callous, egocentric and dishonest (Lilienfeld 1998). There are many parallels between the thinking styles of the criminal personality and that of the psychopath (see Box 5.6). When the life histories of psychopaths are analysed in detail, it becomes apparent that their decision-making over the years shows a strong resemblance to the points raised by Yochelson and Samenow. There are also many similarities to the attribution styles that Sykes and Matza outlined as far back as 1957. In conclusion, it is clear that psychopathy is a case of an extreme form of personality disorder. Hence, in order to understand psychopathy, we first have to develop a good understanding of how psychologists perceive personality.

BOX 5.6: PSYCHOPATHIC THINKING OF THE APPLE MAN?

It has been speculated that Steve Jobs, the co-founder of Apple, although very innovative, had striking characteristics of a thinking psychopath. He treated his friends including colleagues Steve Wozniak (co-founder of Apple) and Daniel Kottke (roommate and Apple employee), and his girlfriend and mother of his child, Chrisann Brennan, callously. He denied paternity of his daughter even when presented with DNA evidence. Jobs' narcissism, perfectionism and need for complete control have led to speculation that he was a narcissistic psychopath. Any disagreement with his views and standards would provoke anger. He always thought he was right and is renowned for making his workers cry by unfounded bullying tactics. It can be argued that Steve Jobs relied on an attribution style of thinking which is representative of the psychopath and overlaps with the thinking errors outlined by Yochelson and Samenow.

SUMMARY

Psychopathy is defined in DSM-5 as a sub-division of ASPD. ASPD in DSM-5 is a personality disorder under Cluster B. It is considered a superordinate personality type meaning it can have trait groupings from other personality disorders such as narcissism. As psychopathy is a sub-division of ASPD, then it too can be considered a superordinate personality type. It is not uncommon to have narcissistic psychopaths. DSM-5 fails to acknowledge psychopathy as independent of ASPD which is why, in order to receive a psychopathic diagnosis, practitioners have to diagnose ASPD beforehand. Using the person–situation division enabled us to address the most ubiquitous trait and situational theories. Eysenck's trait approach to personality outlines three scales: extraversion–introversion, neuroticism and psychoticism. The psychoticism scale is of particular relevance to psychopathy as it defines traits that are consistent with the psychopathic profile. McCrae and Costa developed the five-factor model that includes openness, conscientiousness, extraversion, agreeableness and neuroticism as factors, each containing a cluster of traits. Psychopaths score low on agreeableness and conscientiousness. Agreeableness includes traits such as trust, kindness and prosocial behaviours. High scorers on this tend to be cooperators and show empathy for others. Conscientiousness includes an array of traits such as thoughtfulness, goal-directed behaviours and impulse control. High scorers are mindful of other people. We can see why psychopaths score low on these two factors. Trait theories tailored towards detecting psychopathy were considered. Cooke and Michie's three-factor model was modified from the PLC-SV, a test used to identify psychopaths. They included three factors: interpersonal (arrogant and deceitful style), affective (deficient affective experience) and behavioural (impulsive and irresponsible style). High scores on these are indicative of a psychopathic profile. The dark triad introduced by Paulhus and Williams focuses on three characteristics depicting psychopaths: narcissism, Machiavellianism and psychopathy. High scores on these indicate an individual with psychopathic traits. More recently, the focus has been on the dark tetrad that added sadism. Introduced by Buckels, Jones and Paulhus, this considers everyday sadism where events such as internet trolling, cyberstalking and revenge acts depict a person who is sadistic. The inclusion of sadism is a good measure of delinquency and proclivity. For the situational approach, Mischel's social-cognitive perspective was considered. It highlights the interaction between a person and a situation and how behaviour is inconsistent across different situations. Person variables such as competencies and cognitive strategies vary across individuals but there will be a stable behavioural profile. Therefore, we develop our own repertoire of situation-behaviour relationships, and psychopaths will have one that embraces a psychopathic approach. The overlap between psychopathy and criminality was explored by Yochelson and Samenow using traits associated with criminals. These traits can be seen in psychopaths, such as the need for power and control, acting as predators, egocentricity, selfishness, blaming others and the use of cognitive distortion to change the narrative to suit their perception of events. Yochelson and Samenow also listed a series of crime-related thinking errors, most of which psychopaths succumb to.

FURTHER READING

Gacono, C.B. and Meloy, J.R. (2009). Assessing antisocial and psychopathic personalities. In J.N. Butcher (ed.). *Oxford handbook of personality assessment* (pp. 567–581). Oxford: Oxford University Press.

Kiehl, K. (2015). *The psychopath whisperer: Inside the minds of those without a conscience*. London: Oneworld Publications.

Lynam, D.R., Miller, J.D. and Derefinko, K.J. (2018). Psychopathy and personality: An articulation of the benefits of a traitbased approach. In C.J. Patrick (ed.). *Handbook of psychopathy* (pp. 259–280). New York: The Guilford Press.

Presnall, J.R. and Widiger, T.A. (2012). Personality disorders. In J.E. Maddux and B.A. Winstead (eds.). *Psychopathology: Foundations for a contemporary understanding* (pp. 277–305). Abingdon: Routledge/Taylor & Francis Group.

EXPLANATIONS
DEVELOPMENTAL PATHWAY AND CONTINUITY

Children are like sponges in that they soak up so much information. And learning how to behave appropriately is no exception to this. During the early stages of development, parents socialise their children such that they learn about the world and their place in it. As discussed in Chapter 3, the socialisation process encapsulates society's norms and values that are passed down from one generation to the next by our parents. Socialisation also enables children to learn how to moderate their behaviour so that they can develop into good citizens of society. Behaviour constituting the 'good citizen' is based on an unspoken human moral code. Hence, when a child behaves badly, we often question who is to blame. Did the parents fail to socialise their children appropriately or are these children beyond help? When we ask such questions, the answers become confounded. As we have seen in Chapters 3–5, there are complicated interactions between environmental and biological factors such as parental nurturance and temperamental traits, respectively. Environmental and biological factors not only interact but interact in complex ways. As different aspects of the environment and an individual's biology interact, the causal effects of the antisocial behaviour, for instance, become even more confounded and multi-layered. It's a factor of growing up that children will misbehave. With appropriate parenting, however, guidance on what is morally right will often prevail, and these children develop into law-abiding citizens. There are, however, children who, no matter what form of intervention is used to break the cycle of misbehaviour, will continue to behave antisocially into adolescence and beyond. Such children develop along a disruptive pathway of behaviour and will continue to adopt antisocial values and norms

DOI: 10.4324/9781032221052-6

that fuel and reinforce this developmental trajectory. We may ask, are such children the psychopaths of the future? Or perhaps they are mini-psychopaths already? In order to explore this, it is important first to consider the demographics of such antisocial children. For example, are these children born with underlying conditions that are akin to psychopathy or are they raised to be antisocial?

DEMOGRAPHICS OF CHILDREN WITH ANTISOCIAL BEHAVIOUR

In relation to psychopathy, when we consider the demographics of children with antisocial behaviour, it is important to ascertain the presence of psychopathic traits. There is after all antisocial behaviour, and then, there is antisocial behaviour! Most individuals who behave antisocially are not psychopaths. In fact, it depends on our conceptions of antisocial behaviour and how it sits with other types of negatively perceived behaviours. Taylor (2016) differentiated between criminal, morally offensive, deviant and antisocial behaviour. She argued that specific types of behaviours can crossover into all four categories, or they can be mutually exclusive. For example, an individual who plays their music loudly during the day may well be behaving antisocially, but it is not criminal, morally offensive or deviant. Alternatively, an individual who not only loiters outside the school gates half-dressed and masturbating but takes adolescents' dinner money in exchange for cannabis exhibits criminal, morally offensive, deviant and antisocial behaviour. Hence, considering antisocial behaviour is not enough. We need to consider the presence of other traits associated with psychopathy. This, therefore, implies a checklist of other psychopathic traits such as those outlined in Hare's Psychopathy Checklist: Youth Version (PCL-YV) or those highlighted in the Youth Psychopathic Traits Inventory (YPI; see Chapter 2). In a study by Waller, Dishion, Shaw, Gardner et al. (2016), the early signs of psychopathic traits exhibited in children aged two to four years included:

- No guilt following misbehaviour
- No change of behaviour following punishment
- Selfish and unsharing behaviour
- Telling lies
- Sneaky and manipulative behaviour

According to Waller et al., these traits are a feature of callous-unemotional (CU) behaviour (see Chapters 2–5). Using the YPI, Hillege, Das and De Ruiter (2010) found that traits such as dishonest charm, lying, manipulation, remorselessness, impulsiveness, callousness, unemotionality and irresponsibility were strongly associated with youths who were incarcerated or institutionalised. Moreover, scoring high on CU was more likely to lead to the membership of delinquent and antisocial peers espousing criminal ideals (see Chapter 3). High scorers on the YPI were more likely to be ringleaders who initiated others into behaving antisocially. For our understanding of whether a child has a predisposition for psychopathy, in addition to focusing on the exhibition of antisocial behaviour, we will consider psychopathic personality traits (see Chapter 5).

Deciding on whether antisocial behaviour presents itself as a **disruptive behaviour disorder** (DBD) or as a feature of age-related undesirable behaviour, psychologists have outlined the normative age-related negative behaviour (see Table 6.1). Note that there is an overlap of behaviours occurring across age ranges which eventually decrease in occurrence until eventually dropped at a later age. Additionally, psychologists have introduced three criteria aiding the diagnosis of a DBD:

1. Age of onset: Antisocial behaviour occurring from a very young age is a sign of problems in the future.
2. Frequency of occurrence: Antisocial behaviour that occurs often is a sign of problems in the future.
3. Longevity: Antisocial behaviour that continues over a long period of time is a sign of problems in the future.

Table 6.1 A list of standardised age-related undesirable behaviours in infancy, childhood and adolescence

Age in years	Normative age-related negative behaviours
1½–2	Overactive, demanding attention, defiant, temper tantrums
3–5	Overactive, demanding attention, temper tantrums, negativity, telling lies
6–10	Overactive, temper tantrums, oversensitive, telling lies, achievement problems at school, jealousy
11–14	Temper tantrums, oversensitive, achievement problems at school, jealousy, moodiness
15–18	Achievement problems at school, truancy, using substances, minor transgressions (shoplifting), depressed demeanour

Moffit (1993) highlighted two typologies of adolescent antisocial behaviour. The terms **adolescence-limited** and **life-course-persistent** divide individuals according to the age of onset and the longevity of the antisocial behaviour shown. For example, an individual who began displaying antisocial behaviour from the age of ten which continued into adulthood is classified as life-course-persistent. Those individuals classified as adolescence-limited, alternatively, will begin their antisocial behaviour at a later age and will usually mimic other adolescents behaving in this way to gain rewards – rewards which they too would like to attain. Such individuals, Moffit claimed, are likely to be immature and behave antisocially during their teenage years. As we can see, antisocial behaviour on its own is not a good indicator of psychopathy, especially in the young. Along with the three criteria used to diagnose DBD, antisocial behaviour has been used to diagnose children with one of the two common childhood developmental conditions: **Oppositional Defiant Disorder (ODD)** and **Conduct Disorder (CD)**. Although **Attention Deficit Hyperactivity Disorder (ADHD)** was once considered to be a DBD in DSM-IV-TR, this is no longer the case in DSM-5. We will, however, discuss ADHD here, given the overlap and similarity of behavioural traits.

CHILDHOOD DEVELOPMENTAL CONDITIONS

Oppositional Defiant Disorder (ODD)

The profile of an individual with ODD has five components according to DSM-5: angry/irritable mood, argumentative/defiant behaviour, vindictiveness, disturbed behaviour and behaviour that is exhibited independently from a psychotic diagnosis. Children with ODD can be categorised as showing disruptive behaviour that is mild, moderate or severe. ODD children are typically described as being disobedient, defiant, hostile and misbehaving most of the time (see Figure 6.1). They often have problems at school due to their inability to pay attention and concentrate, which often leads to them being annoyed and frustrated. They tend to be socially isolated as forming and maintaining friendships is challenging. The causes of ODD are diverse and include physiological, genetic and environmental explanations. There is a genetic element to ODD as familial studies show that if a close family member has a behavioural or psychological problem such as

ODD, conduct disorder, attention deficit hyperactivity disorder, personality disorder, depression or anxiety, then the likelihood of having ODD increases. Hence, this means the child is likely to have a genetic predisposition for ODD. Physiological explanations include a variety of factors. For example, van Goozen, Snoek, Matthys, van Rossum et al. (2004) investigated the 'startle reflex' (or blink response) in children with ODD. This involved showing children emotionally laden slides and measuring their startle reflex. Psychologists use the extent to which individuals blink at a distressing event as a measure of feeling stressed and uncomfortable, such that the more blinking that occurs then the more stressed the person is feeling. The startle reflex has also been used as a measure of fearfulness and fearlessness. These children in van Goozen et al.'s study had a low startle response to the emotional slides. Moreover, these children scored high on delinquency. van Goozen et al. found that the higher the delinquency, the lower the startle response (less blinking). They claimed that this suggests low amygdala activity, an area in the brain responsible for processing fear-related and other emotional stimuli (see Chapter 4). In support of this, measures such as heart rate, skin conductance and cortisol (in saliva) levels are also lower in ODD children. Hence, the **'fearlessness theory of antisocial behaviour'**, which was first introduced by Raine in 1993, combines all of these factors together, such that the startle reflex, heart rate, skin conductance and cortisol levels are all low. We would expect these to be high when an individual experiences fear. van Goozen, Matthys, Cohen-Kettenis, Gispen-de Wied et al. (1998) found that in boys with ODD, cortisol levels in saliva decreased when they were scored as aggressively high but anxiously low. Those who scored as aggressively and anxiously high had higher levels of cortisol. This finding suggests that there is a developmental continuity between young individuals with ODD and adults who are antisocial (Taylor and Workman 2018). There are a host of other physiological anomalies such as low serotonin and noradrenalin secretion and brain function such as the control over emotions and motivations. With regard to environmental factors, familial demographics such as marital discord and chaos, inconsistent discipline, neglect, rejection and exposure to violence and substance abuse have been shown to exacerbate ODD and its onset (see Chapter 3). According to Connor (2002), as many as 30 per cent of children with ODD can progress to conduct disorder (CD) if they fail to receive treatment intervention.

Figure 6.1 A boy exhibiting disruptive ODD behaviour by having a screaming tantrum

Table 6.2 The categories of behaviours exhibited by children with CD

Category of symptoms	Description
Aggressive behaviour towards others and animals	Harmful behaviour towards others using intimidation, bullying, cruelty, physical and sexual violations, and weaponry.
Damage to property	Intentional destructiveness to property and causing harm.
Deceitful/devious behaviour	Delinquent acts and lying as a means of attaining goals and renouncing obligations.
Unacceptance and violation of authority and rules	Prior to the age of 13, rules set by parents and other organisations such as school are disrespected.

Moreover, children with ODD tend to exhibit less severe symptoms than those with CD.

Conduct Disorder (CD)

Children with CD portray a catalogue of symptoms that the DSM-5 has grouped into four categories (see Table 6.2).

A study by Fairchild, Hawes, Frick, Copeland et al. (2019) placed the prevalence of CD in school-aged children at three per cent, with it occurring twice as many times in males than females. Blakey, Morgan, Gayer-Anderson, Davis et al. (2021) found the prevalence of CD in children aged 11–16 years in the UK to be five per cent. They also found that such conduct problems occurred more frequently in the inner city as opposed to national samples (16 per cent and five per cent, respectively) and more among boys than girls. The antisocial behaviours expressed by children with CD can range from less serious to more serious. Also, their actions can overlap with normal age-related negative behaviours. Their behaviours can be further divided into behavioural excesses and behavioural deficits. In the case of behavioural excesses, aggression involving physical attacks, verbal abuse, criminal damage, fire-setting and cruelty to animals as well as noncompliance (such as defiant and rule-breaking behaviour) typify the extremes of negative acts exhibited by CD children (see Figure 6.2).

The behavioural deficits support the aforementioned behaviours. Lacking a moral compass where there is little, if any, remorse shown

Figure 6.2 A girl showing her antisocial side that can be seen in individuals with CD

or concern for the welfare of others enables these children to behave negatively. There are behavioural deficits in their social behaviour and ability to perform well academically at school. They often have few friends as forming bonds is difficult, and there is an obvious lack of affection, warmth and cooperation towards others. Behavioural excesses and deficits are considered as problems in the physiological regulation of motivation. Two systems operate together – the **behavioural inhibition system (BIS)** and the **behavioural activation (or approach) system (BAS)**. In the case of BAS, behaviours such as happiness, approach and motor activity are activated which is a good thing but becomes a bad thing when BIS, responsible for moral behaviour, is underactivated. Behaviours associated with CD such as thrill-seeking, fearlessness and insensitivity to punishment are considered to be problems in the regulation of BAS and BIS. The regulation of both BAS and BIS is down to the structure in the brain called the septo-hippocampal area. This regulates fear and anxiety. Hence, a child who constantly seeks the rewards of excitement by indulging in risky behaviour will have an overactive BAS but underactive BIS (thereby subduing fear and anxiety). There are other theoretical approaches to understanding CD such as genetic and environmental.

Is there an easy answer to what causes CD?

The quick answer to the above question is no! But there has been an abundance of research looking into this. Researchers have found a link between a specific type of temperament and CD. In 2003, Keenan and Shaw found that an irritable temperament is common among individuals with CD. Earlier research by Thomas and Chess (1986) indicated that most children can be allocated to one of three types of temperament: 'easy', 'slow to warm up' and 'difficult'. In a longitudinal study involving 136 children aged two years, 65 per cent of children could be classified under three proposed temperaments. Of the 65 per cent, ten per cent of children were classified as 'difficult' as they often had tantrums due to their frustration and negative moods, 15 per cent of children were classified as 'slow to warm up' because they initially had problems adapting to change and showed low levels of activity and 40 per cent of children were classified as 'easy' due to their positivity and easy-going nature. Interestingly, Thomas and Chess found that 70 per cent of the ten per cent classified as 'difficult' children developed problem behaviour such as CD.

These findings raise the question of underlying genetic foundations. As discussed in Chapter 3, the DRD-7-repeat gene is often associated with the development of a difficult temperament. This is not the only gene, however, associated with problematic temperaments. For example, the MAOA gene (see Chapter 4) is associated with aggressive antisocial behaviour and violence (Feresin 2009). This gene codes for an enzyme called monoamine oxidase A, which is responsible for degrading the neurotransmitters noradrenalin, serotonin and dopamine. If there is a mutation in MAOA, the production of the enzyme is depleted, and as a consequence, high levels of the aforementioned neurotransmitters remain. This can cause impulsive behaviour, violence and hypersexuality. Twin studies provide information about the heritability of CD due to there being a higher concordance of antisocial behaviour in identical twins (Moffit 2005; see Chapter 4). It is interesting to note that environmental factors interact with twins who have a predisposition for CD. Maltreatment, for instance, interacted with a predisposition for CD by 24 per cent. This was reduced to two per cent if there was no evidence of a predisposition (Jaffee, Moffitt, Caspi and Taylor 2003), hence a gene-environment interaction. This, therefore, implies that the behavioural symptomology of CD can be attenuated if the right environment is implemented. Implementing the right environment extends to family dynamics. It is well established that a child in a family where there is marital discord and disharmony is likely to have problems with regulating their emotions and with appraising social situations correctly. This often leads to behaving inappropriately and activating hostile and antisocial behaviours to solve social problems. Harsh and physically abusive punishment regimes, poor attachment, and neglectful and rejecting parental interactions can also lead to CD behaviours. Inappropriate behaviour towards social situations occurs not only as a consequence of environmental factors such as parental nurturance but also with problems of executive function. Executive function involves the use of language, memory, attention and thought. Children with poor executive function can find it difficult to solve social problems using a language response, often instead acting out violently. Low success rates for tasks involving executive function are related to deficits in frontal lobe activation (Hobson, Scott and Rubia 2011). Other research has shown that reduced prefrontal brain activity is implicated in emotional regulation in females (aged 15–18 years) with CD (Raschle, Fehlbaum, Menks, Martinelli et al. 2019). Abnormalities of the limbic system such as the amygdala and insula play a pivotal role in the poor processing and regulation of emotions (see Chapter 4). The orbitofrontal cortex and the overlapping brain circuits are involved additionally in reinforcement-based decision-making, which in children with CD would be the excitement and rewards experienced for performing antisocial or callous acts. Hence, the excitement and rewards experienced reinforce the negative behaviour further (Fairchild, Hawes, Frick, Copeland et al. 2019; see Box 6.1).

BOX 6.1: IS THE BAD, BAD CHILD OBVIOUS FROM THE WORD GO?

Lillyth Quillan, the founder of Parents of Children with Conduct Disorder (PCCD), wrote in 2018 about her own experiences of 'parenting a potential psychopath'. Her child was diagnosed with conduct disorder (CD) after exhibiting challenging antisocial behaviour. Despite the definitions of conduct disorder provided, she argued that the diagnosis is merely a way of saying that one's child is likely to grow up to be a psychopath. Quillan's son displayed physically hurtful behaviour towards her when he was merely months of age. This hurting behaviour continued as he got older where he would harm other children. Parents would avoid him when he was in the park, and he was never invited to parties or organised fun activities. Quillan was in contact with other parents who had children with CD who all said the same thing – their children had been violent towards them and to their siblings. And because these children lacked empathy, they would try to manipulate the whole family. One member of the PCCD claimed that her son had punched her in the face and went for his father with a hammer. Quillan herself claimed that her son at just eight months of age would bite her nipple during breastfeeding, causing an immense amount of pain. Even with her yelling in pain, he would smile and laugh and continually repeat the behaviour regardless of how hurtful he was being. She claimed that hurting her was more pleasurable than the reward of food. Eventually, she used formula in a bottle as the experience was unbearable. At 18 years, he has broken the law on numerous occasions (Ridley 2022).

As we can see, disentangling the biological and environmental contributions to CD symptomology is not straightforward. Our last behavioural disorder exhibiting disruptive behaviour is attention deficit hyperactive disorder discussed next.

ATTENTION DEFICIT HYPERACTIVE DISORDER (ADHD)

ADHD has received much attention and has probably been studied more so than the other two conditions. Globally, the prevalence of ADHD is estimated at five per cent, although in some countries, such as the US, it is between eight and ten per cent. As is the case with ODD and CD, more boys are diagnosed with this than girls (2–5:1, respectively). Adults with ADHD in the UK are estimated at three to four per cent, with more males than females at a ratio of 3:1, respectively (National Institute for Health and Care Excellence 2021). There are two sets of symptoms: inattention and hyperactive-impulsivity (see Table 6.3).

Children can exhibit ADHD in one of four ways:

1. ADHD-C is a combination of inattention and hyperactivity/ impulsivity.
2. ADHD-PH is predominantly hyperactive.
3. ADHD-HI is predominantly hyperactive and impulsive.
4. ADHD-I is predominantly impulsive.

Table 6.3 List of ADHD symptoms

Symptoms of inattention

Poor attention to schoolwork details causing careless errors

Unable to maintain attention while performing tasks such as reading, focusing on details and conversation

Appearing not to listen due to difficulty focusing on what is being said

Problems completing tasks and following instructions

Difficulty organising tasks due to poor time management and organisation

Finds sustaining mental effort a problem resulting in unfinished work

Fails to keep tabs on materials needed to complete tasks and activities

Difficulty filtering out unrelated thoughts to the task at hand

Suffers from forgetfulness such as performing a common daily activity

Symptoms of hyperactive-impulsivity

Fidgeting, hand tapping and general restlessness when seated

Finds remaining seated challenging

Active behaviour when inappropriate such as running around the classroom

Fails to perform set activities quietly

Appears to be 'driven by a motor' as cannot be still

Shouts answers to questions out loud in the classroom and completes what people say

Fails to wait for one's turn

Continuously talks

Interrupts others and intrudes by taking over tasks

Hence, in the case of ADHD-C, pretty much all of the symptoms outlined in Table 6.3 are exhibited. For the other forms of ADHD, the symptoms relating to hyperactivity or hyperactivity with impulsivity or impulsivity alone are exhibited. We can therefore assume that children with ADHD present symptoms differently. Some children with ADHD are considered by their peers as the clowns of the classroom (see Figure 6.3). In Box 6.2, we explore the case of a boy who showed behaviour typical of ADHD symptomology.

Figure 6.3 A boy with ADHD acting up in the classroom by balancing a pencil on his nose

---

BOX 6.2: THE CASE OF EE

EE was eight years and eight months of age when he was referred for nuisance behaviour. He was born in China and was an only child to his English and Mandarin speaking parents. There were many complaints from EE's teachers and peers about his behaviour. His behaviour was described as being disruptive in the classroom during his pre-school years. While his teachers did say that EE could pay attention, he would only do so to topics and activities that interested him. He didn't have any friends. When he commenced primary school, his teachers complained that he was inattentive and easily distracted and showed impulsive behaviours. He found it difficult to remain seated and expressed bore-dom during his lessons. As he progressed through primary school, teachers would say that he never submitted his homework on time and was unable to complete his assignments written during class time. He failed to remain focused after playtime and would often be punished by standing in the corner. Interestingly, despite his challenging behaviour, he had the capacity to answer teacher questions. EE's weakest sub-jects were those he found to be boring such as mathematics and the Chinese language, and he managed to provide all kinds of excuses for not completing his work such as having a headache or stomach pains. Eventually, EE was referred for assessment. After completing a battery of tests, EE was not diagnosed with a learning difficulty but did receive a diagnosis of ADHD-C. In other words, he showed ADHD-Inattention and ADHD-Hyperactivity/Impulsivity.

As with ODD and CD, the causes are complex and show an interaction between biological and environmental factors. In 2012, Eme found that 30 per cent of children presenting symptoms of ADHD had experienced some form of traumatic brain injury. Others have shown a decrease in the volume of specific areas in the brain such as the left side of the prefrontal cortex (Krain and Castellanos 2006) implicated in decision–making, moderating social behaviour and the orchestration of profound cognitive behaviour (Yang and Raine 2009). Such problems in the coordination of complex cogni-tive behaviour will make achieving goals difficult – hence, effective executive functioning is challenging for children with ADHD. The area of the brain involved in controlled attention, movement and spatial navigation is known as the posterior parietal cortex that has been found to be 'thin' in ADHD children. Less activity in the frontal-limbic system (which plays an important role in arousal and reward) of the brain is also found in these children. Overall, children with ADHD have problems controlling their activity and picking up on positive reinforcement, which is due to an ineffective inhibitory system. And this, in turn, is accounted for by problems highlighted in these brain areas. Others have highlighted the problems with the **neurotransmitter** pathways of norepinephrine and dopamine in the brain. These pathways are responsible for a number of behaviours relating to motivation, executive function, sensitivity to rewards and control of movement (Chandler, Waterhouse and Gao 2014). Research on fraternal and identical twins (see Chapter 4) demonstrates how ADHD is inherited. Burt (2009) showed that in 75 per cent of cases, children inherited ADHD from their parents. Siblings of those with ADHD are three to four times more likely to also develop the condition. The DRD4 gene of the 7-repeat variant (see Chapter 3) causes deficits of behavioural attention analogous to that seen in children with ADHD (Nikolidis and Gray 2010). In addition to the above biological and genetic factors impacting on ADHD, there are environmental influences found such as the effects of maternal alcohol consumption during pregnancy. This often triggers foetal alcohol spectrum disorders akin to ADHD (Burger, Goecke, Fasching, Moll et al. 2011). Infection and smoking tobacco during pregnancy, and exposure to lead, artificial food colourants and preservatives can all contribute to the development of ADHD symptoms in some children. As discussed in Chapter 3 in relation to psychopathy, ADHD symptomology can be escalated by family factors such as having unaffectionate, critical and disapproving care-givers. Some, researchers such as Weiss and Hechtman (1993) argued that ADHD behaviours induce these responses from parents. The research suggests, however, that environmental factors exacerbate ADHD in children predisposed to gene and biological indicators.

We will return later to the issue of similarity and continuity of these conditions with psychopathy in adulthood. In Chapter 3, we discussed the influence of environmental factors such as attachment and family dynamics on the development of psychopathy. Next, we will focus on famous in-depth longitudinal criminological studies.

FAMILIES WITH A HISTORY OF ANTISOCIAL BEHAVIOUR

The influence of the family on the developing child is important. It provides us with a set of family demographics surrounding the child as it develops into adulthood. Family factors can be compared across a spectrum of family types. Families that endorse antisocial ideals and behave antisocially can be compared to those that don't. Such data can be very informative for ascertaining what it is that leads these families down the path of behaving antisocially, and in some cases, criminally. Although we think of anything to do with the family as being environmentally influenced, there are important gene-environment interactions at play. There are three types of interaction:

1. Passive effects involve providing a home environment that is fitting for the development of a child sharing 50 per cent of its genes with each parent. Hence, parents who play in an orchestra professionally are likely to create a musical home environment such as their children having access to instruments and musical scrolls. Likewise, parents with antisocial behaviour put their children at double risk from genetic and environmental factors for developing an antisocial repertoire.

2. Active effects can be observed when children seek like-minded others – a form of niche picking. This can occur in or out of the home environment. For example, parents or siblings who share similar interests and abilities are likely to be drawn towards each other. And outside of the home, friends fulfil this role. Burt, McGue and Iacono (2009) found that the identical twin with a higher level of antisocial behaviour had deviant friends during late adolescence. Other studies have shown that antisocial behaviour acted as a reliable predictor in the selection of like-minded peers.

3. Evocative effects are studied the most and of interest here. A trait that a child has can be reinforced by the reaction received from others. Thus, this reaction consequently reinforces the expression of that trait. As we have seen in Chapter 3, infants with the DRD4–7R structure of the DRD4 gene are more likely to express a temperament exhibiting problematic and difficult behaviours. This behavioural repertoire is exacerbated by insensitive and unresponsive responses by the care-givers. In this case, the care-givers are reinforcing a problematic temperament of

the future leading to higher levels of psychopathy by 15 years of age (Nikitopoulos, Zohsel, Blomeyer, Buhmann et al. 2014). But with the right nurturance offering sensitive and responsive care, the predisposition for a challenging temperament becomes attenuated or non-existent. The DRD4 gene has received much attention but there have been other genes associated with anti-social and aggressive behaviour. Different forms of the Cate-chol-O-methyltransferase (COMT) and Serotonin transporter (SLC6A4) genes are associated with both youth and adult antisocial and aggressive behaviour. Furthermore, it has been shown that specific types of environments can pacify the extent of aggressive behaviour such as cultural diversity. According to Grossmann and Santos (2016), individualistic cultures highlight the importance of individual rights, autonomy, self-expression and achievement. This is not so for collectivistic cultures where there is a strong emphasis on conformity, social responsibility, harmony and connection with one's society. It could be argued that individualistic cultures encourage individuals to be selfish and behave antisocially.

All three gene effects demonstrate the important role of gene-environment interactions which we cannot ignore when interpreting the impact of family studies for our understanding of antisocial/criminal behaviour. This extends to our understanding of psychopathy. An important study undertaken by Richard Dugdale followed generations of the Jukes family. Dugdale published his findings in an article in 1877 headed, 'The Jukes: A Study in Crime, Pauperism, Disease and Heredity'. The Jukes were notorious in Ulster County, New York, for their generations of deviants. Dugdale stated in 1877 that:

> The nature of the investigation necessitated the study of families through successive generations, to master the full sequence of phenomena and include...facts embraced in the two main branches of enquiry... The heredity that fixes the organic characteristics of the individual, and the environment which affects modifications in that heredity.

> (p. 12)

Dugdale is quite perceptive in acknowledging the gene-environment interaction – you can't have one without the other. He used a longitudinal study approach, and his findings are supportive of genes having passive, active and evocative effects on behaviour, including criminal behaviour (see Box 6.3).

BOX 6.3: DUGDALE'S ANALYSIS OF THE JUKES

A longitudinal methodology traced the Juke family's profile on issues of heredity, education, intelligence, income and criminality. Using a survey and archival information, Dugdale was able to identify links between pauperism and crime, and further links for prostitution and illegitimacy with neglect, misinformation of true parentage and being uneducated. He also claimed that poor decision-making occurred as a consequence of the Jukes being self-indulgent. Dugdale traced the Juke family back to the 1700s. The first member of the family had legitimate and illegitimate children (two boys and six girls). His two sons had incestuous relationships with his two daughters who they then married. It was these two lineages that Dugdale focused on. When Dugdale studied the Juke family, there were 709 members. This number broke down to 540 of Juke blood and 169 through family reconstitutions. There were 535 children all told, with 335 being legitimate, 106 illegitimate and 84 who were unknowns. From his in-depth research, Dugdale concluded that heredity not only had a major impact on physical attributes but on mental capacity also. Combining these two attributes helped shape the future pathway of Jukes. Moral behaviour, he concluded, was shaped by the environment as opposed to physical and mental capacity. Members of the Jukes developed habits that were caused by their environmental experiences – including a 'habit of pauperism'. He highlighted how heredity produces an environment conducive to the perpetuation of that heredity. Finally, Dugdale saw the environment as a factor determining the direction in life an individual takes. Moreover, it is the heredity received which creates and ensures the maintenance of an unchanging environment.

Another similar study was conducted over 100 years later by Brunner, Nelen, Breakefield, Ropers and van Oost (1993). They studied a Dutch family who had a mutated gene associated with criminality.

This mutated gene was known as monoamine oxidase A (MAOA; see Box 4.2). This gene codes for the enzyme monoamine oxidase A (MAO-A; confusingly!). Down the generations of this Dutch family, the males were deficient in MAO-A which led to low levels of serotonin (5-HIAA). Serotonin is a neurotransmitter (see Chapter 4), which plays a major role in mood regulation and explains why low levels of serotonin have been associated with impulsive aggressiveness (in other words, behaving aggressively before thinking). Brunner et al. explained the Dutch family's antisocial behaviour and violence as a consequence of this mutated gene causing a deficit of MAO-A secretion. There have been many other longitudinal family studies that have considered gene-environment interactions, some of which have been discussed previously (see Box 3.5).

Interestingly, a study looking at 'sensitive parenting' found that callous-unemotional behaviours in infants of 24, 36 and 58 months were heightened when there was little sensitivity shown by the care-giver (Wagner, Mills-Koonce, Willoughby, Zvara et al. 2015). This was one of many studies operating under the guise of the Family Life Project (2019) which studied 1,292 children from birth until the first grade. These children were from poor-income families. The aim was to look at various factors during infancy which could be used to predict the presence of CU traits in the first grade. Wagner, Mills-Koonce, Willoughby and Cox (2019), on behalf of the Family Life Project, examined the comments made by care-givers in response to their infants' supposed thoughts and feelings, with the presence of CU traits in grade one. Wagner et al. found that such positive mental state talk was a good buffer from developing CU traits. Another factor that helped to buffer the child from developing CU behaviours is positive reinforcement from the care-giver. Hyde, Waller, Trentacosta, Shaw et al. (2016) used an adoption cohort of 61 families. They found that the antisocial history of the biological mother predicted CU behaviours in infants of 27 months. The positive reinforcement offered by the adoptive mother to infants at 18 months, however, buffered against the high heritability of these CU behaviours. Hence, here we have a case of an evocative gene-environment interaction.

The evidence is robust for there being gene-environment interactions. Regardless of how difficult it is to tease out the factors important for understanding the possible causes of psychopathy, such demographical data will help us to map a progressive trajectory of antisocial/psychopathic behaviour from childhood to adulthood.

CONTINUITY OF ANTISOCIAL BEHAVIOUR FROM CHILDHOOD TO ADULTHOOD

As we have seen earlier in this chapter, disruptive behaviour disorder (DBD) collectively describes children with similar traits to those exhibited by adult psychopaths (see Chapter 5). The traits of psychopathy have been measured in adolescents (Glenn 2019). Glenn discussed how the core socioemotional elements of psychopathy such as callous-unemotional (CU) traits can also be measured in children and adolescents. The CU traits appear to be stable across early development and can be a robust indicator of the extent of future aggressive behaviour in individuals. CU traits, in fact, have been witnessed in toddlers and preschool children (Assary, Salekin and Barker 2015). Traits encapsulated by CU (such as lack of guilt and empathy, non-responsivity to punishment, low fear and proclivity for reward) can be seen in children aged three years. And as has been found in DBDs, the earlier these traits occur, the more severe the antisocial behaviour is likely to be by the age of ten (Waller, Dishion, Shaw, Gardner et al. 2016). A link between CU-related behaviours shown in children aged three to five years was found with ADHD and ODD (Willoughby, Waschbusch, Moore and Propper 2011). Gaysina, Mhango and Muszynska (2022) highlighted the difference between ODD and CD in terms of their correlation with ratings of aggression and delinquency. In the case of ODD, there is a robust correlation with aggressive behaviour. For CD, however, there is a robust correlation with delinquency. Gaysina further reported that these conditions might have a different aetiology and provided the example of CD with ADHD being more heritable than CD *per se*.

As we have seen in Chapters 1 and 2, many experts subscribe to the notion that there are two variants of psychopathy: primary and secondary (Blackburn 1975; Karpman 1941, 1948). Both primary and secondary psychopaths exhibit similar profiles concerning psychopathic traits but show differences in levels of anxiety and general emotional distress. In the case of primary psychopathy, the levels of anxiety are low, unlike secondary psychopathy where it is high (Hicks and Patrick 2006). Both primary psychopathy and secondary psychopathy have been demonstrated in adult populations, but more recently this has been studied in younger population samples. Community, clinic-referred and detained adolescent samples have been considered by various researchers. The findings and trends are conclusive that adolescents mirror adult populations. Adolescent secondary psychopaths, like their adult counterparts, have also experienced a history of abuse and trauma. They show more negative emotions and aggression than primary psychopaths. Furthermore, secondary psychopaths are more likely to experience ADHD. Interestingly, Fanti, Demetriou and Kimonis (2013) found that community-based adolescent secondary psychopaths showed more conduct problems and aggression than those of the primary variant. CU traits are a part of psychopathy, and many studies have focused on these. Docherty, Boxer, Huesmann, O'Brien et al. (2016) were interested in identifying risk factors associated with violent and non-violent behaviours among 799 adolescents averaging 16 years of age. Docherty et al. found a primary CU variant with low anxiety and a secondary CU variant with high anxiety. They also found a third group, which they referred to as the fearful cluster. This cluster had CU traits with higher anxiety than the primary group but lower than the secondary group. Docherty et al. explained the fearful cluster as those who have not completely transitioned to the secondary group. They argued that adolescents in the fearful cluster experience the same adversity and exposure to aggression and violence as those in the secondary cluster, but as yet, they are in the early stages of processing this. Eventually, members of this group are likely to transition into secondary psychopathy. This is because their experience of stressors in their environment acts to increase their levels of anxiety. This study demonstrates the continuity of psychopathy from adolescence to adulthood but can the same be said for children.

Huang, Fan, Lin and Wang (2020) studied 1,861 children aged six to 14 years for the presence of psychopathic tendencies such as CU traits, **conduct problem (CP) behaviours** and anxiety. They found four sub-groups of children:

1. Low risk – low in CU, CP and anxiety
2. Anxious – low in CU and CP but high in anxiety
3. Primary variants with psychopathic tendencies – high in CU and CP but low in anxiety

4. Secondary variants with psychopathic tendencies – high in CU, CP and anxiety

It is of interest to note that the secondary variants exhibited higher levels of CU and CP factors than the primary variants. The finding of increased anxiety is consistent with other research findings (see Figure 6.4).

A multitude of studies have now shown a continuance of psychopathic traits occurring in childhood and adolescence into adulthood. This clearly suggests that psychopathy is not something an individual 'wakes up' to one day in their life, but rather, it is generally a predisposition that starts early on in life. The propensity for this predisposition to develop further is influenced by the individual's environment and culture (as we have seen earlier). The gene–environment interaction is alive and kicking.

WHAT CAN WE SAY ABOUT THE ODD, CD AND ADHD CONNECTION WITH PSYCHOPATHY?

It is easy to see a connection between the symptoms outlined for oppositional defiant disorder (ODD) and conduct disorder (CD) with psychopathy. The callous-unemotional (CU) traits and

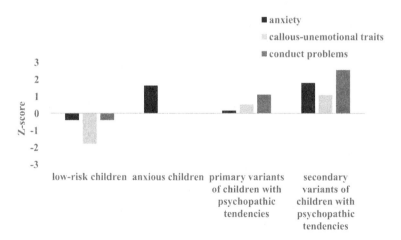

Figure 6.4 The four clusters and anxiety, CU and CP ratings

conduct problems (CP) behaviours are at the core of these two DBDs. Although attention deficit hyperactivity disorder (ADHD) shows some commonality with ODD and CD, many of the behaviours exhibited are due to an inability to pay attention and control motor activity. These symptoms can become majorly disruptive. Depending on environmental factors and the reactions they receive towards their behaviours, however, ADHD symptoms can progress into antisocial behaviour. The progression of ODD to CD is likely, especially if it is left untreated and the environment is predominantly an antisocial one. CD, however, is renowned for being a prerequisite to psychopathy. Many of the symptoms such as CU traits and CP behaviours can be witnessed in adult individuals with psychopathy – both primary and secondary psychopathy. It is such CU traits that enable individuals to commit horrific delinquent acts as juveniles and heinous crimes as adults. A progressive step from juvenile to adult criminality can be seen in certain types of behaviours such as bullying and membership of antisocial gangs.

Bullying

According to Rey, Espino, Ojeda and Mora-Merchán (2022), "Bullying is a psychological problem characterised by repeated aggression toward one or several individuals, which creates a power imbalance between the bully and their victims..." (cited in Smith and Hart, p. 591).

At the heart of this relationship is dominance by the bully and submission by the victim. Bullies exert control over their victims and resort either to direct or indirect forms of aggression. In the case of direct aggression, this can be physical and include behaviours such as punching and kicking or verbal abuse in the form of threats or insults. Indirect aggression can occur through acts such as social exclusion or spreading rumours. Smith (2016) outlined six types of bullying:

1. Physical – punching, kicking
2. Verbal – teasing, insulting
3. Social exclusion – exclusion from others
4. Indirect – spreading rumours
5. Bias or prejudice based – harassment towards specific groups of people
6. Cyberbullying – spreading nasty verbal abuse through texting, emailing, social networking

Bullying behaviour occurs worldwide and can occur as early as four to five years of age. The prevalence of bullying behaviour in children is difficult to ascertain accurately given how studies differ in the methodology used and the different criteria examined. Nevertheless, a report published in 2020 known as Health Behaviour in School-aged Children did use consistent methodology and criteria, finding that bullying varied from 0.3 to 30 per cent depending on the source country (Inchley, Currie, Budisavljevic, Torsheim et al. 2020). Smith (2016) found that the peak age at which bullying occurred was between 11 and 14 years, after which the incidence of bullying declined with an increase in age.

A culmination of factors is responsible for bullying behaviour. As we have seen in Chapter 3, the home and social environment can play a pivotal role in how a child responds socially and emotionally to others. In Chapters 4 and 5, we saw how biological factors can influence a child's temperament and cognition in a way that provokes negativity towards others. The gene-environment interface, however, can characterise a child's bullying behaviour as a consequence of an interaction that is unique to the child in question. Researchers have studied these individual differences, and two key factors that determine the pathway of becoming a bully or victim are empathy and self-esteem. Studies have shown the connection between becoming a bully and having low or no empathy. We have seen in previous chapters and earlier in this chapter that one of the pertinent defining characteristics of psychopathy and conditions such as ODD, CD and ADHD is low or no empathy. In other words, it is an inability to 'feel' the emotions of others (**affective empathy**). Psychopaths can gauge the emotions cognitively of their victims (**cognitive empathy**), as they 'get a high' from torturing them, but they fail to feel what their victims are experiencing. The importance of self-esteem has had mixed findings. There is evidence that victims tend to have low self-esteem while bullies have high self-esteem (Zych, Farrington and Trofi 2019). Self-esteem, however, varies across bullies such that there is a split between those with high and low self-esteem (Tsaousis 2016).

Interestingly, Taylor and Workman (2018) pointed out the similarities in the thinking processes between ODD, CD and ADHD and that of the adult criminal. This conclusion stemmed from the work of Yochelson and Samenow who in 1976 outlined 52 typical errors of thinking seen in the criminal personality (see Chapter 5).

Children with ODD, CD or ADHD make attributions of hostile intent (in an effort to understand why people behave as they do) in the same way as individuals with a criminal personality. In particular, children with CD have emotional, cognitive and behavioural traits in common with adults who are diagnosed with antisocial personality disorder (ASPD). Children indulging in bullying behaviours find it easier to morally disengage (Barchia and Bussey 2007). Morally disengaging makes it easier for bullies to continue their bullying tactics (see Figure 6.5). This is because bullies introduce justifications for their transgressions which support their inability to feel guilt (Bandura 2001). Moral disengagement is a way of thinking that typifies the criminal personality outlined by Yochelson and Samenow. Moreover, Bandura argued that such moral disengagement makes it easier to act even more aggressively and violently.

Sutton and Keogh (2000) examined Machiavellian attitudes among a cohort of children aged nine to 12 years in Scotland. They found that those children who were bullies had Machiavellian attitudes, unlike their non-bullying peers. This finding was also supported in a study conducted in Greece among the same-aged cohort of children (Andreou 2004). CU traits were also found to predict bullying behaviours (Muñoz, Qualter and Padgett 2011). Such findings have a robust link with the traits and behaviours found in adolescents with conduct problems and in adults diagnosed

Figure 6.5 Typical physical bullying by kicking

with psychopathy. In a Swedish study tracking 2,255 twins from adolescence to adulthood, teenage antisocial behaviour was singled out as a key factor predicting adult psychopathy (Forsman, Lichtestein, Andershed and Larsson 2010). This finding supported previous research showing that high scores on psychopathy at the age of 13 were indicative of psychopathy in adulthood. The traits present in children with ODD, CD and ADHD link with being a bully as well as adult psychopathy. This link is supported further in a study by Finger, Marsh, Mitchell, Reid et al. (2008) where children and adolescents exhibiting psychopathic traits (such as CU traits, narcissism, impulsivity and Machiavellianism), ODD or CD had brain anomalies. Using fMRI (to see the brain in action: see Chapter 4), Finger et al. found functional abnormalities akin to adult psychopaths in the orbital and ventromedial prefrontal cortex. These areas of the brain are important in learning and processing information that can be used to anticipate which responses will lead to punishment.

van Geel, Toprak, Goemans, Zwaanswijk et al. (2017) performed **meta-analyses** on youths under the age of 20 for CU traits, narcissism and impulsivity (a typical psychopathic profile) in relation to bullying. Significant correlations across bullying and CU traits, narcissism and impulsivity were found. They concluded that adolescents exhibiting problem behaviours can be identified *via* a combination of these psychopathic markers. Ganesan, Shakoor, Wertz, Agnew-Blais et al. (2021) performed a longitudinal twin study of 2,232 children and obtained reports from the mothers and teachers about bullying behaviour and conduct problems (CPs). Other information about the children's family and temperament at the age of five and their emotional and behavioural problems at the age of 12 and 18 was assessed. Ganesan et al. concluded that CPs and bullying behaviour occurred together during childhood. Interestingly, a study by Ahmed, Metwaly, Elbeh, Galal et al. (2022) found a relationship between ADHD and bullying at school, a finding supporting previous research such as that undertaken among 577 children in the fourth grade at a Swedish school by Holmberg and Hjern (2008). Other studies have shown a link between ADHD, ODD and CD with bullying behaviours.

As we can see, the research triangulates the connection between ODD, CD, ADHD and psychopathy with bullying. Furthermore, the traits and characteristics of ODD, CD and ADHD are closely linked with those of adult psychopathy. The evidence suggests that there is a developmental progression for psychopathy and that bullying behaviour starts young and continues into adulthood as part of an arsenal of behavioural weapons used by psychopathically inclined individuals. Children with psychopathic tendencies who bully can make the lives of their victims a misery. There are, however, cases where bullies take things too far and commit murder (see Box 6.4).

BOX 6.4: SCHOOL BOYS WITH MURDER ON THEIR MINDS

Robert Thompson and Jon Venables (both aged ten) were unpopular children at school. Their peers considered them to be odd and rejected them from many group activities. Rejected children and adolescents tend to be either non-aggressive or aggressive. This clearly has an impact on their social behaviour and the type of peers they are attracted to. For those who are aggressive, the pathway is different. For instance, rejected aggressive children and adolescents will also seek like-minded others. Thompson and Venables saw a common deviancy in each other which created a strong friendship bond between them. They often watched violent videos together and would frequent the shopping precincts when truanting from school. They encouraged each other to be violent. Perhaps if they were not together, the sequence of events in 1993 would not have occurred. They were captured on CCTV leading a toddler of two years (who was discovered to be James Bulger) away from one of the shops in Bootle's (North England) shopping precinct unbeknownst to his mother nearby. Various sightings by witnesses and further CCTV footage spotted the boys holding Bulger's hand and leading him across the town to the railway track where his body was eventually discovered. Bulger had been bullied violently by Thompson and Venables. The bruising on Bulger indicated that he had been violently punched, kicked and stoned after which paint had been thrown on his body. Psychologists deemed Thompson to be the dominant boy in the dyadic friendship and influenced Venables. Their friendship, given their personal characteristics of having CU traits and being Machiavellian, fits the roles of primary (Thompson) and secondary (Venables) psychopaths. Thompson came from a criminal family where his parents and brothers had criminal records. It would be safe to say that Thompson was brought up to have criminal ideals and modelled his behaviour on the criminal members of his family. Alternatively, Venables came from a dysfunctional family where violence was the norm. There was little discipline and few boundaries of what is regarded as acceptable behaviour for Thompson and Venables. Their parents were clearly poor role models and continued the intergenerational transmission of inappropriate socialisation. Bullying a toddler to his death demonstrates a serious deficit in their moral development. Not much is known about Thompson as an adult, but Venables as an adult was imprisoned for downloading child pornography in 2010.

Gang Behaviour

Thornberry, Freeman-Gallant, Lizotte, Krohn et al. (2003) highlighted how peers like to imitate one another, and if they feel bonded together as friends, this imitation could include delinquent behaviours such as stealing and truancy from school. Ray (2018) claimed that having delinquent peers is associated with the development of psychopathic traits and that antisocial behaviour is reinforced by these peers. Furthermore, delinquent peers are more likely to have CU traits. Indulging in delinquency can often lead to an association with other like-minded individuals and to gang membership, a gang with like-minded ideals, norms, values and behaviours (Taylor 2016). It is this like-mindedness that provides members of deviant gangs with a sense of belongingness as an exchange for their loyalty. As Thornberry et al. pointed out, membership to a gang increases the risk of children and adolescents engaging in violent behaviours. The risk of violent behaviour has been reported to be three times higher for gang members than non-gang members. Although the problem of violent gangs with offensive weapons is higher in the

US, members of gangs between ten and 17 years of age and the number of gangs *per se* in Britain have increased in recent years and pose a social problem. There are many reasons why youths join gangs, but Dishion, Nelson and Yasui (2005) listed three contributory factors:

1. Peer rejection
2. Academically failing in the school environment
3. Displaying antisocial behaviour

Wolff, Baglivio, Limoncelli and Delisi (2020) added witnessing adverse events, fighting and experiencing life-threatening situations as factors increasing gang affiliation.

Although, no doubt, there are individuals who become radicalised into joining gangs, the literature seems to suggest that those who become members of antisocial gangs are already inclined to behave antisocially. Researchers have focused on the traits in Factor 1 (Affective/Interpersonal) of the Psychopathy Checklist: Youth Version (PCL-YV; Chapter 2) with members of gangs. Hence, researchers have examined whether the traits of gang members overlap with those seen in psychopaths. Considering typical traits in Factor 1, such as a lack of guilt (Carson, Wiley and Esbensen 2017), low levels of empathy (Lenzi, Sharkey, Vieno, Mayworm et al. 2015) and CU traits (Thornton, Frick, Shulman, Ray et al. 2015), a robust link was found with gang membership. Other traits associated with psychopathy measured in Factor 2 (Antisocial/Lifestyle) have also been demonstrated in gang members such as early antisocial behaviours (Klein and Maxson 2006), impulsivity (Hennigan, Kolnck, Vindel and Maxson 2015) and ineffective anger control (Mallion and Wood 2018). Carson and Ray (2019) even alluded to those scoring high on Factor 2, as being more likely to join a gang. Additionally, it has been argued that gang membership enables individuals to behave antisocially as a consequence of moral disengagement and a diffusion of responsibility. According to Dmitrieva, Gibson, Steinberg, Piquero et al. (2014), leaders of gangs are more likely to have psychopathic traits. This finding, however, is not set in stone as the literature on this is contradictory (see Box 6.5).

BOX 6.5: IS A PSYCHOPATH GANG FODDER?

Carson and Ray (2019) looked at gang trajectories by studying gang members beyond the typical cut-off age of 18 years used in previous research. They continued the age trajectory to 23 years, in the belief that this would provide a greater understanding of how adolescents and young adults become initiated, persist with or desist gang membership. Their data show that there are three different gang membership trajectories. As with previous research, they found a young gang that peaked at mid-adolescence, all-in-all lasting approximately two years. They referred to this group as Adolescent Desister. Another group identified was referred to as Young Adult Desister. In the case of the third gang membership, referred to as Adult Joiner, Persister group, older members continue with the lifestyle afforded by being in the gang. Carson and Ray were also interested to know whether there is a relationship between psychopathy and gang membership. Their findings were not straightforward but indicated that scoring high on Factor 2 was key to desistance from dropping out of the gang. In other words, these individuals were Adult Joiner, Persisters. They enjoyed the gang lifestyle and the rewards and opportunities it provided. These individuals, however, had low scores on Factor 1. Carson and Ray explained this by highlighting how low empathy, CU traits and a lack of guilt are not conducive to a gang lifestyle, thereby making gang membership unattractive. Those high on Factor 1 tend to be uninvolved with peers and prefer to operate alone (Goldweber, Dmitrieva, Cauffman, Piquero et al. 2011). It can work the other way too, as traits such as manipulation, non-accountability and lying are not attractive to other gang members. Moreover, to have such a person as a leader would not be tolerable. Carson and Ray argued that psychopathy *per se* did not predict the longevity of gang membership but rather scoring high on Factor 2 and low on Factor 1 did.

As mentioned in Box 6.5, psychopaths scoring high on Factor 2 but low on Factor 1 are the ones attracted to a gang lifestyle. Hare (1999) claimed that, "Gangs have always provided greater opportunities for young psychopaths. Their impulsive, selfish, callous, egocentric, and aggressive tendencies easily blend in with – and may even set the tone for -many of the gang's activities" (p. 176).

Hare is referring to the 'pulls' of the gang lifestyle – the positive attractions. Hence, individuals are attracted to the excitement, money gains, status and other lifestyle benefits afforded by gang membership. The gang lifestyle provides a way "to fill unsupervised time and spice up otherwise mundane lives" (Densley 2018, p. 10).

SUMMARY

Evidence for there being a developmental trajectory for psychopathy is strong. Numerous studies have shown that children (and in some cases toddlers) can have psychopathic traits which continue into adolescence and further into adulthood. Although children exhibit negative and undesirable behaviours, they generally grow out of this. In fact, developmental psychologists have drawn up a table of normative negative behaviours that occur at different ages of development. It is the children who exhibit these behaviours frequently, early on in development, and continue over a long period of time who can develop conduct problems. Moffit (1993) identified two typologies of antisocial behaviour in youths: life–course–persistent (starts from the age of ten and continues) and adolescence-limited (starts at a later age and mimics others who behave antisocially to attain similar rewards). Some children have been diagnosed with disruptive behaviour disorders (DBD) listed as oppositional defiant disorder (ODD) and conduct disorder (CD). Attention deficit hyperactivity disorder (ADHD), despite not being categorised as a DBD, overlaps with the behavioural traits of ODD and CD. What these disorders have in common are conduct problems and callous-unemotional traits to varying degrees. If left untreated, children with these disorders can exhibit challenging and problematic behaviours that become increasingly more difficult to control with age. Using diagnostic tests such as the PCL-YV, traits typifying psychopathy such as no guilt after a transgression, selfishness, lying, unresponsive to punishment and manipulative behaviour can be seen in children aged two to four years. Other traits including impulsivity, remorselessness, unemotionality and callousness have been found in antisocial and delinquent youths – traits that we see in adult psychopaths. ODD, CD and ADHD have biological underpinnings, and it is argued, underlying genetic causes. Antisocial behaviour appears to run in families as we saw in the Jukes family and has been, in part, explained by three gene-environment interactions: passive, active and evocative effects. Although all three contribute to the development of antisocial behaviour, it is the evocative effect that received the most attention. There have been a number of genes identified which are considered to contribute towards developing antisocial and psychopathic behaviour, in particular, the DRD4–7R structural configuration of the DRD4 gene is found to affect temperament. This, in combination with a difficult upbringing, reinforces the tendency to develop a psychopathic temperament. Studies have connected high CU and CP with primary psychopathy and high CU, CP and anxiety with secondary psychopathy. Moreover, ODD, CD and ADHD have been linked with antisocial behaviour and psychopathy (and even to a primary and secondary divide). Having CU traits is what helps to link children with ODD, CD and ADHD to adult psychopathy. It also links children with CU traits to the propensity to bully and join antisocial gangs.

FURTHER READING

Carroll, A., Houghton, S., Durkin, K. and Hattie, J. (2009). *Adolescent reputations and risk: Developmental trajectories to delinquency.* New York: Springer.

Conkbayir, M. (2021). *Early childhood and neuroscience: Theory, research and implications for practice* (2nd edn.). London: Bloomsbury Academic.

Durbano, F. (2017). *Psychopathy: New updates on an old phenomenon.* London: IntechOpen.

Frogner, L. (2016). *The development of conduct problems in early childhood – the role of psychopathic traits and psychopathic personality.* Örebro, Sweden: Örebro University.

CRIMINAL AND ENTREPRENEURIAL PSYCHOPATHS

When we think about psychopaths frequently, an image of a serial killer comes to mind. It is for this reason we mistakenly consider psychopathy a criminal rather than a personality dimension (see Chapter 5). The reporting of serial murder and other heinous homicides exaggerates the number of psychopaths who actually contravene the law. Proportionately, there are relatively few psychopaths who commit crimes; but because of their personality characteristics such as callous-unemotional traits, when they do contravene the law, their acts are execrable enough to break the human moral code (known as *mala in se* acts). There are many, however, who successfully and discreetly navigate society without ever getting into trouble (see Chapter 8). Family, friends and peers of the psychopath might notice a slight edge to their temperament but consider this a small price to pay for their other good attributes. Some psychopathic individuals are extremely innovative and creative. These individuals run businesses successfully and are founders of companies that go on to create useful things for society. Despite these positive contributions to society, however, such individuals often have a cruel side to the way in which they interact with their employees. We can refer to successful innovative individuals as these as entrepreneurs. Do entrepreneurs have some of the traits of a psychopath? Do they harbour the characteristics encapsulated in the dark triad? In this chapter, we will explore the seemingly disparate lifestyles of the psychopath – a criminal or entrepreneurial lifestyle. We will also consider why it is that given a similar personality profile, some psychopaths will commit crimes while others will be enterprising.

DOI: 10.4324/9781032221052-7

CRIMINAL PSYCHOPATHS

Criminal psychopaths, in part, are a product of their personality make-up, which makes it easy for them to commit *mala in se* crimes such as homicide, arson and acts of a sexual nature. These types of crimes are personal acts that are often committed without any empathy or respect for their victims. In the case of serial murder, the atrocities inflicted on victims show extreme violence and deviance. When we consider the way in which Jack the Ripper killed and eviscerated his female victims in the White Chapel area of London during the 19th century, we see a violent individual with an aberration of thought. He not only murdered his victims but used a specific method of targeting and killing them; in other words, he had a *modus operandi* **(MO)** that sets him apart from other killers. The way in which he carried out his crimes was similar across victims. There were set behaviours committed by Jack the Ripper which helped to serve his emotional needs such as selecting female victims and employing extreme violence to deface them. These behaviours cumulated to create Jack the Ripper's own idiosyncratic criminal signature. Criminal psychopaths, in particular those committing serial murder, often have their own signature. What they have in common despite these differences, however, is the ability to debase and dehumanise their victims without any empathy, remorse or guilt. This places them in a communal space where their personality traits coincide.

We often consider criminal psychopaths to be unsuccessful. In the scheme of things, they are unsuccessful. There are, however, criminals who live successful lives and are good at evading capture. Success very much depends on the nature of criminal activity considered. We could argue that even psychopathic serial killers are successful, given how long it takes for the police to apprehend and bring them to justice – it can take many years. Furthermore, even if we use the FBI 'organised' and 'disorganised' classifications to separate the well-planned killer from the chaotic serial killer, respectively, the detection and apprehension of the most disorganised of serial killers can take many years. This in itself suggests that all serial killers have elements of an organised MO but can vary in the level of disorganised crime-scene traits (Taylor, Lambeth, Green, Bone et al. 2012). Hence, even criminal psychopaths can be successful (at what they do, evading capture and, it can be argued, living a successful life-style). What we can say is that those criminal psychopaths who end up incarcerated serving a lengthy sentence are the unsuccessful ones.

Some of the most heinous criminal acts are committed by psy-chopaths. Such acts more often than not involve the torture of victims, non-consensual deviant sexual violations and violent deaths (Toates and Coschug-Toates 2022). Even in death, many of these victims are violated, often sexually as a means of satisfying the kill-er's necrophilia. In cases of erotophonophilia (lust murder), sexual sadism and erotic homicide are apparent among individuals embrac-ing this form of paraphilia (Taylor 2016). Such individuals are also very likely to have psychopathic traits. There are many examples of criminal psychopaths but here we will focus on violent sexual serial killers and white-collar criminals. These two seemingly unrelated types of criminals are united by their callous–unemotional (CU) traits. These two categories of criminals operate very differently, but despite their different MOs, their underlying psychopathic traits enable them to be unemphatic towards their victims. Serial kill-ers are often personable as they are in physical contact with their victims thus causing both physical and emotional harm. Alterna-tively, **white-collar criminals** are more likely to be impersonable as they operate from a distance, thereby inflicting emotional harm that could lead to physical problems.

DEFINITION OF SERIAL KILLING AND WHITE-COLLAR CRIMES

It is worth spending some time defining serial killing and white-collar crimes in order to understand why these seemingly unrelated criminal activities are committed by individuals with the same underlying personality traits – that is, traits depicting a psychopath. Also, what is it that separates serial killing from other killing? If you remove a one-off murder from the equation, we are left with the categories of mass killing, spree killing and serial killing. And the perpetrators of these killings are referred to as mass murderers, spree murderers and serial murderers, respectively. In the case of mass murderers, we have examples such as the Columbine High School shootings of 1999 in the US, the Dunblane School shootings of 1996 in the UK and the Temple Military Base in Bloemfon-tein murders of 1999 in South Africa. What these events all have in common is that "one explosive event" (Leyton 1986, p. 18) had occurred where many people were killed within a short time frame in the same area by one individual. An example of spree murderers is the partners in crime, Peter Grundling and Charmaine Philips. In 1981, they murdered many people during a three-week time frame in different places such as Durban, Bloemfontein and Melmoth. According to Holmes and Holmes (2001) to qualify as a spree murderer, there are normally three different locations where killings occur which implies that these murders are separate events. Finally, to qualify as a serial murderer, Resler, Burgess, Douglas, Hartman et al. (1986) claimed that at least three separate killings in different locations over a defined 'emotional cooling-off period' (hence a temporal segregation between murders) must occur. Additionally, it is argued by Hickey (2002) that a pattern should emerge from the victims and crime scene leading to a clear MO and signature. It is important to highlight at this point in time that both mass and spree killers can also be psychopaths and that not all serial killers are psychopaths. We have chosen to focus on serial killers as one example of criminals who are enabled to kill in the most deplorable of ways by their psychopathic traits (see Boxes 7.1 and 7.2).

BOX 7.1: BELLFIELD, A KILLER WAITING FOR VICTIMS TO ALIGHT THE BUS

Levi Bellfield worked as a nightclub bouncer and a wheel clamper but was also a drug dealer. He had a history of violent behaviour, entertained male chauvinistic attitudes and was renowned as a bully. With this life history, Toates and Coschug-Toates (2022) considered him to be a prime suspect for psychopathy. At the age of 12, Bellfield had a girlfriend who was two years older than him. Although her strangled body was found two days after she went missing from school, Bellfield who was suspected of her murder was never officially investigated. By the age of 13, he had two convictions for burglary. Given his tall and muscular stature due to steroids, the job of a bouncer was apt. He used alcohol and drugs that helped escalate his sexually abusive language to females, some of whom were underaged. Additionally, he would use date rape drugs to undermine his victims. Bellfield had two long-term relationships that ended in violence towards them because he had gotten them pregnant. In both cases, he punched, kicked and raped them. Interestingly, like his girlfriend he had when he was 12 years old, these women were blonde and were forced to dress up in schoolgirl uniforms. It was clear that Bellfield was attracted to under-aged girls as his next girlfriend bore testament to – she was 15 years old. He wanted her to have sex with a friend, but she refused. This caused him to be angry and violent towards her as his authority and control were questioned. In 2003, Bellfield struck a blonde woman called Marsha with a blunt weapon to the head. She died. In 2004, a blonde called Kate who alighted the bus was run over but survived her injuries. A blonde called Amélie was battered over the head again with a blunt weapon. She died. It was the next murder of a 13-year-old girl by the name of 'Milly' Dowler that gripped the nation and led to Bellfield's apprehension and conviction and sentencing of life imprisonment. She wore a school uniform, and her body was found naked some 25 miles away from her home. Bellfield had serious anger issues but "kept his anger-based desire and sex-based desire apart" (Toates and Coschug-Toates 2022, p. 267).

BOX 7.2: UNTERWEGER, THE VIENNA WOODS KILLER

Jack Unterweger born in 1950 is considered as Austria's highest rank serial killer. His killings extended from Austria to Prague in Czechia and Los Angeles in the US. Unlike Bellfield, Unterweger was an intellectual and considered in Austrian society to be a well-acclaimed author and playwright. He had another side to him, however, where he was violent, indulged in burglary, theft and fraud, a pimp and perfected the art of manipulation. He even broadcasted on radio about the murders (which he was committing unbeknownst to the police) which led to police cooperation. Unterweger never knew his American dad and was transferred to the care of his drunken grandfather at the age of two while his mother remarried. He sought the affection of his mother, but his grandfather famously said she was a "tramp with no time for you" (Leake 2008, p. 9). From the age of 23 to 24, there were complaints over Unterweger's sexual assaultive behaviour.

His sexual behaviour was violent and involved the use of ligaments to tie his girlfriends' and friends' hands behind their backs. His first murder occurred when he was 24 years by strangling 18-year-old Margaret Schäfer using her bra. He was caught and convicted in 1976 and spent 15 years of his life sentence imprisoned. Supposedly redeemed, he was released from prison as a bit of a celebrity. It was while in prison that he learned to read and write and wrote novels, poems and plays. His book *Endstation Zuchthaus* (Terminal Prison) won a literary prize in 1984. Unterweger left prison in May 1990, but it was not long after that a prostitute was found strangled with her underwear – a very similar MO was used. Seven more prostitutes were found murdered in the same way and disposed of in the Vienna woods. Unterweger by now was a reporter and made himself the key journalist investigating these murders. This led to a five-week spell in the US, writing about the poor conditions endured by prostitutes in Los Angeles. During his time there, three prostitutes were found strangled by their own bras – the same MO as Unterweger's previous kills. Crime linkages were made between the murders in Austria, Czechia and the US and Unterweger's presence at the time of these murders. He was eventually arrested in Miami, US, in 1992. Unterweger was extradited to Austria and convicted on 29 June 1994. That night he hung himself in his cell. It was said this was his best murder yet.

White-collar crimes are very different from serial killing. The term white-collar crime was coined by American sociologist/criminologist Edwin Sutherland in 1939. Sutherland highlighted how white-collar criminals were of a respectable social standing; thus, white-collar crimes were "committed by a person of respectability and high social status in the course of his occupation" (1983, p. 7). From this definition, there are three underlying aspects: the crime, the perpetrator and the crime being related to the perpetrator's occupation. There has been some controversy over Sutherland's definition of white-collar criminals, in particular his reference to high social status. Taylor (2016) suggested that Sutherland's main objective was to highlight crimes that have often escaped the notice of the criminal justice system. Furthermore, Sutherland highlighted the fact that those occupying positions of power are more likely to commit criminal acts of a different genre to the common street crimes accessible to the lower classes. Retribution and justice, he argued, are more commonly reserved for the latter genre of crime when in fact white-collar crimes are often equally as serious and harmful. Interestingly, Williams (1997) pointed out that Sutherland included crimes of theft and fraud which were considered at the time to be criminal acts by both the lower-middle and lower classes. Williams claimed that what linked these criminal acts was the place in which they occurred – the workplace. These are all associated with an individual's occupation. Sutherland also paid heed to the importance of the violation of trust and suggested that this could occur by:

- Abusing power for self-gain or an advantage
- Disabling and eliminating the opposition
- Violating rules and regulations causing harm to the public (*mala prohibita* crime)

Edelhertz (1970) introduced a modified definition of white-collar crimes which was less restricted by social class. "…illegal acts committed by nonphysical means…by concealment or guile, to obtain money or property, to avoid the payment or loss of money or property…obtain business or personal advantage" (p. 3). He went on to say that "…character of white-collar crime must be found in its *modus operandi*…its objectives rather than the nature of the offenders" (p. 4).

This implies that criminally-minded individuals' choice of crime is influenced by the resources they have access to. Hence, white-collar criminals are more likely to operate at a higher level of difficulty as the nature of these criminal acts often entails ways of circumnavigating the legal system. Nevertheless, white-collar crimes can vary from low-level fraud to complicated acts of insider trading and embezzlement. There are many cases of white-collar criminals (see Box 7.3).

In recent years, there has been a shift towards stealing an unsuspecting individual's photograph from their 'Facebook' or 'Instagram' portfolio. This is then used to create a portfolio of a non-existent individual which can be picked up by a dating web app. In the UK, in the county of Hampshire, Richard Dexter was sentenced to four and a half years in prison after conning 'Tinder' user, Amrita Sebastian out of £141,500 (Morris 2022). As is often the case with such fraudsters, they supply their unsuspecting victim with a made-up narrative to encourage them to depart with their money. In this case, Dexter claimed he was due a windfall from investments made towards bio-pharmaceutical technology. He duped Sebastian into parting with her cash in a series of payments to pay for equipment needed. He made exaggerated claims such as having bought an air balloon because he could. This case is slightly different from other cases of this nature, simply because Sebastian had met Dexter in 2015. He promised he would pay out £100,000 over the next 15 months. Despite making a series of payments to him and feeling that something was not right, she claimed she felt "trapped" and was hoping that she would be refunded by the profits he made. This is an interesting case, as there is some background to his personality. For example, his own grand-mother claimed that Dexter would consistently ask her to transfer £10 due to his card not working. A businessman who Dexter was in contact with claimed that he lied but was good at charming people and was likeable. [A 'likeable rogue' is often how such psychopaths are described, at least at first.] In court, it became apparent that he had many unpaid debts to his close friends. Judge Timothy Mousley QC referred to Dexter as dishonest and uncaring towards his victims. The use of false information and identity theft is not an uncommon criminal activity (see Box 7.4).

BOX 7.3: A UK AND A US WHITE-COLLAR CASE

In the UK, Robert Maxwell was known for his British Printing Cor-poration and the Mirror Group Newspapers. He appeared to be a successful newspaper tycoon but there were questions asked about the financial security of his publication empire. *The Daily Mail, Sunday Mirror, New York Daily News, Daily Record* and *The People* newspa-pers were some of his main publications that he was responsible for. Maxwell did have money problems, and in order to cover the repay-ments of his various bank loans, he would shift money across his companies as a delaying tactic. But the true depth of his embezzle-ment only became apparent after he was found drowned in 1991. His fraudulent activities were on a very large scale and brought his whole empire into disrepute (which his sons would later try and resolve). The nature of his embezzlement involved the theft of monies and properties from his own employees. He embezzled pension funds, some £400 million from 32,000 of his employees in order to keep his newspaper empire afloat. The Department of Trade and Industry released the Maxwell Report in 2001. The Honourable Sir Thomas and Turner (1992) concluded that, "the most important lesson from all the events is that high ethical and professional standards must always be put before commercial advantage..."

Hare (1993) claimed that white-collar crimes are far more likely to be committed by those individuals with psychopathic traits. This equally applies to our next white-collar criminal from the US.

In 1987, John Grambling Jr. defrauded many banks. By borrowing large amounts of money without evidence of collateral, he managed to convince bank managers to lend him millions of dollars. He was very convincing and exuded the skills of manipulating his victims by using charm and deceit and appearing as trustworthy in his high-brow suit. His personality traits overlap very well with the traits seen in psychopaths and the criminal personality type (see Chapter 5). Grambling Jr. used the same MO towards his sister where he exploited her into signing her mortgage over to him – a sum of $4.5 million – and yet remaining liable.

Despite white-collar criminals having superior executive functioning and a heightened ability to process information (Raine, Laufer Yang, Narr et al. 2012), they demonstrate callous-unemotional traits that are characteristic of psychopaths. Other biological commonalities with psychopaths have also been found (see Chapter 4).

The evidence for the psychopathic nature of white-collar criminals is mounting. This comes from personality research, such as the 'dark triad' (see Chapter 5) and assessments to detect psychopaths as seen in the PCL-R introduced by Hare (see Chapters 1 and 2). There is evidence of white-collar criminals having superior executive functioning when compared to other psychopathic criminals, which might explain their choice of criminal activity. In some respects, we could say that white-collar crimes are more high-brow due to their often more complex *modus operandi*. In order to execute these crimes, a level of attention to detail and knowledge is essential. And having superior executive function enables such individuals to perform the essential attention to detail required. While white-collar criminals are not in direct physical contact with their unsuspecting victims, their actions nevertheless cause considerable distress to those who fall foul of scam activities. White-collar criminals often have the dark triad traits that suggest a callous and unemotional interior.

BOX 7.4: NUNN AND MCCREESH – CASES OF PSYCHOPATHY?

A man's picture was shown in a glossy brochure where he was happily smiling at the investment bond, he made in the Blackmore International Group. This picture was a case of identity theft and was used as a ploy to encourage people to invest in this company. The photograph was tracked down using a reverse image search and was part of a stock photo base. He was an ex-head of the KGB in one scam and a pastor of a local church in another. The brochure was very convincing and performed its task of 'catfishing' for potential individuals to invest in a residential property scheme consisting of luxury flats and houses in the UK by buying bonds. This was sold as a good investment that would result in an annual payback return of ten per cent in interest payments. The Blackmore International Group was co-founded by Phillip A. Nunn and Patrick M. McCreesh who considered themselves as the directors. Over 2,000 investors bought bonds using money from their pensions culminating in 46 million pounds. They were told that their money was protected by an insurance scheme that had a guarantee on it. It became apparent to the investors that their money returns were overdue. When one investor emailed McCreesh, he received a response that 'fobbed' him off. In Manchester on April 2020, Blackmore International collapsed. Investors lost their money, but how and why? The company was based in Costa Ricca and what Nunn and McCreesh did was to take 5.5 million pounds in fees for themselves from the investment pot instead of investing in the property market. The story doesn't finish here. After the administration of Blackmore International, they created Blackmore Global. Again, there were many investors in the offshore investment scheme. The money went to the Virgin Islands which is a tax haven. Nunn and McCreesh paid themselves out a hefty fee which left investors high and dry. In Gibraltar, they set up a company called Aspinal Chase Limited, where they made a pay out to themselves of 2.2 million pounds before winding the company up. McCreesh denied everything when approached by investigators. Nunn, however, was found to be operating a well-being and positive energy website with 67,000 followers from around the world – places like Australia, Norway, Beirut and India! The investigation into Nunn and McCreesh is ongoing.

ENTREPRENEURIAL PSYCHOPATHS

When we consider white-collar criminals, we think of individuals who have contravened the law – (*mala prohibita* in particular). There are of course psychopathic individuals who work in organisations, but instead of outrightly contravening legal legislation, they bend the rules without breaking them and create a bullying environment for their employees. We can consider these individuals as **entrepreneurial psychopaths**.

While the incidence of psychopathy in the general population is relatively low, the number of psychopaths in the corporate world is noticeably higher. Babiak and Hare (2007) found that between three and 25 per cent of executives have psychopathy – a figure that is much higher than the general population. Babiak and Hare (2007) referred to such individuals as 'snakes in suits'. The role of business leader and chief executive officer (CEO) are positions that appeal to the 'corporate psychopath'. It has been estimated that one in 25 bosses have psychopathic traits (Babiak, Neumann and Hare 2010). Babiak et al. gave 203 corporate professionals a number of assessments to complete, including the PCL-R and a Psychopathy Checklist: Screening Version (PCL:SV). The results confirmed that in this sample, there were more psychopaths than that found in community samples. Scores from the PCL-R and PCL:SV were corroborated by in-house ratings of high charisma, creativity and good strategic thinking but negatively with ratings of responsibility, being a team player and management skills. CEOs, they argue, no longer contribute to charities but instead are led by stock markets and make money *via* insincere, remorseless, shameless and truthless methods of operating.

Dutton (2016) reviewed the traits of politicians and world leaders and claimed these traits overlapped with psychopathic serial killers. He claimed that past and present leaders can be defined according to three categories of characteristics: fearless dominance, self-centred impulsivity and cold-heartedness. These characteristics are typical of psychopaths. Kets de Vries (2012) introduced the term '**Seductive Operational Bully' (SOB)**. Individuals classified as SOBs thrive in organisational settings where there is status, power and money to be had. They are good at avoiding incarceration in prison or psychiatric facilities because they are able to bend the rules so as not to be criminally accountable. According to Kets de Vries SOBs typify the psychopath by being outwardly charming and confident but inwardly a 'cold fish' devoid of any guilt or remorse or shame, and most importantly, any empathy. SOBs are good at presenting themselves as competent, confident and successful, which accounts largely for their ascent to top executive positions within organisations. Organisations priding themselves on risk-taking approaches to business, or who particularly appreciate executives with a cool demeanour in times of pressure with a keenness for domination and competitiveness, attract psychopaths at their peril. For it is more often than not that these individuals will eventually bring their organisation to its knees and quite often get away with doing so. This is the world of the entrepreneurial psychopath who isn't quite a criminal but does things that are on the borderline of being illegal. The entrepreneurial psychopath can walk in many spheres of life as we will see later, but there are some areas that enable and even encourage them to operationalise their plans – the corporate world.

Interestingly, Renata Schoeman highlighted five psychopath subtypes associated with the corporate world (see Table 7.1).

Despite these trait setbacks, Schoeman argued that some of these psychopaths can be successful in business. The cost of this, however, is their creation of a **toxic work environment**, often leading to employee discontentment, conflict and stress, days off on sick leave and loss of staff members. Schoeman (2019) claimed that:

> Emotional stress can also cause or aggravate physical illnesses such as gastrointestinal problems (such as irritable bowel syndrome) and cardiovascular problems (such as hypertension), while victims of workplace bullying had double the risk of considering suicide in the five years following.

> (News24).

Table 7.1 List of the five sub-types of psychopaths outlined by Schoeman

Subtypes of psychopaths	Description
Primary	Exhibit CU traits, no fear, anxiety, guilt or remorse and yet they do not take risks. They are good at directing their manipulative behaviour *via* socially accepted means.
Secondary	Exhibit emotional instability and whose traits demonstrate an aggressive, hostile, impulsive and self-destructive profile. They embrace risky decision-making.
Distempered	Have a low tolerance for boredom and find dangerous sports and activities exciting. They are also likely to be aggressive and violent due to being 'hotheads'.
Charismatic	They tend to be charming, pathological liars and manipulative. This masks their antisocial predispositions and often allows them to get away with things.
Egocentrically-impulsive	They are good at bending the rules to help achieve personal gains. They lie and manipulate and find it a challenge to make commitments and oversee long-term goals. They rationalise their aggressive acts and blame others for their failings.

From the descriptions of these sub-types of psychopath, it appears that secondary and distempered psychopaths would least suit an executive role within an organisation. Primary, charismatic and ego-centrically impulsive sub-types all have the ability to manipulate others in common; however, primary and charismatic individuals probably fit in best with a competitive organisation. In the case of primary psychopaths, their reluctance to take risks bodes well with avoiding sticky situations, whereas for charismatic psychopaths, their charm allows them to lie their way out of the mess. Support for this arises from Akhtar, Ahmetoglu and Chamorro-Premuzic's (2013) study. They were interested to see if there is a relationship between entrepreneurship and subclinical psychopathy. By considering the competencies, behavioural tendencies and activities and achievements of entrepreneurial working adults, they were able to develop a model revealing the relatedness of these individuals with primary and secondary psychopathic characteristics. A positive relationship was found with primary but not secondary characteristics. SOBs described by Kets de Vries most likely overlap with Schoeman's primary, charismatic and egocentrically impulsive sub-types of psychopath. With the use of bullying tactics to discombobulate their employees, SOBs are good at achieving what they want by not breaking the law in any obvious way (see Figure 7.1).

OTHER SPHERES OF THE WORKFORCE WHERE ENTREPRENEURIAL PSYCHOPATHS CAN LURK

A questionnaire called the Business Scan was developed by Babiak and Hare in 2006. The Business Scan measures four areas:

1. Personal style
2. Emotional style
3. Organisational effectiveness
4. Social responsibility

It is not designed to measure criminal factors but more as an investigative tool to isolate non-incarcerated white-collar psychopaths. It compares leadership traits with psychopathic traits such as charismatic versus superficial charm or ability to influence

Figure 7.1 Bullying gestures in the workplace by an entrepreneurial psychopath

versus manipulation, respectively. The overlap between leadership and psychopathic traits is vast. Harper (2022) highlighted how the 'ability to take risks' is an entrepreneurial trait, whereas 'impulsivity' is an irresponsible characteristic of the psychopath. 'The Great British Psychopath Survey' asked volunteers to elicit information about their employment and themselves. From this information, it was possible to separate high from low scorers for psychopathy. The results were interesting and showed a difference of career choices based on a high or low score for psychopathy. These findings were ranked and reported by Dutton in 2013 (see Figure 7.2).

Figure 7.2 List of careers attracting individuals with high or low psychopathy scores

Careers pertaining to low scores of psychopathy fit in with the notion of caring or teaching roles that require empathy and understanding of others. The creative artist is often referred to as a sensitive role in connection with his or her emotions. It is not surprising to see that CEOs, lawyers and salespersons make the list of high scorers, but some of the other careers are very unexpected. A clergy person and police officer and a chef? A clergy person is one of the high psychopathy scorers and is unexpected, and there is no reasonable explanation for this. A chef in the high-scoring career categories might be explained away by the desire to be a creative cook and become a renowned brand name – perhaps but don't criticise the chef at any rate! A police officer is also a surprise given their role as a protector of the peace. However, there is a saying 'that it takes a thief to catch a thief'. Could this be an insightful adage – meaning that you have to have the theory of mind of a potential criminal in order to anticipate their next action? The Metropolitan Police in England have been heavily criticised in recent years for, amongst other things, their heavy-handedness against protestors and attendees of vigils. There was an outcry against the Metropolitan Police Commissioner Cressida Dick for her failure to root out the culprits that brought the rest of the force into disrepute. It was the Major of London, Sadiq Khan, who put the commissioner on notice. In February 2022, she resigned. It was reported by an independent police watchdog that between 2016 and 2018 there was a toxic culture within the Metropolitan police where a group of officers shared sexist, racist and homophobic messages with 19 other officers (Police and Crime Correspondent, Vikram Dodd 2022). In March 2021, however, the Metropolitan Police were in trouble again after the kidnap and murder of Sarah Everard (see Box 7.5).

Wayne Couzens, it would appear, exemplifies the profile of a psychopath and provides support for Dutton's report in 2013. We have to be careful, however, when dividing careers up in this way as there are cases of criminal psychopaths who occupy the 'caring careers' – Dr Shipman, for example, who watched as many as 250 of his patients die while he injected them with a fatal dose of morphine. As a rule of thumb, entrepreneurial psychopaths do not commit crimes but rather will create a toxic environment for their employees and can cause years of stress and misery for those unfortunate to be in their path (see Boxes 5.6 and 7.6).

BOX 7.5: WAYNE COUZENS – THE LONDON METROPOLITAN POLICE OFFICER WHO USED HIS POSITION TO RAPE AND MURDER SARAH EVERARD

The high rate of psychopathy among police officers is disturbing (see Figure 7.2). One police force that has faced more than its fair share of criticism over the last 30 years is the London Metropolitan in the UK. Following criticisms of institutional racism during the 1990s, the 'Met' subsequently were also criticised by official watchdogs for bullying, homophobia and misogyny. In 2021, their standing fell to an all-time low when one of their officers was found guilty of the kidnap, rape and murder of 33-year-old Sarah Everard. That man was 48-year-old Wayne Couzens, a married man with two children. Described by his mother-in-law as 'a wonderful family man', it turned out that he was anything but. At the trial, it was revealed that Couzens had used his status as a police officer to 'arrest' and handcuff Everard in a premeditated attack. After murdering her, Couzens attempted to burn her body before leaving it in a bag in the countryside. In summing up, the judge, Lord Justice Fulford, noted that, while Couzens had pleaded guilty, he showed 'no genuine contrition'. He sentenced Couzens to a full life tariff meaning he joined a select group of around 60 killers in the whole of England and Wales who are considered to pose such a danger to the public that they can never be released.

Clearly, Couzens murder of Sarah Everard was an appalling crime, but we have to ask does this make him a psychopath? The majority of people who have committed murder have not been diagnosed as psychopathic (Taylor 2016). Some committed their crimes in the heat of the moment and later show great remorse, likewise for those 'high' on drugs or inebriated when committing a violent attack. But in Couzens' case, the rape and murder were planned meticulously and involved deception and manipulation of his victim. These acts were committed cold-bloodedly, and as was clear at the trial, Couzens showed no remorse, only self-pity. Given his behaviour, it might be surmised that it would be difficult to build an argument that his behaviour was not that of a psychopathic individual.

BOX 7.6: THE ANDREW CARNEGIE STORY

Andrew Carnegie was born in 1836 in Fife, Scotland, and went to Pennsylvania with his family at the age of 12. He came from a poor background – the son of a Scottish weaver – and yet he transformed his life in a classic story of rags-to-riches. He was known for helping those less fortunate than himself. He was renowned as the 'father of philanthropy' and made millions of dollars in the American steel industry during the 1800s. His wealth was vast. It was reported that he had given away about $350 million to charities and organised more than 2,800 public libraries. Despite this generosity, Carnegie had a dark side to his personality. His employees and work contacts claimed he could be ruthless and cruel. In Les Standiford's book, *Meet you in Hell*, Carnegie is described as Machiavellian, and in his effort to exploit, his workforce would be a brutal boss. Despite coming from a Scottish family who knew about the rights of workers, he mistreated his employees badly. One example is when he argued with the Knights of Labor and the Amalgamated Iron and Steel Workers (trade union) at his Edgar Thompson Works in Pennsylvania in 1883 for a cut in their wages of 20 per cent. They were forced to accept this as his counterargument was that the plant would shut down otherwise. Three years later, the plant was closed, and 1,600 men lost their jobs only ten days before Christmas. And yet in 1885, he agreed on individual contracts with the men to come back to work there with an increase of 33 per cent to their wages. He did manage to get rid of the trade union at the plant. He was certainly a mixed blessing. Standiford (2006) claimed that while Carnegie was ambitious, talented and worked hard, he had a tendency to be unethical and morally compromised – hence a conflicting combination of traits. He was generous and contributed to many charities, and sometimes to his employees, but more often than not he was brutal towards his workers. Even a close work associate, his company chairman, by the name of Henry Clay Frick, took the blame for an uprising at the Homestead where armed guards brought in by Frick shot 12 people dead. Carnegie told Frick to deal with the situation and was happy to disassociate himself from Frick. And yet, Carnegie was touched by an incident in 1904, where 180 Americans were trapped in a Pennsylvanian coal mine due to a fire outbreak. All died (barring one miner) including two 'heroes' who tried to rescue them. Carnegie donated what amounted to $100 million in today's currency in recognition of US and Canadian heroes. Ever since then, this legacy continues as the Carnegie Hero Medal where thousands of people have been awarded the medal for their heroism. Carnegie was a man of many contradictions.

Our next individual of interest is someone you would least expect to be an entrepreneur with possible psychopathic traits. L. Ron Hubbard was a science fiction writer who also published books that purported to provide a metaphysical account of how the mind and body are connected. He espoused a pseudoscientific ideology in order to set guidelines of how to behave (see Box 7.7).

BOX 7.7: L RON HUBBARD – INVENTING A RELIGION TO MAKE A FORTUNE?

Lafayette Ronald Hubbard was born in Helena, Montana, in 1911. In his teens, he began to write science fiction and served as a naval officer during the Second World War. While he rose to command two ships, he was removed from this position on both occasions due to complaints about his disorganised and unpredictable behaviour. Following the war, he returned to science fiction writing at which he proved to be prolific, churning out dozens of books and 100s of short stories. Hubbard once stated to a friend that 'if you want to get rich, then start a new religion', which he duly did. In 1950, he published a book entitled *Dianetics: The Modern Science of Mental Health*. In it, Hubbard claimed that he had developed new theories concerning the human mind and its capacities. In particular, Hubbard claimed that our brains record all of the bad things that happen to us as 'engrams', and these can later cause many physical and emotional problems. By 'auditing' ourselves (essentially, plugging into a primitive lie detector), we can regress back to examine these engrams and in doing so 'clear' them. Despite being re-hashed Freudian gobbledegook, during the early 1950s, Dianetics sold in enormous numbers and brought Hubbard a good return. Then in 1954, Hubbard set up the Church of Scientology. This 'Church' was based around Hubbard's notion that our true selves were spiritual 'thetans', immortal entities that had existed for billions (or possibly trillions of years – Hubbard was inconsistent on this, but in either event, the time scale is much longer than the actual age of the universe). These thetans had created the physical world, and having become trapped in our bodies, then forgot they had such god-like powers. This absent-mindedness of the thetans could, however, be overcome in each person *via* many (expensive) sessions of auditing until the church member was clear and able to reach their full potential. The Church of Scientology made Hubbard enormous wealth as he rapidly become a multimillionaire. In January 1986, Scientology leaders announced that Hubbard had chosen to 'drop his body' and continue his work on another plane of existence. In other words, he had died. All of this bizarre background information raises the question, was Hubbard a genuine, but deluded, man or was he a psychopathically manipulative one? A number of events in his life provide us with clues. First, while in the navy, his commanding officers summed up his behaviour in the following report:

> This officer is not satisfactory for independent duty assignment. He is garrulous and tries to give impressions of his importance. He also seems to think he has unusual ability in most lines. These characteristics indicate that he will require close supervision for satisfactory performance of any intelligence duty.
>
> (Miller 1987)

Second, his second wife Sara (whom he married while still married to his first wife Margaret), in filing for divorce in 1951, claimed that he subjected her to beatings, sleep deprivation and strangulation. Third, it is well documented that he regularly made false claims about his life and, in particular, his time in the armed forces (including the fact that he cured himself of blindness). Such stories were used to impress his followers. Fourth and finally, towards the end of his life, when his wealth was estimated to be over $200 million, the IRS considered indicting him for tax fraud (Miller 1987). None of this proves beyond doubt that L Ron Hubbard was a psychopath. But if he wasn't, then he was pretty good at imitating one.

Although we have divided this chapter into criminological and entrepreneurial psychopaths, and in particular have included serial killers and white-collar criminals and entrepreneurial psychopaths separately, we need to consider the question of just how different these individuals actually are. Because the MO of serial killers is quite different from white-collar criminals, we need to ask do their psychopathic personality traits differ? The quick answer is no. The personality traits are the same in that there are callous and unemotional (CU) traits, manipulation, narcissism and the propensity to hurt/harm others. What of our entrepreneurial psychopaths do they too have the same traits but use them differently by putting them to 'good use'? They do have superior executive functioning after all (as indeed do white-collar criminals). This might help to account for their ability to control their propensity to take unfounded risks as we saw in Schoeman's primary sub-type. Perhaps, however, the inclination for entrepreneurial psychopaths to attenuate or eliminate some of their natural predispositions such as CU and Machiavellian traits is simply too difficult. These traits are expressed in the form of bullying tactics towards employees, which is encapsulated by Kets de Vries' (2012) Seductive Operational Bully (SOB).

SUMMARY

Psychopathy, as we have seen in previous chapters, is often associated with criminality. While psychopathy is a personality dimension, many heinous crimes are committed by individuals who are psychopaths. In the case of serial killing, the crimes committed generally involve severe violence and deviance towards the victims. The *modus operandi* (MO) of serial killers involves violence and aggressive acts towards their victims prior, during and after death. The question posed is what enables these killers to commit such atrocities, and the simple answer is their personality traits. The callous and unemotional (CU) traits of the psychopath play a big part in disengaging them from the feelings of their victims. Their propensity towards impulsive and aggressive behaviour only adds to the way in which their MO plays out. Of course, there are other types of shocking crimes but here we primarily focused on this form of homicide. Harm to victims need not only be of a physical nature involving close contact but can cause emotional harm and occur from a distance. White-collar crime is an example of individuals causing extreme psychological stress and harm to their unsuspecting victims. The term white-collar criminal was introduced by Sutherland as a means to describe an individual of respectable social standing who commits crime related to his/her occupation. Sutherland's white-collar criminal includes crimes of theft and fraud committed by lower-middle and lower classes. These white-collar crimes often cause psychological harm to their victims, and the fraud and scams committed are often callous and cruel causing extreme stress and adversity. White-collar criminals exhibit CU traits and have superior executive functioning. This superior ability enables them to circumnavigate the legal system. Despite operating from a distance of their victims, their CU traits, ability to manipulate and charm are used to con people. There is evidence of some entrepreneurs showing psychopathic traits. Such individuals also have a superior executive functioning, but they would seem to also have the ability to be creative and have good problem-solving skills. Babiak and Hare found that between three and 25 per cent of executives are psychopaths. They referred to them as 'snakes in suits'. Many of these executives and CEOs are obsessed with making money for the company and often act in shameless, insincere, remorseless and ruthless ways. Others have described these individuals as having typical psychopathic characteristics captured by the term 'Seductive Operational Bully' or SOB. SOBs thrive in an organisational environment and have little empathy for their workforce, nor do they treat them very well. The entrepreneurial psychopath may have the same underlying traits as their criminal counterparts but tend not to break the law. Instead, they may bend the rules, but more often than not will discombobulate their employees. Schoeman claimed that this behaviour towards their employees creates a toxic environment with a high rate of staff discontentment and days off sick. From Schoeman's descriptions of her five sub-types, such entrepreneurs are most likely to be primary, charismatic or egocentrically impulsive psychopaths. There are other careers that attract psychopaths such as lawyers, journalists, surgeons and police. Careers that tend not to attract psychopaths include the caring professions such as doctors, nurses, charity workers and teachers.

FURTHER READING

Babiak, P. and Hare, R.D. (2019). *Snakes in Suits: Understanding and surviving the psychopaths in your office*. New York: HarperCollins Publishers.

Body, C. (2011). *Corporate psychopaths organisational destroyers*. London: Palgrave Macmillan.

Standiford, L. (2006). *Meet you in hell: Andrew Carnegie, Henry Clay Frick and the bitter partnership that transformed America*. New York: Crown Publication.

Toates, F. and Coschug-Toates, O. (2022). *Understanding sexual serial killing*. Cambridge: Cambridge University Press.

PSYCHOPATHS LIVING AMONG US

We previously considered both criminal and entrepreneurial psychopaths. These two groups of individuals differ from one another by virtue of their likelihood of committing a crime. In contrast to criminal types, entrepreneurial psychopaths tend to stay within the law, but they can make life a misery for others. We consider here those psychopaths who 'successfully' navigate our world and hence have a higher likelihood of interacting with us. Interestingly, Hervey Cleckley in 1946 described how typical psychopaths often integrate successfully among us where, for example, they: "…outstripped 20 rival salesmen over a period of 6 months, or married the most desirable girl in town, or, in a first venture into politics, got himself elected into the state legislature" (p.22).

This statement implies that such individuals can live among us unnoticed and be successful. As we are going to see in this chapter, there are psychopaths who occupy leadership positions such as rulers of countries who for many years cause hardship to the people they govern. Some of these rulers cause a change of ideology in the country they lead or implement a totalitarian grip over their countryfolk. For other psychopaths, the desire to leave an imprint of their creativity and a kind of entrepreneurialism can be used as a means of abusing people. This can go unnoticed for many years, but their psychopathic traits can lead them to contravene the law and even be incarcerated. So, the once successful psychopath living among us can slip up and become noticed for what they are. The lifestyle of most psychopaths living among us, however, tends to be one of a non-incarcerated existence. Although we will consider ruthless leaders and some highly successful profiles, the aim of this

DOI: 10.4324/9781032221052-8

chapter is to introduce the 'everyday' psychopath. But how can we spot these individuals?

HOW CAN WE DETECT EVERYDAY PSYCHOPATHS?

An interesting study about non-institutionalised psychopaths was conducted by Catherine Widom in 1977. The method for attracting individuals with typical psychopathic traits involved placing an advert in the Boston counterculture newspaper for volunteers to participate in an experiment. The advert stated the need for, "charming, aggressive, carefree people who are impulsively irresponsible but are good at handling people and looking out for number one". As many as 23 males and five females aged between 19 and 47 years responded to the advert. They were subjected to a series of tests including a biographical interview and the Eysenck Personality Inventory (see Chapter 5) that measured for socialisation, empathy and Machiavellianism. There was also a delay of gratification task. Widom concluded from the results that all the volunteers had fulfilled the criteria for psychopathy. In other words, the volunteers exhibited personality traits consistent with incarcerated psychopaths. This implies that the description in the advert had attracted individuals who were psychopaths. Furthermore, this was confirmed by their test results. It also demonstrates that they had the same psychopathic traits as those psychopaths who are incarcerated, but somehow were able to remain crime-free. In 2001, Ishikawa, Raine, Lencz, Bihrle and Lacasse recruited three groups of men (16 unsuccessful [incarcerated] and 13 successful [non-incarcerated] psychopaths and 26 controls). All were subjected to a series of psychophysiological measures taken under controlled emotional situations in addition to a series of reasoning ability and memory-related tests. Interestingly, the **successful psychopaths** exhibited heightened cardiovascular stress reactivity when compared to both **unsuccessful psychopaths** and controls. They also performed better on tests measuring reasoning ability (such as the Wisconsin Card Sorting Test [WCST]). They concluded that the successful psychopaths demonstrated social anxiety and were better able to modulate their impulses. They further concluded that it was this ability to control their impulses and to experience social anxiety that helped them to live crime-free lives. Lilienfeld and Watts

(2021), among other researchers, speculated that a preponderance of individuals with psychopathic traits can be found disproportionately across professions. As we previously discussed in Chapter 7, there are professions that attract psychopathic individuals, such as business, law enforcement and politics. Lilienfeld and Watts added to the list special operations military services, firefighting and high-risk sports. They argued that such individuals are likely to have psychopathic traits without being the classic psychopath.

But just how common is psychopathy in the population? This was a question addressed by Sanz-Garcia, Gesteira, Sanz and Garcia-Vera in 2021. They performed a meta-analysis on 15 studies (one study with two samples, hence adding to 16 samples), which totalled 11,497 individuals. They analysed the data and concluded that the rate of psychopathy in the general adult population was 4.5 per cent (this is higher than other studies suggest; see Chapter 1). What they did was interesting and deserves an in-depth review. The breakdown of the 11,497 individuals came from seven samples of university students which translated to 43.75 per cent of the total samples. Six samples were community-based adults that comprised 37.5 per cent of the total samples. Of the remaining three samples, individuals were recruited from a variety of organisations – comprising 18.75 per cent of the total samples. These studies were from different countries:

- US – five samples (31.25 per cent)
- UK – three samples (18.75 per cent)
- Australia – two samples (12.5 per cent)
- Sweden – two samples (12.5 per cent)
- Canada – two samples (12.5 per cent)
- Portugal – one sample (6.25 per cent)
- Belgium – one sample (6.25 per cent)

These were then divided into three categories: North America, mainland Europe and UK-Australia. Psychopathy was measured using self-reporting, clinical ratings or an interview. In the case of clinical ratings, Hare's Psychopathy Checklist-Revised (PCL-R) or the Psychopathy Checklist: Screening Version (PCL-SV) was used. In the case of self-reporting, the Levenson Self-Report Psychopathy (LSRP) scale was used (see Chapter 2). Of the 15 studies, 12 studies were conducted between 2010 and 2021 and three studies between 1994 and 1995. Sanz-Garcia et al. found that the prevalence rates of psychopathy across the 16 samples for the general population ranged from 0 to 21 per cent translating to a combined prevalence of 4.5 per cent. Unsurprisingly, those recruited from a variety of organisations had the highest prevalence of psychopathy at 12.9 per cent. For the university students, this was just over eight per cent, whereas for community-based adults, this was just under two per cent. Of importance here is the finding that sex was the only variable significantly related to the prevalence of psychopathy. In fact, males were twice as likely to exhibit psychopathic traits. Other factors such as the country of origin, measures used and sample type had less of an impact on psychopathy prevalence rates.

Hassall, Boduszek and Dhigra (2015) compared business with psychology students for psychopathy. In line with findings from Smith and Lilienfeld (2013), the prevalence of psychopathy tends to be higher in the financial sector, so it made sense to consider students embarking on a career in business studies. 263 final year university students from a UK university participated in Hassall et al.'s study – 148 studying psychology and 115 studying business. All were tested for psychopathy, and their score comparisons revealed a preponderance of psychopathic traits among business undergraduates. Furthermore, being male and exhibiting antisocial behaviour was negatively related with successful academic grades.

Other researchers have looked at the relationship between the four main factors of psychopathy (interpersonal, affective, impulsivity/lifestyle and antisocial) on professional/monetary and romantic success. In a sample of 304 males with a mean age of 48, Ullrich, Farrington and Coid (2008) considered psychopathic personality traits and life success. Their hypothesis was that there are specific psychopathic traits that can have beneficial influences on life success. Ullrich et al., however, failed to find a significant association between psychopathic traits on life success for either status and wealth or successful intimate relationships. What they did find, however, was that typical psychopathic personality traits are strongly associated with life failure.

Lilienfeld, Watts and Smith (2015) introduced three models to account for differences in the expression of psychopathy-related traits in individuals, which might explain why some psychopaths are failures in life while others are successful:

1. Differential severity (DS): Those exhibiting psychopathy-related traits differ only in the intensity of their expression. Hence, in the case of successful psychopaths, they have all the traits, but some express them to a lesser degree.
2. Differential configuration (DC): The constellation of psychopathy-related traits differ in successful psychopaths which alters any behavioural outcomes. In this model, it is suggested that successful psychopaths have some of the classic psychopathic traits but also some additional traits, including self-discipline, conscientiousness and a level of agreeableness that buffers them from negative outcomes.
3. Moderated expression (ME): This model makes the link between the classic psychopathic traits and external factors that can have a moderating effect. External factors can be classed as protective factors, such as having a positive childhood within a functioning family environment and good bonding and attachment with care-givers. Having an intact executive functioning (organised in thought, planning ability and good memory) and effective autonomic responsivity (ability to experience fear and stress) are additive factors to the mix, which can collectively mediate psychopathic traits and create socially acceptable responses to situations. This can ultimately negate the likelihood of engaging in antisocially driven behaviours.

It has been argued that all three models are not antagonistic and instead can operate together. The reasoning behind all three models is supported ideologically and empirically (see Chapters 3–6). The combination of these models can also be used to account for why it is often difficult to spot the psychopath who adapts easily and integrates well among us. But there are ways of detecting the everyday psychopath who lives among us.

TELL-TALE SIGNS OF THE EVERYDAY PSYCHOPATH

In Babiak and Hare's (2019) revised edition of 'Snakes in Suits', they discuss how we can understand and survive the psychopaths present in the offices in which we work. These psychopaths are not your regular entrepreneurial psychopaths, but people we are likely to meet and associate with. Babiak and Hare stated that:

> Some psychopaths live in society and do not technically break the law – although they may come close, causing problems in hidden economic, psychological, and emotionally abusive ways...not make warm and loving parents, children, or family members...not make reliable friends or coworkers...take advantage...abuse the trust and support of friends and family.

> (2019, p. 21)

Importantly, for Babiak and Hare, we are unlikely to know when we are in contact with a psychopath often until it is too late. These 'successful' psychopaths are so well integrated that we fail to notice whether our boss, colleagues, marital partner, friends or neighbours are manipulating us for their selfish purposes while the going is good. While we have good tests for psychopathy, enticing your boss or colleague to take the assessment is not really a likelihood. There are tell-tale signs, however, which become apparent when you know what to look out for (see Box 8.1).

BOX 8.1: THE PSYCHOPATH'S TRACES OF THE REAL DEAL

For a number of reasons, spotting a psychopath is not always an easy task. For example, they are often skilled at 'reading people', working out their vulnerabilities and 'pushing their buttons'. It can also be difficult because they have good communication abilities and a chameleon-like nature—which they use to 'blend in'. The one feature, however, that can give the psychopath away is the motivation and ease with which they can callously take advantage of other people to achieve what they want. As part of the typical psychopath's personality make-up is their lack of empathy, Machiavellian manipulation of others and narcissism (see Chapter 5). Psychopaths who are good at communication and are reasonably educated will use their polished skill of manipulation to get what they want. Those without these skills are more likely to resort to bullying tactics, such as coercion, aggression and intimidation. So, your boss who makes unreasonable demands and wants you to bypass regulations in order to get something done quickly, but you refuse, is more likely to intimidate you in front of others to make you look foolish and incompetent. This is not the sign of a good boss and suggests a person who is passing the 'buck' of responsibility to you. Even individuals who have good communication skills and are well educated will resort to these baseline psychopathic tactics when challenged. Narcissism is a personality characteristic of many psychopaths as they like to pride themselves on their superiority over others and take the credit for other people's achievements. Narcissism is in itself also one of many types of personality disorder. Often, narcissistic individuals have a profound difficulty in coming up with a range of options to solve problems. They can be considered as inflexible and unimaginative, and therefore closed-minded and staid. If they are not the centre of attention, they will do and say things so that they are. These traits coupled with psychopathy, the 'dark triad' (see Chapter 5), can be a tell-tale sign of an individual housing psychopathic tendencies. If, for example, you are in conversation with the boss about an idea for a marketing venture and your colleague intervenes and convinces your boss that it was his idea and the pair of you were discussing this earlier, then you might have a narcissistic psychopath on the team.

There are other tactics used by psychopaths to consider. According to Babiak and Hare, there are three phases of approach by the psychopath:

- Phase 1 – Assessment
- Phase 2 – Manipulation
- Phase 3 – Abandonment

In Phase 1, psychopaths are in an information–gathering mode where the data they collect informs them about the individuals they are assessing. Psychopaths enjoy toying with people and the challenge of conning and manipulating them. In fact, Babiak and Hare argued that the primary motivators of the typical psychopath are manipulating and toying with others. It is through the constant observation and assessment of individuals as potential victims that the psychopath can successfully weigh up a person's value and use-fulness to them, as well as their susceptibility to being manipulated and conned. Value and usefulness can be ascertained through an individual's position and influence within a company for instance. An individual's position does not have to necessarily be high up in the ranks. Someone who has access to company files, IT or security could serve a useful purpose when the time is right. Additionally, Babiak and Hare claimed that psychopaths are very adept at analys-ing an individual's emotional vulnerabilities and their psychological defence and coping mechanisms used in times of stressful situa-tions. The typical psychopath appears confident and successful, but this outward persona is a disguise to cover up an individual liv-ing the parasitic lifestyle. By this, they refer to an individual who cleverly 'uses' a colleague's ideas to impress the boss or uses col-leagues, friends and family as a source of endless financial support. The emotional and psychological impact their demands have on others fails to be registered by the psychopath who has a deficit of feelings such as empathy, guilt or remorse. Cheating or manipulat-ing others and the system to attain qualifications is often the route they take to succeed instead of 'hard grafting'. This strategy is, in part, down to a low threshold for monotony which makes doing the work long-term arduous. Coupled with being egotistical and condescending, they can often be considered as charming and, in some cases, charismatic. Hence, finding a suitable person to fulfil their needs, however temporary, becomes an important feature of Phase 1, the assessment.

Now that the psychopath has done his or her homework on which individuals are likely to be useful, Phase 2 becomes enacted. They will manipulate these individuals using their skilled ability to make a good impression. Making a good impression, according to Babiak and Hare, involves techniques of managing how they appear to others that can rely on ingratiation, putting on the charm and developing a trusting relationship. And what is this trust based on? It is based on a convinc-ing narrative created through lying. Psychopaths are pathological liars and are very good at it. They are able to convince others to believe what they say and can achieve this even when the facts of the situ-ation suggest a fiction. Allied with their cunning ability to control and manipulate their selected 'victims', they can make their 'victims' doubt their own truths. Babiak and Hare also highlighted the psychopath's ability to pass on accountability and responsibility to someone else – usually the person they have identified as useful to them. By putting the blame onto someone else, the psychopath can use this as a self-promotion tactic (see Box 8.2).

BOX 8.2: THE MULTI-FICTITIOUS DAVE

In Babiak and Hare's 'Snakes in Suits', there is a running account throughout a fictitious character known as Dave. Dave applies for a post at Garrideb Technologies, a high-tech company in the US that is successful but wants to expand the production of their products. Dave appears polished and competent with a tailor-made curriculum vita. He impresses the interview panel and the vice president of the company. Without further checks into his career history, Dave is given the post despite the HR director wanting to discuss his candidacy. On his first day there, Dave arranged to see Jack Garrideb at the expense of having lunch with one of his line managers called Frank. Frank was later surprised to see Dave in the CEO's office. There were occasions when Dave had confrontations with security over insisting on parking in the reserved visitor's spot and announcing his importance at a meeting. Dave showed his manipulative nature by ensuring he met with the employee of the month, Dorothy, whose ideas and her skill at report writing he would later use. Dave charmed the colleagues he thought would be useful. Frank relied on Dave to present data and information for a presentation he was to give – he did so but ensured Frank took an incomplete draft with him on his travels. Only when Frank arrived did he realise it was incomplete and what was there was plagiarised and started to rewrite it himself. The next day Dave had secretly emailed the report to the boss, John (see Figure 8.1). John informed Frank that the presentation was a winner and Dave had sent it to him and even acknowledged thanks to himself on behalf of Frank! We are already seeing Dave trying to make his mark at the expense of others such as Frank. Once confronted, Dave said that Frank had dropped the USB containing the final document and made out that he had saved the day. Dave had previously written a substandard interim report which Frank had confronted him over. When confronted, Dave ranted but eventually submitted an improved report and his later reports were also good – step in Dorothy whose writing skills were useful to Dave. Dave was playing people against one another so that the work atmosphere became toxic. He even blamed Dorothy for sloppy work but also spread rumours that her line manager was holding her back. The fact that Dorothy was writing his reports came to the fore. It was not long after that Frank received complaints about Dave and the many transfers requested by employees working with him. Frank went to John and they decided to have Dave's curriculum vita checked. It materialised that his qualifications were a fiction. HR wanted to check his credentials before he was offered the post, but John and Frank were taken in by Dave's charm – typical of the psychopath. By the time John and Frank pieced all the information together and went to see Jack Garrideb, it was too late. Dave was there shaking Jack's hand and was promoted while Frank was offered a retirement package. After a year, Dave was a vice president and Dorothy his secretary. Although this is a fictitious case invented by Babiak and Hare, the character portrayed is far from fictitious. Psychopaths really do operate in this way – assessment, manipulation and abandonment.

During Phase 3, the selected 'victim' has exhausted his or her utility and is no longer of any use and is abandoned. A person who experiences this abandonment has no idea that this is coming. The psychopath just leaves. This can occur in the workplace or in a romantic relationship. As a consequence of their capacity to behave callously and an inability to form robust social attachments, abandoning someone, whether a partner or colleague, is simple.

These three phases ultimately have an effect on the psychopath's lifestyle. They often have a stream of failed short-term relationships and numerous spawned partners and leave behind their children. These relationships might have been plagued with physical and sexual abuse and emotional intimidation. In relation to their careers, psychopaths will often have disconnected goals, a fake curriculum vita and a series of random jobs.

Figure 8.1 Could this be Dave?

Thus far, we have discussed the psychopath who we may encounter in everyday life, but we need also to consider those who we are unlikely to encounter but will nevertheless affect our lives considerably.

EVERYDAY PSYCHOPATHS WE ARE UNLIKELY TO ENCOUNTER BUT WILL IMPACT ON OUR LIVES CONSIDERABLY

Our political leaders make decisions that will affect us from the top on down. We become familiar with our political leaders on a daily basis through the multitude of media outlets operating within our society. For most of us, however, it is very unlikely that we will ever meet our politicians in the flesh. Despite this, more recently, there has been a plethora of research examining the personality of our political leaders from past to present day (Antonakis, House and Simonton 2017; Costa Lobo 2018; Nai and Maier 2018). Joly, Soroka and Loewen (2018) found that low agreeableness (see Chapter 5) is key to electoral success. Scoring high on openness (Scott and Medeiros 2020) and extraversion (Nai 2019) tends to hinder electoral success. What facilitates success for candidates is high levels of conscientiousness and psychopathy (Nai 2019). It is a two-way process, however, as voting also depends on the personality of voters. While conscientiousness correlates positively with conservatism, openness correlates positively with liberalism (Hirsh, DeYoung, Xu and Peterson 2010). This suggests that high scorers on conscientiousness tend to place more importance on social norms and to valuing a sense of order which makes them more conservative. This contrasts with high scorers on openness who are more receptive to unconventional social behaviour and to less orthodox policies associated with liberalism or the left. Jonason (2014) found that both psychopathy and narcissism are linked with political conservatism of the voter. Studies have considered previous US Presidents for their personality traits. Charisma is a trait that facilitates economic performance, while conscientiousness promotes an outstanding president. Those exhibiting boldness make for better leadership in times of crisis, and narcissism helps drive the president to take risks, be bold and imaginative (Watts, Lillienfeld, Smith, Miller et al. 2013). For Watts et al., however, having too much narcissism and psychopathy can lead to a low moral compass enabling ineffective policy to pass in order to maintain political success. Nai and Toros (2020) considered the recent rise of the **autocratic strongmen** who promote traditional and nationalistic ideologies with destabilising effects. An example of this at the time of writing is Vladimir Putin, leader of the Russian Federation. The need to expand the boundaries of Russia and make it great by invading its neighbour Ukraine is a prime example of the autocratic strongman causing destabilisation throughout the world. Such problematic behaviour has happened many times in our history (see Box 8.3; Figure 8.2).

In Nai and Toros' study, the personality profile of 157 political figures worldwide was compared over a period of three years. They profiled the personality of these figures which included 14 who were considered to exhibit autocratic tendencies such as Vladimir Putin and Donald Trump. The Big Five and the Dark Triad (see Chapter 5) were used as measures of personality across both the autocratic and non-autocratic leaders; however, this was achieved not by administering these tests but through expert scholar assessments. Nai and Toros were interested in the 14 autocrats elected between 2016 and 2019, and hence, there are many more autocratic leaders who were excluded on the grounds of being in power before these dates.

The following autocratic leaders include:

- Andrej Babiš of Czech Republic
- Jair Bolsonaro of Brazil
- Rodrigo Duterte of the Philippines

- Recep Tayyip Erdoğan of Turkey
- Nikola Gruevski former Prime Minister of the Republic of Macedonia
- Benjamin Netanyahu of Israel
- Narendra Modi of India
- Viktor Orbán of Hungary
- Vladimir Putin of the Russian Federation
- Matteo Salvini former Deputy Prime Minister of Italy
- Serzh Sargsyan former President of Armenia
- Heinz-Christian Strache former Vice-Chancellor of Austria
- Donald Trump former President of the US
- Aleksandar Vučić former President of Serbia

There has been scandal and controversy associated with all 14 autocratic leaders.

BOX 8.3: PSYCHOPATHIC HEADS OF STATE?

Throughout this book, we present vignettes of case studies of psychopathic individuals. Many of these have profound negative effects on those they come into regular contact with. In some cases, however, the psychopathic individual may have profound negative effects on thousands or even millions of people. This is the case, arguably, for heads of state who demonstrate psychopathic traits (Nai and Toros 2020). Here we present a series of descriptions of the behaviour of heads of various states covering the last 100 years. We do not know for certain that any of them was (or is) a psychopath as they do not generally open themselves up to psychiatric assessment. We feel, however, that in each case there is at least evidence of psychopathic like actions. You might like to consider each and decide whether or not you would perceive them as psychopathic. We begin with arguably the most notorious figure of the 20th century.

Adolf Hitler (Adolf Schicklgruber 1889–1945): Hitler became the leader of the Nazi Party in 1921 and German Chancellor in 1933. In 1924, he published *Mein Kampf*, a book that presented a racist view of human nature with his own people – the Arians as the superior race. He later made it mandatory that newlyweds had to buy a copy of this book which inflated his royalty payments greatly. Through his invasions of many

European countries (including Austria, France, Poland and Demark), he initiated the Second World War leading to the death of around 40 million people. Additionally, he initiated the 'final solution' (the Holocaust) that led to the deaths of around six million Jews and others he considered to be 'subhuman'. While he could be charming and charismatic, he was also egocentric, impulsive, cold and calculating.

Mao Zedong (1893–1976): In 1949, Mao founded the People's Republic of China. He then set about reshaping China by taking the industry into state ownership and organising farmers into state-controlled 'collectives'. In 1958, Mao introduced the 'Great Leap Forward' that involved moving millions of people around supposedly to improve industry and agriculture. In reality, agricultural output declined rapidly, and millions died of famine. Then in 1966, Mao introduced the 'Cultural Revolution' that involved purging those he perceived as negative about his revolution. This led to the death of around 1.5 million people. Mao's original aims may have been to improve the lives of the working people, once he gained power; however, he insisted the masses read his work and sang songs that glorified him by placing his portrait throughout China. His purges saw many innocent people imprisoned or executed suggesting he was prone to paranoia and self-obsession.

Pol Pot (Saloth Sar 1925–1998): Pol Pot became the leader of the communist party known as the Khmer Rouge in Cambodia during the 1970s. In 1975, following the capture of the Cambodian capital, Phnom Penh, Pol Pot reset the calendar to 'Year Zero' and established a communist state where no one was allowed to own money or property and all religions were abolished. Many of those who resisted were murdered or detained. During Pol Pot's leadership of Cambodia, many thousands died of starvation. Interestingly, Pol Pot was generally described as courteous and quietly spoken by those who met him. He was said to have demonstrated apparent charismatic warmth to those he came into personal contact with. Despite this, he glorified violence, and it is believed that around one million people died under his leadership. When in 1997, the Vietnamese invaded Cambodia, they overthrew the Khmer Rouge and sentenced Pol Pot to life under house arrest where he died in 1998.

Saddam Hussein (Saddam Hussein Abd al-Majid al-Tikriti 1937–2006): Saddam became president of Iraq following his displacement of the previous leader al-Bakr in 1979. He then ruled the country as a despot for more than 20 years. Among his many acts of tyranny were the suppression of the northern Iraqi Kurdish people in 1988 when chemical weapons were used to kill almost 200,000 individuals and his invasion of neighbouring Kuwait in 1990 in order to take over the oil reserves. This latter action led to a six-week Persian War where many people lost their lives. He appears to have been a man with unconstrained aggression and pathological narcissism. Throughout his life, Saddam appears to have lacked remorse for any of his actions. In 2006, he was found guilty of crimes against humanity and hanged on 30 December 2006.

Donald Trump (1946–): Trump became the 45th President of the United States in 2017. Although democratically elected, his presidency polarised the American populace. One reason for this is the many allegations of misconduct that have been labelled against him. Many believe he regularly made (and continues to make) false claims and promoted conspiracy theories. These include claims that President Obama was not born in the United States and that many citizens who voted for Trump had their votes removed. The *Washington Post* has claimed that, during his presidency, he made a total of over 30,000 false or misleading statements. Trump has also been accused of sexual misconduct and misogyny. Over 20 women have made claims of sexual harassment or assault. At the time of writing, none of these allegations has been proven, but a locker room recording exists of Trump making lewd and boastful comments about his treatment of women. He once described himself as a 'very stable genius...who is like, really smart'. Some might beg to differ.

Vladimir Putin (Vladimir Vladimirovich Putin 1952–): Putin, the former KGB officer, in effect has ruled Russia for over 20 years. During this period, he is believed to have been involved in the assassination of dozens of critics of his regime. This list includes exiled Alexander Litvinenko *via* polonium poisoning and former politician Boris Nemtsov who was shot several times near the Kremlin. Both men had spoken out against Putin. In February 2022, Putin ordered the invasion of Ukraine resulting in the deaths of thousands of Russian and Ukrainian people. This act has been considered to constitute a war crime by a number of Western leaders. Putin projects a 'strong man image' who never exhibits remorse or responsibility for any of his unethical actions. He is highly autocratic and authoritarian. (Note that a predecessor of his, Joseph Stalin, is discussed in Chapter 9.)

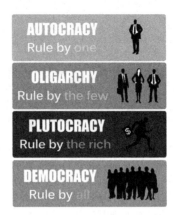

Figure 8.2 Definitions of the different types of leadership

Nai and Toros (2020) found that for extraversion, the autocrats as a group score high on extraversion and conscientiousness but low on agreeableness. Interestingly, Donald Trump had the highest score for extraversion and the lowest for conscientiousness and agreeableness out of all the 14 autocrats. He also scored the lowest for emotional stability (neuroticism) unlike Vladimir Putin who scored the highest. When the dark triad was considered, all of the autocratic leaders scored high on narcissism and psychopathy. Taking Donald Trump as an example, he scores the highest of all the autocratic leaders for narcissism and Machiavellianism and the second highest for psychopathy. First place for psychopathy is taken up by Nikola Gruevski who was allegedly involved in covering up murders while he ruled Macedonia. The personality profiles for non-autocratic leaders contrast with these autocrats. They score higher on agreeableness and emotional stability and lower on extraversion, psychopathy, narcissism and Machiavellianism. There was no difference between the two types of leaders for conscientiousness and openness. Regarding the findings for the dark triad, there are no surprises found and in fact support previous research (Hodson, Hogg and MacInnis 2009; Jones and Figueredo 2013).

The policies and acts passed by the government seriously impact on our lives on a daily basis. They also impact on us when the decisions they make are flawed or corrupt. As we have seen, autocratic leaders act in ways to promote themselves and in so doing can introduce policies that are detrimental to 'Joe Public', that's us. Donald

Trump failed to put safeguards in place to prevent the spread of COVID-19 when it was clear that the virus was particularly virulent and posing a threat to the American people. In fact, the US has the highest COVID-19 deaths in the world. Moreover, Donald Trump suggesting that the ingestion of bleach could help to kill the virus given that it kills germs on our worktops is dangerous advice. Is this a caring President? We also have Vladimir Putin who claimed that (at the time of writing) there are Nazis in the Ukraine which he intends to obliterate by a 'special military operation' – there is still a war raging on Ukraine soil. Vladimir Putin's 'special military operation' is affecting the global supply and price of crude oil and gas around the world – hence, we are all affected by his actions.

There are other everyday psychopaths we are unlikely to encounter but who still can have an influence on our lives – discussed next.

EVERYDAY PSYCHOPATHS WE ARE UNLIKELY TO ENCOUNTER BUT ARE LIKELY TO INFLUENCE US

Entertainment is very much a part of our lives where we read about celebrities across different media, watch a programme on the television, a DVD or a film at the cinema or see a play or musical at the theatre or hear bands performing on stage. We are more likely to see our favourite bands and actors from a distance but less likely to meet them in the flesh. The entertainment world is not exempt from having flawed individuals with personality disorders like psychopathy. There have been a number of actors and directors described by others, including colleagues, friends and family, as exhibiting psychopathic traits, such as Charlie Chaplin. Charlie Chaplin, for example, was described by his own children as being angry and violent which made them fear him. Colleagues such as assistant director Robert Florey described him as a "tyrannical, wounding, authoritative, mean, despotic man". Some have described him as having a **narcissistic personality disorder**, either way he appears to have exhibited traits of psychopathy. Although difficult people, they have not necessarily committed any crime and are considered to be successful psychopaths. There are some, however, who have been very successful during their acting career but have fallen from grace by virtue of being caught out for what they really are. Bill Cosby famous American comedian and actor was accused by 60 women of sexual offences ranging from groping, drugging and then sexually assaulting and raping them. These accusations stem back to the 1960s. He was described by his accusers as a sociopath and serial rapist. Many women accused him of sexual misconduct in 2014 and 2015 and this became part of the #MeToo movement. It was not until 2018 that he was sentenced to three-to-ten years in a state prison. Cosby, however, was granted an appeal by the Pennsylvania Supreme Court in 2019. It was found by this court in 2021 that an agreement with a previous prosecutor meant that Cosby's conviction was overruled. The implications of this is that he cannot be tried again on the same charges. Some celebrity predators, however, have not been as fortunate (see Box 8.4; Figure 8.3).

BOX 8.4: HARVEY WEINSTEIN – THE SHERIFF OF HOLLYWOOD – UNTIL THE LAW CAUGHT UP?

As a major film producer, Harvey Weinstein was highly successful. With his brother Bob, Weinstein set up the film company Miramax in 1979. Miramax went on to produce a series of highly successful films including *Pulp Fiction, The English Patient* and *Shakespeare in Love*, which between them went on to win 81 Academy Awards ('Oscars'). His success in the film industry led to him being mentioned in 34 acceptance speeches at the Oscars (this places him equal second [with God] behind Steven Spielberg with 43 mentions). In addition to his movie success, Weinstein was also financially successful amassing a fortune estimated to be around 240 million dollars. But, in addition to the highly successful film producer, there was another Harvey Weinstein. In 2017, more than 80 women came forward and accused him of a wide range of sex crimes from sexual harassment to rape. These acts would occur when Weinstein invited young women (usually actresses or models) into his hotel room to discuss how he might 'help their careers'. If they agreed, he would then ask them to give him a massage or share a shower with him. In either event, Weinstein would progress these activities onto sexual assault or rape. At his trial in 2020, through his solicitors, he suggested that all sexual activity was consensual and took no responsibility for his actions. The jury did not believe him; he was found guilty and sentenced to 23 years incarceration. Clearly, Weinstein's behaviour was repugnant, but the question is, was it the behaviour of a psychopath?

You may recall Hare's checklist from Chapter 2 that includes features such as grandiosity, lack of remorse, lack of empathy, deceitfulness and manipulation in addition to general antisocial behaviour. Considering each of these in turn, Weinstein, when challenged, regularly boasted he was 'the sheriff of Hollywood' who could not be touched by the authorities. This is clearly a grandiose claim, and arguably, this overblown self-belief was part-and-parcel of his downfall since his confidence led him to believe he could assault women with impunity. With regard to lack of remorse, it is apparent from his trial that he did not consider he had done anything wrong (which also demonstrates his deceitfulness). As far as manipulation is concerned, the Italian model Ambra Gutierrez secretly recorded Weinstein swearing on his children's lives that, if she joined him in the shower, he would 'not do anything to her'. The reality of course is that this was a manipulative lie. Finally, with regard to antisocial behaviour in general, Weinstein was frequently observed belittling and bullying those who worked for him, and his business practices were regularly underhand (not to mention the small matter of multiple sex crimes). Putting all of this together, it is clear that Weinstein was certainly a psychopath and a 'successful' one at that. That is, the Sheriff of Hollywood until the real Sheriff caught up.

Figure 8.3 The Harvey Weinstein mugshot

SUMMARY

While most of us are aware of the trait descriptions of psychopaths, we remain vulnerable to their exploitative tactics. Why is that we might ask? The answer is simple, we have difficulty identifying them until it is too late. This is why researchers have resorted to focusing on the everyday psychopath who lives and operates around us. The method of attracting potential psychopathic individuals to participate in experiments about them is to appeal to their typical psychopathic personalities by requesting for volunteers fitting the advertised descriptions. This method has proven to be a successful one. It informs researchers of the prevalence of psychopathy in the community across both sexes. It also provides data from psychophysiological tests about emotions, memory and reasoning ability. It also provides comparative data across successful and unsuccessful psychopaths and controls, such as there being a heightened cardiovascular stress reactivity and social anxiety among successful psychopaths. Successful psychopaths are better able to modulate their impulses and anxieties than unsuccessful psychopaths, which may account for why they can live a crime-free lifestyle. By comparing and analysing studies across many countries, the prevalence of psychopathy in the community ranged from 0 to 21 per cent, hence averaging a combined prevalence of 4.5 per cent. However, the prevalence of psychopathy among people working in organisations was higher at 12.9 per cent. Other studies have found a higher prevalence of psychopathy among undergraduates studying business studies than those studying psychology for instance. The differences in the expression of psychopathic traits have been explained using the 'differential-severity', 'differential-configuration' and 'moderated-expression' models. Although different, it has been argued that the explanations from these three models can operate together. Babiak and Hare have been advocates for ways in which we can identify the successful psychopath who lives among us by knowing what to look for. They outlined three phases that successful psychopaths adopt as a means to achieving their goals. In Phase 1, assessment, they collect information about individuals they are in close contact with, whether they be work colleagues, friends or family. By assessing individuals, they can form a guide to the person's value and usefulness to them. They can also pinpoint their vulnerabilities and susceptibility to manipulation.

This takes us to Phase 2, manipulation. Psychopaths are expert at portraying themselves in a positive light. They are pathological liars and find it easy to say the things you want to hear. By doing this, they gain the trust of others, which makes the manipulation of others simple. In Phase 3, abandonment, individuals who have served their purpose and are no longer needed are dropped. The everyday psychopath can affect our lives in different ways, such as through government and the entertainment industry. Autocratic leaders have been found to possess psychopathic traits. The Big Five reveals scores of low agreeableness and emotional stability, while the Dark Triad shows high levels of narcissism, Machiavellianism and psychopathy. Across the entertainment industry, there have been notable famous figures such as actors, directors and comedians who exhibit typical psychopathic traits, in particular narcissism. Some of those, however, who successfully hid their criminal inclinations for many years have finally been discovered and now disgraced with prison sentences.

FURTHER READING

Ferguson, K. (2022). *My Life with a Sociopath: It could happen to anyone*. London: Chronos Publishing.

Gillespie, D. (2017). *Taming toxic people: The science of identifying and dealing with psychopaths at work and at home*. Sydney: Macmillan Publishers Australia.

Kennedy, T.D., Anello, E., Sardinas, S. and Woods, S.P. (2021). *Working with psychopathy: Lifting the mask*. Cham, Switzerland: Springer.

Lobaczewski, A.M. (2022). *Political Ponerology: The science of evil, psychopathy, and the origins of totalitarianism*. Otto, NC: Red Pill Press.

CAN THEY CHANGE THEIR SPOTS?

Having examined the historical roots, and classification systems for psychopathy in addition to social, developmental and biological explanations of the condition, it is fair to say that there remains a rather large elephant in the room. Or perhaps a leopard? Just how do we treat it? Indeed, can it be treated successfully? Is it the case that, unlike other psychopathological conditions, these leopards simply cannot, and will not, change their spots? This view of the immutability of the disorder is widespread and long-standing (see, for example, Cleckley 1941a; Hecht, Latzman and Lilienfeld 2018; Losel 1998; Salekin 2002). It is fair to say that there are two reasons why this view prevails. First, in order for psychotherapeutic treatments to work a client needs to form some type of interpersonal connection with the therapist. Unfortunately, psychopaths appear to be, by and large, simply unable to form such emotional connections (Hecht, Latzman and Lilienfeld 2018). Moreover, given they rarely report feelings of guilt and shame or take personal responsibility for their actions, they are unlikely to be motivated to change (De Lisi 2019; Viding 2019). Finally, given they are prone to deception and manipulation, it is often difficult to determine whether or not they have modified their internal state or overt behaviour following treatment. Each of these factors, arguably, creates barriers to successful treatment (Hecht, Latzman and Lilienfeld 2018). Second, most forms of treatment that have been subjected to analysis suggest moderate to low success rates. You will note, however, that embedded in the last statement of 'moderate to low success rates' is the notion that some demonstrate a degree of success. This raises two questions. Which forms of treatment show some degree of success and why? In order

DOI: 10.4324/9781032221052-9

to answer these questions, we need to consider the main forms of treatment and their reported success rates. As with adult personality disorders in general, we can divide treatments into psychotherapeutic and biological. We will consider each in turn. Prior to this, however, given the adage 'prevention is better than cure', we will first examine the notion that it might be possible to reduce the likelihood of antisocial behaviour progressing towards psychopathy during childhood.

CHILDHOOD INTERVENTIONS

As we saw in Chapters 3–6, there is strong evidence that early childhood experiences can have a profound effect on the development of psychopathic traits. In some well-documented cases, however, individuals who are prone to antisocial behaviour from an early age can develop into responsible individuals in maturity provided they receive appropriate adult guidance (Polaschek and Skeem 2019; Taylor and Workman 2018). This opens the door to the possibility of planned childhood interventions provided such individuals can be identified early on. While children cannot be diagnosed with psychopathy, it is known that those with callous-unemotional (CU) traits are significantly more likely to develop this disorder in adulthood (Wilkinson, Waller and Viding 2015). Such children are generally diagnosed with a disruptive behaviour disorder (that is, a DBD such as oppositional defiant disorder [ODD], conduct disorder [CD] or attention deficit hyperactivity disorder [ADHD]; see Chapter 6). Hence, children who have had one of these diagnoses and who are high on CU traits are considered to be at elevated risk of psychopathy in adulthood ('at risk'). Some studies have identified 'at risk' children and reported on the efficacy of early interventions. Such interventions mostly involve parental-focused approaches, that is, training parents to improve their interactions with their offspring, such as consistently rewarding good behaviour. In reviewing interventions for childhood antisocial behaviour, Wilkinson et al. found that children high in CU traits generally had worse outcomes than those scoring low on CU traits. Despite this, where families were provided with behavioural therapies and emotion recognition training, even in children with high levels of CU, some degree of improvement was often observed (Wilkinson, Waller and Viding 2015). Despite this finding, most studies are difficult to evaluate given they lack control groups (that is, a matched group that did not receive interventions). This lack of control groups makes conclusions difficult to draw (see below).

One study by McDonald, Dodson, Rosenfield and Jouriles (2011), which did, however, include a control group, examined a parenting intervention programme known as 'Project Support'. The participants consisted of the mothers and offspring of 66 families living in domestic violence shelters where at least one child from each (aged between four and nine years) had exhibited clinical levels of conduct problems. Half were randomly assigned to Project Support and half (the control group) to continued traditional child service support. Those families in the Project Support condition received two types of support: first, parent training that involved child management skills such as appropriate listening, reprimanding and praising; and second, emotional support for the mothers. Over a period of 20 months, each child was assessed on six occasions. McDonald and co-researchers found that children who took part in Project Support demonstrated significantly greater reductions in psychopathic-type behaviours than those in the control group. This is an important finding for two reasons. First, it demonstrates that interventions for children of this age range can reduce the risk of becoming psychopathic later in life, and second, it is the first to make use of a randomised control group. This latter point may arguably have moral connotations, but it does mean that the results are more reliable than studies that lack a control group. It might, for example, be argued that without a control group, any improvements noted as children mature could be down to the fact that many children 'grow out' of disruptive behaviour disorders rather than reaching the criteria for adult psychopathy (see Chapter 6).

It appears that provided parental support is offered at the appropriate age, then at-risk children can take a different path in later life. Such forms of support invariably take up a fair amount of time and resources and are generally quite intensive (the McDonald study, for example, used a number of support workers and took place over 20 months). Of course, we have to bear in mind that in McDonald et al.'s study, while the Project Support group improved overall, not all of the at-risk children improved in a substantial way, and we do not know how long lasting such improvements were. It is possible that this variability in levels of improvement might reflect those on the primary or secondary path to psychopathic traits (see Box 9.1).

BOX 9.1: PRIMARY AND SECONDARY PSYCHOPATHS – WHICH IS THE MOST 'TREATABLE'?

You might recall from Chapters 1, 2 and 5 that some experts divide psychopathy into primary and secondary classifications. While there is debate about this bifurcation, many experts perceive a clear distinction between the two (Del Gaizo and Falkenbach, 2008; Mealey 1995; Morrison and Gilbert 2001). To recap, primary psychopathy, which is believed to involve a genetic predisposition, is characterised by low anxiety, callousness and manipulativeness. In contrast, secondary psychopathy, which is believed to be the outcome of a highly aversive upbringing, is characterised by high anxiety and impulsivity. In reviewing the evidence of the effectiveness of treatments, Taylor (2016) suggested that, because primary psychopathy is largely genetically influenced, interventions are unlikely to have a high rate of success. In contrast, for those with the secondary sub-type, being more malleable, she is more hopeful. In effect, she argues that, because the second sub-type is largely environmentally influenced by altering the environment (via, for example, forms of psychological therapy), it might be possible for children to 'unlearn' inappropriate response to others. While we do not explicitly make this distinction throughout our discussion of treatments in this chapter, this distinction is worth bearing in mind.

ADULT PSYCHOLOGICAL INTERVENTIONS

Despite the study described above, it is relatively rare for someone who is at risk of developing psychopathic traits to be identified and initiatives to aid prevention put in place during childhood. Hence, researchers and clinicians have made efforts to apply psychological treatments to adults identified as psychopathic (or, as is often the case, those with antisocial personality disorder). In evaluating the efficacy of such treatments, Hecht, Latzman and Lilienfeld (2018) divided them into three main forms of intervention:

- Cognitive-behavioural approaches
- Psychodynamic approaches
- Therapeutic community approaches

We consider each in turn.

COGNITIVE-BEHAVIOURAL APPROACHES

As with all treatments, those which can broadly be brought under the umbrella term of 'cognitive-behavioural' are based on a theoretical approach, in this case the conception of behaviour and internal states as being the product of learning through life experiences. This being the case, then through these forms of 'talking therapy' people can overcome their problematic behaviour by changing the way they think. In a sense, because the behaviour is learned, such learning can be attenuated or even reversed using one of the various forms of cognitive-behavioural approaches. Although the term covers a range of different related forms of therapy, the most common form used today is **cognitive behavioural therapy** or 'CBT'. In a word, CBT is all about changing or challenging current distortions of thought and developing strategies that address the symptoms of a disorder. In order to do this, it seeks to break the cycle of negative or inappropriate thoughts leading to inappropriate feelings, leading to inappropriate behaviour, which, in turn, leads to negative thoughts and so on in a cyclical manner (see Figure 9.1). This differs from traditional psychotherapies in that, rather than considering unconscious meanings that supposedly underpin behaviour (see below), it is very much about current conscious thoughts. While CBT is most often used to treat depression or anxiety (where it appears to have a high success rate), it has also been utilised for personality disorders including psychopathy.

The question is how effective are CBT and other cognitive-behavioural approaches in treating psychopathy? There is a limited amount of research which has concluded that CBT can be effective. In 1997, for example, Hughes, Hogue, Hollin and Champion reported nine psychopathic inpatients at a secure hospital who received group work, designed to alter cognitive and emotional states. All nine patients subsequently showed significant improvements in attitudes and reductions in impulsivity. This appears to be an indication of success for cognitive-behavioural therapy. We need to bear in mind, however, that all of the participants scored lower than 30 on the PCL-R scale (see Chapter 2); hence, they were not the most severely psychopathic. Also, due to their deviousness, it is always possible that such individuals are particularly adept at appearing to show improvements. Very few overall analyses have been undertaken to determine the success rate of cognitive-behavioural therapies. In 2002, however, Randy Salekin pooled together

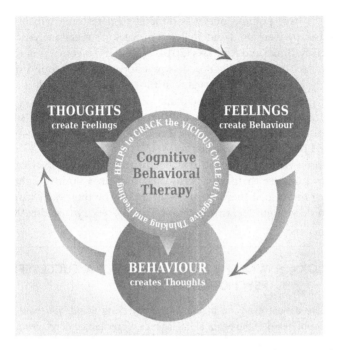

Figure 9.1 Cycle diagram of how cognitive behavioural therapy involves altering the negative cycle of thoughts, feelings and behaviour

a number of studies that can be considered as broadly cognitive-behavioural therapies and compared these with psychoanalytic and other therapies (see later) to determine the relative rate of success. He found a notable reported success rate of 62 per cent for cognitive-behavioural approaches. These were compared with a 20 per cent success rate in control groups not receiving therapy. (Note that the term success rate refers to decreases in criminality and antisocial behaviour, likewise for the other therapies discussed below.) These figures sound impressive and might be taken to suggest that our misgivings about the efficacy of treatments for psychopathy may be misplaced. In fact, Salekin's findings have been criticised on a number of grounds (Harris and Rice 2006). On the one hand, Salekin's meta-analysis only included five cognitive-behavioural studies, and each of these had a small sample size (one apparently had only three participants). On the other hand, as Hecht, Latzman and Lilienfeld

(2018) have pointed out, it is difficult to determine which forms of therapy were used and analysed in Salekin's meta-analysis. More recently, Bonta and Andrews (2017) considered reconviction rates in high-risk offenders diagnosed as psychopathic. They found significantly lower reconviction rates in those high-risk offenders whose therapists had spent a considerable amount of time using cognitive and behavioural techniques. This suggests that there can be success, at least for some cases, but we should not expect cognitive-behavioural therapy to be a 'quick fix'.

One problem with the concept of treating psychopaths is that many consider their own personality traits in a positive light. This being the case, if they are successful in life, by their own standards, then they might feel that treatment is unnecessary (see Box 9.2).

BOX 9.2: WAS THE REAL JAMES BOND A 'SUCCESSFUL PSYCHOPATH'?

Like almost everyone in the English-speaking world, you have no doubt heard of the fictional intelligence officer James Bond. Through the books of Ian Fleming and the series of blockbuster films, Bond has entered our consciousness as a tough, courageous, charismatic, womanising, licenced to kill spy. You may not, however, have heard of Wing Commander Forest Frederick Edward Yoe-Thomas. Yoe-Thomas was one of the few men to have fought in both World Wars where he demonstrated many acts of extreme heroism for which he was awarded numerous medals for gallantry. But perhaps the most interesting thing about him is that he is believed to be the real figure on which Fleming based his fictional character Bond (Lilienfeld, Watts and Francis 2015). During both wars, Yoe-Thomas was captured and subsequently escaped. During the First World War, he was captured by the Russians and escaped by strangling a guard with his bare hands. During the Second World War, he acted as an intelligence officer and regularly escaped attention by donning a series of disguises and pretending to be a Nazi sympathiser. His list of courageous acts includes leaping from moving trains, refusing to talk when tortured and leading groups of prisoners in daring escapes. These are the sort of escapades that most men can only dream of. But there was also another side to Yoe-Thomas. Like Bond, he could be ruthless and a notorious womaniser. Also, like Bond, he regularly violated the rules of the British intelligence service, such as carrying arms on occasions when he was not permitted to do so. Following the war, he married, but as an unfaithful husband, he treated his wife in a callous manner. Because of these features, some experts consider that Yoe-Thomas might have been a successful psychopath, also known as a subclinical or adaptive psychopath. If this is the case, then is it possible that, given the 'right' environment (e.g., during wartime), people with psychopathic traits might be useful to society (albeit perhaps less so to the enemy or to their romantic partners)?

PSYCHODYNAMIC APPROACHES

Today, there are many forms of psychodynamic treatment, all of which can be traced back to Sigmund Freud's original **psycho-analysis**. In this case, the client lies down on the couch, while Freud (largely out of view) encourages him or her to make 'free associations'. Such associations indicate inner conflicts and repressed drives, which when brought into conscious awareness, can then be addressed (see Figure 9.2). Psychoanalysis, as a therapeutic technique, is based on the notion that people have both conscious and unconscious processes and that many of our emotional issues are due to unresolved unconscious processes from our past (and in particular, from childhood) which lead to repressed conflict. By bringing these repressed conflicts into the conscious part of our minds, we can then overcome them and improve our mental well-being. In order to achieve this, it is crucial that the client forms a strong and trusting relationship with the therapist. It is worth pointing out at this point that the plethora of psychodynamic approaches can differ quite widely, and many have diverged from Freud's original approach. Despite this, the general importance of repressed unconscious conflict and forming a strong relationship with the therapist remain central features to the majority. Given that, as briefly flagged up earlier, people with psychopathic traits are, by definition, not good at forming trusting relationships, we might ask is it feasible to expect psychoanalysis to work for them? Very few studies have

Figure 9.2 Reconstruction of Freud's set-up for psychoanalysis

considered the efficacy of psychoanalytic treatments, but, perhaps surprisingly, one which did, suggested it can be quite effective. As a part of his 2002 meta-analysis, Salekin considered 17 studies that made use of such forms of therapy. He reported a success rate of 52 per cent. So, contrary to popular opinion, might psychoanalysis be the solution to psychopathy? Unfortunately, Salekin's findings with regard to psychoanalysis have been criticised on a number of grounds (Hecht, Latzman and Lilienfeld 2018). On the one hand, of the 17 studies, only one involved a scientifically controlled design. On the other hand, detail of the form of psychoanalysis used is missing from the meta-analysis (to be fair to Salekin, this is because the original studies lacked detail). Such problems, critics have argued, make Salekin's conclusions that psychoanalysis can be effective in treating psychopathy open to question (Hecht, Latzman and Lilienfeld 2018). This does not mean of course that none of the clients in these 17 studies showed any signs of improvement, only that it is difficult to establish the true success rate.

THERAPEUTIC COMMUNITY APPROACHES

The notion of **therapeutic communities** was first developed and used by Maxwell Jones in 1952. The idea here is that psychopathic inmates should be allowed to develop responsibility for their own actions and behaviour through a supportive environment. Prison staff, rather than directing these problematic inmates, not only act as positive role models but also address challenging behaviour. The reason it is called a therapeutic community approach is, in part, due to the fact that daily meetings are held with all staff and inmates present to make democratic decisions including rule formation and conflicts discussed. In Rappoport's (1960) words, this approach perceives the 'community as doctor'. This form of therapy has been used quite widely, and a degree of success has been documented (Copas and Whiteley 1976). They have, however, also attracted a degree of criticism (Hecht, Latzman and Lilienfeld 2018). One problem is that therapeutic community studies (rather like cognitive-behavioural and psychodynamic ones) lack detailed descriptions of procedures, and they vary greatly from one setting to another. In his meta-analysis, Salekin found a 25 per cent success rate for therapeutic community approaches. This might sound quite positive, but we have to bear in mind that control groups, where no intervention was applied, demonstrated a success rate of 20 per cent. (Incidentally, a 20 per cent success rate is suggestive that, following prison or secure unit incarceration, one in five psychopaths appears to reduce their disturbing behavioural patterns. This does not of course mean they have been 'cured'.) In addition to these issues, at least one study has suggested that therapeutic community approaches can actually make psychopaths worse: a situation known as an **iatrogenic** outcome. Rice, Harris and Cormier (1992), in a retrospective analysis of data from the 1960s, examined a sample of over 300 individuals incarcerated for serious crimes who had taken part in a maximum-security therapeutic community programme. Approximately half of the group were diagnosed as psychopathic and the remaining half were diagnosed as non-psychopathic. Astonishingly, ten years later, while those in the non-psychopathic group were found to have reduced rates of violence and recidivism, those in the psychopathic group showed elevated levels of violent recidivism. Rice et al. suggested that both psychopaths and non-psychopaths learned *via* their therapeutic communities to better understand the feelings of others and how to use emotional language. However, whereas the non-psychopaths used their new abilities to shift their behaviour towards prosocial responses, the psychopaths used their new skills to better manipulate and exploit others.

In summary, some studies suggest around 20 per cent of psychopaths show fewer incidents of problematic behaviour following psychology-based treatments. Due, however, to a lack of detail for such studies, the efficacy of these therapies is difficult to determine (see Box 9.3).

BOX 9.3: JOSEPH STALIN: WAR-TIME LEADER (AND PSYCHOPATH?) WHO LED ONE OF THE AUTHORS TO STUDY PSYCHOLOGY.

Many years ago, as a student, one of the writers of this book (LW) wrote an essay about the infamous Soviet Union leader Joseph Stalin. The essay title was 'Why did Stalin's purges take place?', and it was an assignment for a history module as part of a foundation year of a degree. To provide some background, Stalin was born into a poor and dysfunctional family in Georgia in 1878. Following a childhood and adolescence which were notable mainly for a series of petty crimes, Stalin became prominent in the formation of the Communist Party (the Bolsheviks) that eventually came to control Russia, which, with its satellite states, went on to form the Soviet Union. By 1924, Stalin had managed to become the leader of the Soviet Union, and during the 1930s, he instigated a series of 'purges' to eradicate 'enemies of the working class'. Such purges involved exiling millions to Gulags in Siberia and having around 800,000 executed. Many of these were exiled or sentenced to death on trumped-up charges of disloyalty to the Soviet Union. So, the task of my aforementioned essay was to explain why Stalin engaged in such purges. Given this was a history assignment, I initially considered the difficulties that Stalin faced in order to maintain power and the problems of keeping the Union together. However, having recently read a book about psychopaths, I realised that Stalin's behaviour perfectly fitted the profile of a primary psychopath. He was callous, dishonest, suspicious, uncaring and self-centred. He could also be charming, and during the Second World War, he proved to be a brilliant strategist. In fact, it can be argued that Stalin's leadership was a major factor in the defeat of the Nazis. (Note that this was considered so important that a proportion of the Russian people still revere him today; see Figure 9.3.) When he died in 1952, many people wept openly (while others celebrated in private). A real 'mixed blessing' but arguably the profile of a highly intelligent and manipulative psychopath. When I received my essay back from the history tutor, he told me that it was a highly original answer, but one which 'contained perhaps too much psychology and not enough history'. It didn't receive a good grade. But his feedback was also a major factor in my decision to study psychology. Hence, were it not for Joseph Stalin one of us would probably not have studied psychology and would certainly not have gone on to co-author the book you are now reading. Maybe he wasn't all bad.

Figure 9.3 Admirers of Joseph Stalin carrying his portrait through the streets of Sevastopol to mark the anniversary of the Soviet Union's victory in the Second World War

BIOLOGICAL APPROACHES

As we saw in Chapter 4, in recent years great strides have been made in our understanding of the biological bases of psychopathy. To recap, there is evidence that a number of quite specific brain regions differ both in function and in structure in people with the disorder. These include the amygdala, hippocampus and other parts of the limbic system, the paralimbic and prefrontal cortex. Additionally, hormonal and neurotransmitter abnormalities have been identified in people who have psychopathic traits. In particular, it has been suggested that there are imbalances in levels of circulating testosterone and cortisol, especially in the case of those who show callous-unemotional aspects of psychopathy. Moreover, elevated levels of the precursor to testosterone, dehydroepiandrosterone (DHEA), in relation to cortisol have been found in juveniles who demonstrate psychopathic traits. While such findings are in no way straightforward, they have been found in a number of studies giving them a degree of validity.

The finding of biological-based differences in people diagnosed with psychopathy opens the door to the possibility of biological interventions. Clearly, the notion of making changes to a person's biology is one that raises moral issues. Do we have the right to alter brain chemistry or function in dangerous criminal psychopaths? No doubt most people who live in liberal democracies would baulk at such a notion. But what if neuroscientists could make changes with the participants' permission and such changes could be made with little or no physical stress? This might sound like science fiction, but you might be surprised to learn that just such techniques already exist.

REPETITIVE TRANSCRANIAL MAGNETIC STIMULATION AND TRANSCRANIAL DIRECT STIMULATION

Repetitive transcranial magnetic stimulation (rTMS) is a revolutionary technique that can alter both brain function and structure through repeated treatment. It is a non-invasive, low-risk tool that targets an area of the brain with a series of painless magnetic pulses in order to repeatedly excite or suppress that area (Glenn and Raine 2014; Konikkou, Kostantinou and Fanti 2020). Bursts of pulses are generally used over a period of around 40–50 minutes, and after several treatments, it is claimed they can lead to long-lasting (possibly permanent) changes. In recent years, rTMS has been used to help alleviate a number of disorders including depression and emotional processing problems (Glenn and Raine 2014). Some studies, which involve the use of rTMS over areas of the prefrontal cortex, have demonstrated its use can improve the nature of emotional processing and of moral judgements that people make (Tassy, Oullier, Duclos et al. 2012).

One recent study, which made use of individuals diagnosed with antisocial personality disorder, showed that, following rTSM treatment over the dorsolateral prefrontal cortex, such individuals were then better able to identify happy and painful emotions in others (Konikkou, Kostantinou, and Fanti 2020). This does not, of course, mean they will react more appropriately to such emotional states. A development out of rTSM has, however, gone even further.

While there is some evidence that rTMS can lead to lasting changes in internal states, in recent years a newer modified experimental form of brain stimulation known as **transcranial direct current stimulation** (tDCS) has led to a great deal of excitement among neuroscientists. In tDCS, rather than discrete pulses, a continuous low-intensity electrical current is passed between two electrodes (anode and cathode) to stimulate a specific brain region for a period of time. In one specific study, Choy, Raine and Hamilton (2018) randomly assigned 81 participants to one of two groups:

1. Experimental group – received tDCS over the dorsolateral prefrontal cortex (N 39)
2. Control group – received a 'sham treatment' – led to believe they had received tDCS (N 42)

The day after receiving treatment, those in the experimental group showed a lower level of intention to commit aggressive acts. This was assessed by hypothetical vignettes describing two types of aggression – physical assault and sexual assault – followed by their ratings of moral wrongfulness. Participants in the experimental group reported being less likely to commit aggressive acts and judged aggressive acts as more morally wrong when compared with the control group (see Figures 9.4a and 9.4b). This suggests that stimulating this area of the prefrontal cortex can lead to a lowering of aggressive and morally dubious behaviour. This experimental evidence can be seen as astonishing proof that non-invasive brain stimulation might reduce aggressive behaviour and even alter, in a positive way, moral beliefs. We need to bear in mind, however, that the individuals who took part in Choy et al.'s study were drawn from the general populace and were not identified as psychopathic. Also, we are dealing with a relatively small sample and a short time frame. You may recall from Chapter 4 that biologically based findings frequently have caveats associated with them. Both rTMS and tDCS are exciting developments that if used on a large sample of people with psychopathic traits over a lengthy time period might conceivably be a ground-breaking form of treatment. Such studies have not yet been conducted. Is it possible that criminal psychopaths who receive one of these non-invasive biological treatments will then show reduced levels of recidivism? This is clearly a case of watch this space.

HORMONE TREATMENT

As we saw in Chapter 4, there is evidence that two particular hormones may be unbalanced in people with psychopathic traits: testosterone and cortisol. The former is related to dominance and competitiveness

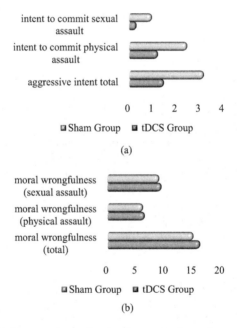

Figure 9.4 (a) A comparison of levels of aggressive intent in experimental and control groups (Based on Choy, Raine and Hamilton 2018); (b) A comparison of perceptions of moral wrongfulness in experimental and control groups (Based on Choy, Raine and Hamilton 2018)

and the latter to stress responses (such as fight, flight or freeze). It has been suggested that, rather than psychopaths simply having too much testosterone and too little cortisol, it is the ratio of these two chemicals which is unbalanced. This raises an important question. If we could alter this balance, perhaps by increasing circulating levels of cortisol, might this reduce psychopathic traits? The argument here is that psychopaths, in general, show a lack of fear and inhibition. Interestingly, one study which involved a number of preschool children, who were at risk of antisocial behaviour found that, following a 22-week family-based intervention, they demonstrated increased levels of cortisol (Brotman, Gouley, Huang, Kamboukos et al. 2007). Furthermore, the children's levels of aggressive response were lowered as their cortisol levels increased. This is, arguably, a positive finding. We have to bear in mind, however, that we are dealing here with very young children, none of which would have been classified as psychopathic at this age. As Andrea Glenn and Adrian Raine have documented, another important potential hormone treatment for antisocial behaviour is oxytocin. Oxytocin (OT) is an important hormone involved in our social relationships (see Chapter 4). It is known to be involved in attachment processes and in general social facilitation. So, it might be argued that treatment with this particular hormone could be beneficial to those with psychopathic traits. Interestingly, a review by Guastella and MacLeod in 2012 found that when oxytocin was administered (in short bursts of nasal spray) in combination with emotional training, it enhanced the effectiveness of such training. This sounds very promising, but as Bakermans-Kranenburg and van IJzendoorn (2013) have pointed out, that while there is evidence OT leads to improvements in social cognition in general, it does so within a social context. In other words, OT treatment is unlikely to be effective in the absence of family-based interventions. It may be effective, however, in enhancing the effects of such social interventions.

Hence, there is some indirect evidence that, if we can increase levels of cortisol or oxytocin during childhood, we might be able to nullify at least some of the traits of psychopathy (especially if this is accompanied by appropriate family-centred therapy). These findings raise an important question. Is it possible that we might be able to attenuate negative behaviour through altering hormone levels in adults? Some recent studies have suggested that this might be possible, although, when it comes to a possible 'cure', it is clear that such studies are only just beginning to scratch the surface (see Box 9.4).

BOX 9.4: ALL YOU NEED IS LOVE? CAN SNIFFING OXYTOCIN REDUCE SOME PSYCHOPATHIC RESPONSES?

If oxytocin is the 'love hormone' (see Chapter 4), then is it feasible that administering this chemical might reduce some aspects of psychopathy? Astonishingly, one recent preliminary study has provided evidence that this might just be the case. Psychiatrist and researcher Ronald Rijnders from the Netherlands Institute of Forensic Psychiatry and Psychology led a team that considered whether dominant psychopaths might become less so following a single administration of a nasal spray containing oxytocin. Rijnders and his team assessed the level of dominant gaze in 21 psychopathic patients (and a control group of 24 non-psychopaths) before and after the administration of oxytocin. The task measured how long it took individuals to avert their gaze when looking at neutral, happy and angry faces. (Note that this gaze aversion technique is a well-established method of assessing dominance and that psychopathy is positively associated with dominant behaviour.) This administration of oxytocin abolished the relationship between psychopathy and dominance in a second gaze avoidance task that followed the oxytocin treatment (Rijnders, Dykstra, Terburg, Kempes et al. 2021). Clearly, this is an early indication of a reduction in dominance which is only one feature of psychopathy in a small sample. Hence, further research is needed. It is, however, an indication that the so-called love hormone might at least reduce some psychopathic responses. Perhaps it's a little premature to suggest that, in the words of Lennon and McCartney, all you need is love.

We began this final chapter by outlining the widespread view that psychopaths are untreatable. While it is a truth universally acknowledged that this personality disorder presents great challenges, we feel that progress during this century suggests there are grounds for optimism. We have seen how early family interventions can reduce psychopathic traits in later life. We have also seen that, between them, psychological therapeutic techniques and innovative biological-based ones can make a difference even for adults who have been diagnosed with this serious personality disorder. In conclusion, the best way to treat the development of psychopathic traits appears to be to start early and combine psychosocial therapies with biologically based ones. For adults, however, a cure is an unlikely outcome – but attenuating behaviour through making good behaviour preferable to psychopaths does seem attainable, at least for some. Perhaps with a combination of biological and psychological treatments, some diagnosed with psychopathy (or at least ASPD) can gravitate towards more positive social responses. Perhaps at least some of these leopards can change some of their spots and maybe, if identified early on, some will even grow up to be spotless.

SUMMARY

There is a widespread view that psychopathy is untreatable. Despite this, a number of interventions have been applied to this disorder. Children who have a disruptive behaviour disorder and who score high on callous–unemotional traits are considered to be at risk of developing psychopathy in adulthood. One of the most commonly used interventions for such children addresses family interactions. Parenting interventions frequently involve teaching the parents child management skills such as appropriate listening, reprimanding and praising skills. When such interventions are put in place, further development of antisocial behaviour can be curtailed at least for some. Adult interventions include psychological and biological treatments. Psychological treatments include cognitive-behavioural, psychodynamic and therapeutic community approaches. In the case of cognitive-behavioural approaches, the aim is to break the cycle of inappropriate thoughts leading to inappropriate feelings, leading to inappropriate behaviour. Psychodynamic approaches involve bringing unconscious repressed conflicts into the conscious part of a person's mind so that they can be resolved, with this in turn, leading to improvements in mental well-being. Finally, therapeutic communities, which are often used in secure units, consist of all staff and inmates coming together to make democratic decisions about rule formation and conflicts discussed. In terms of the success rate for each of these forms of therapy, one meta-analysis suggested that cognitive-behavioural approaches have a success rate of 62 per cent, psychodynamic 52 per cent and therapeutic communities 25 per cent (all compared to a 20 per cent improvement rate in those not receiving therapy). Such figures have, however, been questioned on the grounds that they generally lack control groups and very few provide methodological detail. Biological treatments include forms of transcranial magnetic stimulation and direct current stimulation. These non-invasive techniques involve passing a current through areas of the brain (in particular parts of the prefrontal cortex) and are currently experimental. They have, however, led to some promising results with indications of reductions in aggressive and antisocial responses. Other biological treatments involve altering levels of the hormones oxytocin and cortisol. Once again, these are largely experimental, but there is some evidence that increasing both of these hormones can reduce indications of antisocial behaviour.

FURTHER READING

De Lisi, M. (2019). *Routledge international handbook of psychopathy and crime.* Abingdon, Oxon: Routledge.

Glenn, A.L. and Raine, A. (2014). *Psychopathy: An introduction to biological findings and their implications.* New York: New York University Press.

Polaschek, D.L.L. and Skeem, J.L. (2018). Treatment of adults and juveniles with psychopathy. In C.J. Patrick (ed.). *Handbook of psychopathy* (pp. 710–31). New York: Guilford Press.

Thomson, N.D. (2019). *Understanding psychopathy: The biopsychosocial approach.* Abingdon, Oxon: Routledge.

GLOSSARY

Affectional bond: The attachment behaviour that an individual has for another person. Most frequently used in the case of care-giver-child relationships.

Affective empathy: The ability to recognise and share feelings with others.

Agreeableness: A personality trait in which a person demonstrates warmth, sympathy and cooperativeness.

Antisocial personality disorder (ASPD): A personality disorder where the individual has serious deficits in guilt, shame and empathy. They may also have a callous disregard for the rights of others. Some consider 'psychopathy' as a severe form of ASPD.

Attention deficit hyperactivity disorder (ADHD): A disorder characterised by an inability to sit still and concentrate for any length of time.

Autocratic strongmen: An authoritarian political leader who bends the political system to their needs.

Behavioural activation system (BAS): A neuropsychological motivational system that is activated by reward signals. It generally triggers approach.

Behavioural inhibition system (BIS): A neuropsychological system that is activated during negative events. It generally triggers avoidance.

Bronfenbrenner's Developmental Ecosystem Model: An ecological model of child development where there are five levels of external influence on a child during development. These move out from the most intimate (the microsystem) via the mesosystem, ecosystem and macrosystem to the least intimate, the chronosystem.

Callous–unemotional traits (CU): Traits that constitute a temperamental dimension featuring little or no empathy and a disregard for the feelings of others. One of the main features of psychopathy.

Candidate gene studies: Studies that examine genetic variations in a limited number of genes in order to identify a specific gene for a particular trait.

Cognitive behavioural therapy: A form of therapy that attempts to modify negative thoughts, beliefs and behaviours.

Cognitive empathy: The ability to understand the mental state of another.

Conduct disorder (CD): A childhood disorder characterised by repeated behaviour patterns that transgress social norms for a child of that age.

Conduct problem behaviours (CP): This describes a series of behavioural problems that are disruptive and negative. Such behaviours typify children and adolescents with a disruptive behavioural disorder.

Conscientiousness: A personality trait in which a person demonstrates diligence and dependability.

Criminal psychopaths: People diagnosed as psychopathic who engage in criminal activity.

Dark triad: The term used to describe a triad of personality traits consisting of Machiavellianism, narcissism and psychopathy. People who have the dark triad have a callous disregard for the rights of others.

Disruptive behaviour disorder (DBD): A series of disorders whereby children and teenagers exhibit a range of socially undesirable behaviours.

DSM-5: The fifth edition of the Diagnostic and Statistical Manual of Mental Disorders. Published by the American Psychiatric Association in 2013, the DSM-5 attempts to classify all mental and personality disorders.

Entrepreneurial psychopaths: People who demonstrate psychopathic behaviour patterns generally within a work setting but who remain within the letter of the law. Often demonstrate manipulation and callous disregard for their work colleagues.

Extraversion–introversion: One of the big five personality factors. In this case, the extent to which an individual is an outgoing sensation seeker.

Fearlessness theory of antisocial behaviour: The notion that psychopathy is related to a neuropsychological deficit in the ability to experience fear.

Five-factor model (FFM): A well-accepted model of personality that suggests we can outline a person's personality by measuring five dimensions: extraversion, openness, agreeableness, conscientiousness and neuroticism.

Frequency-dependent selection (FDS): A state where the success of a phenotype (in terms of survival and reproduction) is dependent on the frequency of other local phenotypes.

Genome-wide association studies: A branch of genetics research that involves scanning the whole genome in large samples in order to detect specific gene variations.

Group socialisation theory (GST): Judith Harris' theory that a child's peers have more of an impact on the development of their personality than the parents.

Iatrogenic: The side effects of a treatment including the feedback from a clinician.

Insecure anxious-resistant: An attachment style where the child is reluctant to move far from the care-giver. Becomes unlikely to explore the environment and becomes 'clingy'.

Insecure avoidant: A form of attachment where the child, lacking sensitive responses from the parent, becomes emotionally independent.

Insecure disorganised/disoriented: An attachment style where the child develops a poor bond with the care-giver. This generally leads to ambiguous responses to parents.

Integrated emotion system theory: The notion that psychopathic people have a dysfunctional amygdala such that they are unable to respond appropriately to the distress of others.

Intraorganismic organisation: The infant is born equipped with a biological mechanism adapted for the formation of social bonds, one of which is the attachment to the care-giver.

Life history theory (LHT): An approach that seeks to understand the way in which organisms allocate time and effort to different activities such as growth, learning and reproduction during their lifetime.

Meta-analyses: The pooling and analysing of the data from a number of separate studies in order to reveal overall trends.

Mismatch hypothesis: The notion that many aspects of human life are better suited to our ancestral past rather than to our lifestyle today. Proposed because the rate of evolutionary change is unable to keep up with changes we have made to our environment.

Modus operandi (MO): The distinctive method of operating, especially in relation to crime.

Narcissistic personality disorder: A personality disorder where an individual maintains a grandiose self-image and craves admiration from others.

Neuroticism–emotional stability: One of the big five personality factors. The extent to which an individual has negative emotional reactions, such as anxiety and depression, to events.

Openness: A personality trait in which a person is receptive to new ideas, opinions and arguments. Involves being a good listener and a lack of dogmatism.

Oppositional defiant disorder (ODD): A type of disruptive behaviour disorder that is typified by defiant, angry and vindictive behaviour.

Paralimbic cortex: An area of the cortex that lies close to, and has connections with, the limbic system.

Person-situation debate: A debate concerning the extent to which individuals have enduring personality traits and the extent to which their apparent personalities are reactions to specific situations.

Polygenic: A characteristic that is coded for by more than one gene.

Polymorphic: Existing in more than one form. Often used to refer to different varieties in a population or to genetic variation.

Primary (or idiopathic) psychopath: This sub-type of psychopath exhibits antisocial behaviour and is unable to regulate this due to a lack of feelings of guilt or a conscience. Primary psychopaths fail to experience affective empathy but can fake empathy by relying on their intact cognitive empathy. They are considered to be true psychopaths. The term idiopathic was used by Karpman but describes the same phenomenon.

Proximate: A level of explanation that makes use of the immediate causes of behaviour or internal states (see **ultimate**).

Psychoanalysis: A term, coined by Austrian psychiatrist Sigmund Freud, used to describe a form of treatment for psychiatric disorders. It involves bringing unconscious memories and emotions into consciousness, thereby helping people to recover.

Psychopathy: A personality disorder that is characterised by disinhibited, self-centred, callousness and antisocial behaviour. People with psychopathy also lack empathy and remorse.

Psychopathy Checklist-Revised (PCL-R): An assessment tool used primarily in forensic settings to diagnose psychopathy in adults.

Psychopathy Checklist: Screening Version (PCL-SV): An assessment tool used to assess the presence and severity of psychopathic traits primarily in non-forensic settings.

Psychopathy Checklist: Youth Version (PCL-YV): An assessment tool used to diagnose psychopathy in 12–18-year-olds. It can also provide an understanding of which factors might contribute towards latent adult psychopathy and antisocial behaviour.

Psychosocial acceleration theory: A theory developed by Belsky, Steinberg and Draper, which proposes that deviant behaviours are in reality adaptive responses to a harsh upbringing.

Psychoticism–self-control: The extent to which an individual is prone to risk-taking and antisocial behaviour.

Repetitive transcranial magnetic stimulation (rTMS): The use of magnetic fields to send electrical pulses to areas of the brain in order to improve mood or behaviour. Generally used over a number of sessions.

Secondary (or symptomatic) psychopath: This sub-type of psychopath shows a similar pattern of behaviour to the primary psychopath, but the underlying cause is based on psychosis or neurosis. Some argue that the secondary psychopath is actually a sociopath. The term symptomatic was used by Karpman but describes the same phenomenon.

Securely attached: An attachment style where a child feels comforted by the care-giver and develops a healthy bond with them.

Seductive operational bully (SOB): An individual who may be superficially charming, but lacks conscience, empathy, guilt or remorse. Generally applied to the workplace where their deceitful behaviour frequently causes damage to their work colleagues and to their organisations.

Social–cognitive perspective: A view of learning that emphasises the social context in which learning takes place. Suggests individuals are influenced by their environment when learning, but also that they are able to influence this environment. Particularly associated with Albert Bandura.

Socialisation: The process where a person learns to adopt the behaviours and attitudes of the group to which they belong. Generally, they do so in order to gain approval from other group members.

Sociopathy: A controversial term that describes behaviour broadly similar to psychopathy. Suffers from being used as having a different meaning by different experts. Some experts consider sociopaths are more erratic and less organised when compared with psychopaths, but that they also have a degree of empathy. Others use the term as a synonym for secondary psychopath.

Successful psychopaths: Psychopathic individuals who, while demonstrating deceit, callousness and impulsivity, are successful in their endeavours. Generally have good or superior cognitive functioning. Mostly non-criminal.

Superordinate personality type: This describes an overarching personality type from which other personalities can be a part of. This means that a superordinate personality can also subsume some of the trait clusters apparent in other personality types.

Super trait: A trait that is made up of a number of more specific sub-traits. An example of this is agreeableness that can be subdivided into traits such as kind, warmth, cooperativeness and well-mannered.

Therapeutic communities: An approach to mental illness, drug abuse and personality disorders in which an entire 'community' is involved. (Note that a community can mean a psychiatric hospital or prison.)

Toxic work environment: A working environment where personal conflicts are commonplace. Generally associated with toxic managers who are motivated by and emphasise personal gain rather than encouraging a congenial and cooperative working environment.

Transcranial direct current stimulation (tDCS): Non-invasive electrical stimulation of specific brain areas in order to alter the activity of these areas.

Ultimate: A level of explanation that seeks to answer the function that a particular behaviour or internal state serves. Generally considered on an evolutionary timescale.

Unsuccessful psychopaths: Those psychopaths who are brought to justice due to their underlying cognitive and emotional deficits.

White-collar criminals: Individuals who engage in crime within the workplace. Generally involves no direct violence but rather involves criminal business practices.

REFERENCES

Ahmed, G.K., Metwaly, N.A., Elbeh, K., Galal, M.S. and Shaaban, I. (2022). Prevalence of school bullying and its relationship with attention deficit-hyperactivity disorder and conduct disorder: A cross-sectional study. *The Egyptian Journal of Neurology, Psychiatry and Neurosurgery*, 58(1), 60, 1–10.

Ainsworth, M.D.S. (1967). *Infancy in Uganda*. Baltimore, MD: John Hopkins.

Akhtar, R., Ahmetoglu, G. and Chamorro-Premuzic, T. (2013). Greed is good? Assessing the relationship between entrepreneurship and subclinical psychopathy. *Personality and Individual Differences*, 54(3), 420–25.

Alzeer, S.M., Michailidou, M.I., Munot, M. and Kyranides, M.N. (2019). Attachment and parental relationships and the association with psychopathic traits in young adults. *Personality and Individual Differences*, 151, 109499.

American Psychiatric Association (2013). *Diagnostic and Statistical Manual of Mental Disorders: DSM-5* (5th edn.). Washington, DC: American Psychiatric Association.

Andershed, H.A., Kerr, M., Stattin, H. and Levander, S. (2002). Psychopathic traits in non-referred youths: Initial test of a new assessment tool. In S. Blaauw (ed.). *Psychopaths: Current international perspectives*. The Hague: Elsevier.

Andreou, E. (2004). Bully/victim problems and their association with Machiavellianism and self-efficacy in Greek Primary School Children. *British Journal of Educational Psychology*, 74, 297–309.

Antonakis, J., House, R.J. and Simonton, D.K. (2017). Can super smart leaders suffer from too much of a good thing? The curvilinear effect of intelligence on perceived leadership behavior. *Journal of Applied Psychology*, 102(7), 1003–21.

Assary, E., Salekin, R.T. and Barker, E.D. (2015). Big-five and callous-unemotional traits in preschoolers. *Journal of Psychopathology and Behavioral Assessment*, 37(3), 371–79.

Augustyn, M.B., Ward, J.T. and Krohn, M.D. (2017). Exploring intergenerational continuity in gang membership. *Journal of Crime and Justice*, 40(3), 252–74.

Babiak, P. and Hare, R.D. (2006). *Snakes in suits: When psychopaths go to work*. New York: Regan Books.

Babiak, P. and Hare, R.D. (2007). *Snakes in suits: When psychopaths go to work.* New York: Regan Books.

Babiak, P. and Hare, R.D. (2019). *Snakes in Suits: Understanding and surviving the psychopaths in your office* (Rev edn.). New York: HarperCollins.

Babiak, P., Neumann, C.S. and Hare, R.D. (2010). Corporate psychopathy: Talking the walk. *Behavioral Sciences and the Law*, 28(2), 174–93.

Baglivio, M.T., Wolff, K.T., DeLisi, M. and Jackowski, K. (2020). The role of Adverse Childhood Experiences (ACEs) and psychopathic features on juvenile offending criminal careers to age 18. *Youth Violence and Juvenile Justice*, 18(4), 337–64.

Bakermans-Kranenburg, M.J. and van Ijzendoorn, M.H. (2006). Gene-environment interaction of the dopamine D4 receptor (DRD4) and observed maternal insensitivity predicting externalizing behavior in preschoolers. *Developmental Psychobiology*, 48(5), 406–09.

Bakermans-Kranenburg, M.J. and van IJzendoorn, M.H. (2013). Sniffing around oxytocin: Review and meta-analyses of trials in healthy and clinical groups with implications for pharmacotherapy. *Translational Psychiatry*, 3(5), e258. https://doi.org/10.1038/tp.2013.34.

Bamvita, J-M., Larm, P., Checknita, D., Vitaro, F., Tremblay, R.E., Côté, G. and Hodgins, S. (2017). Childhood predictors of adult psychopathy scores among males followed from age 6 to 33. *Journal of Criminal Justice*, 53, 55–65.

Bandura, A. (2001). Social cognitive theory: An agentic perspective. *Annual Review of Psychology*, 52, 1–26.

Barchia, K. and Bussey, K. (2007). The psychological impact of bullying on victims, bullies and student defenders. *Australian Journal of Psychology*, 236. Australian Psychological Society Conference (42nd), Brisbane.

Barkow, J.H. (1989). *Darwin, sex, and status: Biological approaches to mind and culture.* Toronto: University of Toronto.

Barkow, J.H., Cosmides, L. and Tooby, J. (1992). *The adapted mind: Evolutionary psychology and the generation of culture.* Oxford/New York: Oxford University Press.

Belsky, J. (2005). Differential susceptibility to rearing influence: An evolutionary hypothesis and some evidence. In B. Ellis and D. Bjorklund (eds.). *Origins of the social mind: Evolutionary psychology and child development* (pp. 139–63). New York: Guilford.

Belsky, J., Houts, R. M. and Fearon, R.M.P. (2010). Infant attachment security and timing of puberty: Testing an evolutionary hypothesis. *Psychological Science*, 21, 1195–201.

Belsky, J., Steinberg, L. and Draper, P. (1991). Childhood experience, interpersonal development, and reproductive strategy: An evolutionary theory of socialization. *Child Development*, 62, 647–70.

Benning, S.D., Patrick, C.J, Bloningen, D.M., Hicks, B.M. and Iacono, W.G. (2005). Estimating facets of psychopathy from normal personality traits. *Assessment*, 12(1), 3–18.

Blackburn, R. (1975). An empirical classification of psychopathic personality. *British Journal of Psychiatry*, 127, 456–60.

Blackburn, R. and Coid, J.W. (1998). Psychopathy and the dimensions of personality disorder in violent offenders. *Personality and Individual Differences*, 25, 129–45.

Blackburn, R. and Coid, J.W. (1999). Empirical clusters of DSM-III personality disorders in violent offenders. *Journal of Personality Disorders*, 13(1), 18–34.

Blair, R.J.R., Mefert, H., Hwang, S. and White, S.F. (2018). Psychopathy and brain function: Insights from neuroimaging research. In C.J. Patrick (ed.). *Handbook of psychopathy* (pp. 401–21). New York: The Guilford Press.

Blair, R.J.R., Mitchell, D. and Blair, K. (2005). *The psychopath: Emotion and the brain*. Malden MA: Blackwell.

Blais, J., Elliott, E. and Forth, A.E. (2014). A meta-analysis exploring the relationship between psychopathy and instrumental versus reactive violence. *Criminal Justice and Behavior*, 41, 797–821.

Blakey, R., Morgan, C., Gayer-Anderson, C., Davis, S., Beards, S., Harding, S., Pinfold, V., Bhui, K., Knowles, G. and Viding, E. (2021). Prevalence of conduct problems and social risk factors in ethnically diverse inner-city schools. *BMC Public Health*, 21(849), 1–13.

Boeree, C.G. (1998). *Hans Eysenck (1916–1997) (and other temperament theorists)*. http://www.ship.edu/~cgboeree/eysenck.html

Bonta, J. and Andrews, D.A. (2017). *The psychology of criminal conduct*. New York: Routledge.

Book, A. and Quinsey, V. (2004). Psychopaths: Cheaters or warrior-hawks? *Personality and Individual Differences*, 36, 33–45.

Book, A., Visser, B.A., Volk, A., Holden, R.R. and D'Agata, M.T. (2019). Ice and fire: Two paths to provoked aggression. *Personality and Individual Differences*, 138, 247–51.

Bowlby, J. (1944). Forty-four juvenile thieves. *International Journal of Psychoanalysis*, 25, 1–27.

Bowlby (1969). *Attachment and loss: Attachment* (vol. 1, p. 129). New York: Basics Books.

Bretherton, I. (2005). In pursuit of the internal working model construct and its relevance to attachment relationships. In K. E. Grossmann, K. Grossmann and E. Waters (eds.). *Attachment from infancy to adulthood: The major longitudinal studies* (pp. 13–47). New York: Guilford Publications.

Bronfenbrenner, U. (1977). Toward an experimental ecology of human development (p. 514). *American Psychologist*, 32(7), 513–31.

Bronfenbrenner, U. (1979). *The ecology of human development*. Cambridge, MA: Harvard University Press.

Brotman, L.M., Gouley, K., Huang, K., Kamboukos, D., Fratto, C. and Pine, D.S. (2007). Effects of a psychosocial family-based preventive intervention on cortisol response to a social challenge in preschoolers at high risk for antisocial behavior. *Archives of General Psychiatry*, 64, 1172–79.

Brunner, H.G., Nelen, M., Breakefield, X.O., Ropers, H.H. and van Oost, B.A. (1993). Abnormal behaviour associated with a point mutation in the structural gene for monoamine oxidase A. *Science*, 262(5133), 578–80.

Buckels, E.E., Jones, D.N. and Paulhus, D.L. (2013). Behavioral confirmation of everyday sadism. *Psychological Science*, 24, 2201–9.

Burger, P.H., Goecke, T.W., Fasching, P.A., Moll, G., Heinrich, H., Beckmann, M.W. and Kornhuber, J. (2011). How does maternal alcohol consumption during pregnancy affect the development of attention deficit/hyperactivity syndrome in the child. *Fortschritte der Neurologie-psychiatrie*, 79(9), 500–6.

Burt, S.A. (2009). Rethinking environmental contributions to child and adolescent psychopathology: A meta-analysis of shared environmental influences. *Psychological Bulletin*, 135(4), 608–37.

Burt, S.A., McGue, M. and Iacono, W.G. (2009). Nonshared environmental mediation of the association between deviant peer affiliation and adolescent externalizing behaviors over time: Results from a cross-lagged monozygotic twin differences design. *Developmental Psychology*, 45(6), 1752–60.

Buss, D.M. (2019). *Evolutionary psychology: The new science of the mind* (6th edn.). New York: Routledge.

Carson, D.C. and Ray, J.V. (2019). Do psychopathic traits distinguish trajectories of gang membership? *Criminal Justice and Behavior*, 46(9), 1337–55.

Carson, D.C., Wiley, S.A. and Esbensen, F-A. (2017). Differentiating between delinquent groups and gangs: Moving beyond offending consequences. *Journal of Crime and Justice*, 40(3), 297–315.

Cauffiel, L. (1992). *Forever and Five Days*. London: Kensington Publishing Corporation.

Chandler, D.J., Waterhouse, B.D. and Gao, W-J. (2014). New perspectives on catecholaminergic regulation of executive circuits: Evidence for independent modulation of prefrontal functions by midbrain dopaminergic and noradrenergic neurons. *Frontiers in Neural Circuits*, 8(53), 1–10.

Chegeni, R., Pallesen, S. and Sagoe, D. (2021). Aggression and criminality in androgen abusers. *Current Opinion in Endocrinology and Diabetes and Obesity*, 28(6), 615–24.

Chisholm, J.S. (1996). The evolutionary ecology of attachment organization. *Human Nature*, 7, 1–38.

Choy, O., Raine, A. and Hamilton, R.H. (2018). Stimulation of the prefrontal cortex reduces intentions to commit aggression: A randomized, double-blind, placebo-controlled, stratified, parallel-group trial. *The Journal of Neuroscience*, 38, 6505–12.

Cima, M. and Raine, A. (2009). Distinct characteristics of psychopathy relate to different subtypes of aggression. *Personality and Individual Differences*, 47(8), 835–40.

Cleckley, H. (1941a). *The mask of sanity*. St. Lous, MO: Mosby.

Cleckley, H. (1941b). The so-called psychopathic personality, with special emphasis on his status in the selective service. *Journal of the Medical Association of Georgia*, 30, 466–72.

Cleckley, H. (1946). Psychopath: A problem for society (p.22). *Federal Probation Journal*, 10, 22–28.

Coid, J., Yang, M., Ullrich, S., Roberts, A. and Hare, R.D. (2009). Prevalence and correlates of psychopathic traits in the household population of Great Britain. *International Journal of Law Psychiatry*, 32(2), 65–73.

Connor, D.F. (2002). *Aggression and antisocial behavior in children and adolescents: Research and treatment*. New York: Guilford Press.

Conradi, H.J., Bortien, S.D., Cavus, H. and Verschuere, B. (2015). Examining psychopathy from an attachment perspective: The role of fear of rejection and abandonment. *The Journal of Forensic Psychiatry and Psychology*, 27(1), 92–109.

Cooijmans, K.H.M., Beijers, R., Brett, B.E. and de Weerth, C. (2021). Daily skin-to-skin contact in full-term infants and breastfeeding: Secondary outcomes from a randomized controlled trial. *Maternal and Child Nutrition*, 18(1), e13241.

Cooijmans, K.H.M., Beijers, R. and de Weerth, C. (2022). Daily skin-to-skin contact and crying and sleeping in healthy full-term infants: A randomized controlled trial. *Developmental Psychology,* 58(9), 1629–38.

Cooke, D.J. and Michie, C. (2001). Refining the construct of psychopathy: Towards a hierarchical model. *Psychological Assessment*, 13(2), 171–88.

Copas, J.B. and Whiteley, J.S. (1976). Predicting success in the treatment of psychopaths. *British Journal of Psychiatry*, 129, 388–92.

Cosmides, L. and Tooby, J. (1992). Cognitive adaptations for social exchange. In J. Barkow, L. Cosmides and J. Tooby (eds.). *The adapted mind* (pp. 163–228). Oxford/New York: Oxford University Press.

Costa, B.D.J., Azevedo, M.D.C., Relva, I.C. and Simões, A.M. (2022). Relationship between psychopathic traits and moral sensitivity in a university student sample. *Legal and Criminological Psychology*, 27, 216–33.

Costa, P.T. and McCrae, R.R. (1992). *Revised NEO Personality Inventory (NEO-PI-R) and NEO Five-Factor Inventory (NEOFFI) professional manual* (p.6). Odessa, FL: Psychological Assessment Resources.

Costa Lobo, M. (2018). Personality goes a long way. *Government and Opposition*, 53(1), 159–79.

Coyne, S.M. and Thomas, T.J. (2008). Psychopathy, aggression, and cheating behavior: A test of the Cheater-Hawk hypothesis. *Personality and Individual Differences*, 44, 1105–15.

Daly, M. and Wilson, M. (1983). *Sex, evolution and behavior*. Boston, MA: Willard Grant Press.

De Lisi, M. (2019). *Routledge international handbook of psychopathy and crime*. Abingdon, Oxon: Routledge.

Del Gaizo, A.L. and Falkenbach, D.M. (2008). Primary and secondary psychopathic traits and their relationship to perception and experience of emotion. *Personality and Individual Differences*, 45, 206–12.

Del Giudice, M. and Belsky, J. (2011). The development of life history strategies: Toward a multi-stage theory. In D.M. Buss and P.H. Hawley (eds.). *The evolution of personality and individual differences* (pp. 154–76). Oxford: Oxford University Press.

Deng, J., Wang, M-C., Shou, Y., Lai, H., Zeng, H. and Gao, Y. (2020). Parenting behaviors and child psychopathy: A regression mixture analysis. *Current Psychology*, 41(6), 3585–96.

Densley, J.A. (2018). Gang joining. *Oxford Research Encyclopedia of Criminology and Criminal Justice*, 10.

Dishion, T.J., Nelson, S.E. and Yasui, M. (2005). Predicting early adolescent gang involvement from middle school adaptation. *Journal of Clinical Child and Adolescent Psychology*, 34(1), 62–73.

Dmitrieva, J., Gibson, L., Steinberg, L., Piquero, A.R. and Fagan, J. (2014). Predictors and consequences of gang membership: Comparing gang members, gang leaders, and nongang affiliated adjudicated youth. *Journal of Research on Adolescence*, 24, 220–34.

Docherty, M., Boxer, P., Huesmann, L.R., O'Brien, M. and Bushman, B.J. (2016). Exploring primary and secondary variants of psychopathy in adolescents in detention and in the community. *Journal of Clinical Child and Adolescent Psychology*, 45(5), 564–78.

Dodd, V. (2022). Met officers joked about raping women, police watchdog reveals. *The Guardian*. https://www.theguardian.com/uk-news/2022/feb/01/met-officers-joked-raping-women-police-watchdog-racist

Dugdale, R. (1877). *The Jukes: A study in crime, pauperism, and heredity* (p.12). New York: Putnam.

Dutton, K. (2013). *The wisdom of psychopaths: What saints, spies, and serial killers can teach us about success*. London: Arrow Books.

Dutton, K. (2016). Would you vote for a psychopath? *Scientific American Mind*, 27(5), 50–55.

Eagly, A.H. (1995). The science and politics of comparing women and men. *American Psychologist*, 5, 145–58.

Eagly, A.H. and Wood, W. (1999). The origins of sex differences in human behavior: Evolved dispositions versus social roles. *American Psychologist*, 54, 408–23.

Edelhertz, H. (1970). *The nature, impact and prosecution of white collar crime* (p.3). Washington, DC.: National Institute of Law Enforcement and Criminal Justice.

Eme, R. (2012). ADHD: An integration with pediatric traumatic brain injury. *Expert Review of Neurotherapeutics*, 12(4), 475–83.

Epstein, S. (1983). A research paradigm for the study of personality and emotions. In M.M. Page (ed.). *Personality: Current theory and research* (p.112). Lincoln: University of Nebraska Press.

Eysenck, H.J. (1952). *The structure of human personality*. London: Methuen.

Eysenck, H.J. (1970). The classification of depressive illness. *British Journal of Psychiatry*, 117, 241–50.

Fagan, J. and Tyler, T.R. (2005). Legal socialisation of children and adolescents. *Social Justice Research*, 18(3), 217–41.

Fairchild, G., Hawes, D.J., Frick, P.J., Copeland, W.E., Odgers, C.L., Franke, B., Freitag, C.M. and De Brito, S.A. (2019). Conduct disorder. *Nature Reviews Disease Primers*, 5, 43.

Falkenbach, D.M., Reinhard, E.E. and Zappala, M. (2021). Identifying Psychopathy subtypes using a broader model of personality: An investigation of the Five Factor Model using model-based cluster analysis. *Journal of Interpersonal Violence*, 36(15, 16), 7161–84.

Fallon, J. (2013). *The psychopath inside: A neuroscientist's personal journey into the dark side of the brain*. New York: Penguin.

Family Life Project Key Investigators. (2019). Parenting and cortisol in infancy interactively predict conduct problems and callous–unemotional behaviors in childhood. *Child Development*, 90(1), 279–97.

Fanti, K.A., Demetriou, C.A. and Kimonis, E.R. (2013). Variants of callous-unemotional conduct problems in a community sample of adolescents. *Journal of Youth and Adolescence*, 42(7), 964–79.

Fanti, K.A. and Kimonis, E.R. (2017). Bullying and victimization: The role of conduct problems and psychopathic traits. *Journal of Research on Adolescence*, 22(4), 617–31.

Farrington, D.P., Coid, J.W., Harnett, L.M., Jolliffe, D., Soteriou, N., Turner, R.E. and West, D.J. (2006). Criminal careers up to age 50 and life success up to age 48: New findings from the Cambridge Study in Delinquent Development (2nd edn.). *Home office research study 299*. London: Home Office Research, Development and Statistics Directorate.

Feresin, E. (2009). Lighter sentence for murderer with 'bad genes'. *Nature, News*[online], 30 October. http://www.nature.com/news/2009/091030/full/news.2009.1050.html

Finger, E.C., Marsh, A.A, Mitchell, D.G., Reid, M.E., Sims, C., Budhani, S., Kosson, S.S., Chen, G., Towbin, K.E., Leibenluft, E., Pine, D.S. and Blair, J.R. (2008). Abnormal ventromedial prefrontal cortex function in children with psychopathic traits during reversal learning. *Archives of General Psychiatry*, 65(5), 586–94.

Flowers, A. (1993). *Blind Fury*. New York: Windsor Publishing.

Fonagy, P. (2010). Attachment and personality pathology. In J.F. Clarkin, P. Fonagy and G.O. Gabbard (eds.). *Psychodynamic psychotherapy for personality disorders: A clinical handbook* (pp. 37–87). Washington, DC: American Psychiatric Publishing Inc.

Forsman, M., Lichtestein, P., Andershed, H. and Larsson, H. (2010). A longitudinal twin study of the direction of effects between psychopathic personality and antisocial behaviour. *Journal of Child Psychology and Psychiatry*, 51(1), 39–47.

Forth, A.E., Kosson, D.S. and Hare, R.D. (2003). *Hare Psychopathy Checklist: Youth Version*. Toronto, ON: Multi-Health Systems.

Fowles, D.C. and Dindo, L. (2006). A duel-deficit model of psychopathy. In C.J. Patrick (ed.). *Handbook of psychopathy* (pp. 14–34). New York: Guilford Press.

Furr, R.M. and Funder, D.C. (2021). Persons, situations, and person–situation interactions. In O.P. John and R.W. Robins (eds.). *Handbook of personality: Theory and research* (pp. 667–85). New York: The Guilford Press.

Ganesan, K., Shakoor, S., Wertz, J., Agnew-Blais, J., Bowes, L., Jaffee, S.R., Matthews, T. and Arseneault, L. (2021). Bullying behaviours and other conduct problems: Longitudinal investigation of their independent associations with risk factors and later outcomes. *Social Psychiatry and Psychiatric Epidemiology*, 56, 2041–52.

Gaysina, D., Mhango, W. and Muszynska, S. (2022). Life course mental health and adolescent age at first birth: Findings from a British Birth Cohort. Presented at European Conference S2–10-E3.

Ghaderi, D., Amirsardari, L. and Agashteh, M. (2019). Comparison of personality traits between psychopathic prisoners, non-psychopathic prisoners, and non-prisoner patients. *Jentashapir Journal of Health Research*, 10(2), e12494.

Giammanco, M., Tabacchi, G., Giammanco, S., Di Majo, D. and La Guardia, M. (2005). Testosterone and aggressiveness. *Medical Science Monitor*, 11, 136–45.

Glenn, A.L. (2019). Early life predictors of callous-unemotional and psychopathic traits. *Infant Mental Health Journal*, 40, 39–53.

Glenn, A.L., Kurzban, R. and Raine, A. (2011). Evolutionary theory and psychopathy. *Aggression and Violent Behavior*, 16, 371–80.

Glenn, A.L. and Raine, A. (2014). *Psychopathy: An introduction to biological findings and their implications*. New York: New York University Press.

Godar, S.C., Fite, P.J., McFarlin, K.M. and Bortolato, M. (2016). The role of monoamine oxidase A in aggression: Current translational developments and future challenges. *Progress in Neuro-Psychopharmacology and Biological Psychiatry*, 69, 90–100.

Goldweber, A., Dmitrieva, J., Cauffman, E., Piquero, A.R. and Steinberg, L. (2011). The development of criminal style in adolescence and young adulthood: Separating the Lemmings from the Loners. *Journal of Youth Adolescence*, 40, 332–46.

Grossmann, I. and Santos, H.C. (2016). Individualistic cultures. In V. Zeigler-Hill and T.K. Shackelford (eds.). *Encyclopaedia of personality and individual differences*. New York: Springer.

Guastella, A.J and MacLeod, C. (2012). A critical review of the influence of oxytocin nasal spray on social cognition in humans: Evidence and future directions. *Hormones and Behavior*, 61, 410–18.

Hagen, E.H. (1999). The functions of postpartum depression. *Evolution and Human Behavior.* 20, 325–59.

Hall, J.R., Benning, S.D. and Patrick, C.J. (2004). Criterion-related validity of the three-factor model of psychopathy: Personality, behavior, and adaptive functioning. *Assessment*, 11(1), 4–16.

Hare, R.D. (1980). A research scale for the assessment of psychopathy in criminal populations. *Personality and Individual Differences*, 1, 111–19.

Hare, R.D. (1991). *Manual for the revised Psychopathy Checklist* (1st ed.). Toronto, ON, Canada: Multi-Health Systems.

Hare, R.D. (1993). *Without conscience: The disturbing world of the psychopaths among us.* New York: Guilford Press.

Hare, R.D. (1999). *Without conscience: The disturbing world of the psychopaths among us* (p.176). New York: Guilford Press.

Hare, R.D. (2003). *The Hare Psychopathy Checklist – Revised* (2nd edn.). Toronto, Canada: Multi-Health Systems.

Hare, R.D. (2005). Without conscience: Understanding and treating psychopaths. *Seminar Presentation at Lancaster*, Pennsylvania, July 7–8.

Harper, A. (2022). The benefits of psychopathy for business and capitalism. Owlcation. https://owlcation.com/social-sciences/The-Benefits-of-Psychopathy-for-Business-and-Capitalism

Harris, G.T. and Rice, M.E. (2006). Treatment of psychopathy. In C.J. Patrick (ed.). *Handbook of psychopathy* (pp. 555–72). New York: Guilford Press.

Harris, J.R. (1995). Where is the child's environment? A group-socialisation theory of development. *Psychological Review*, 102(3), 458–89.

Harris, J.R. (1998). *The nurture assumption: Why children turn out the way they do.* New York: Simon and Schuster.

Hart, S.D., Cox, D.N. and Hare, R.D. (1995). *Manual for the Hare Psychopathy Checklist: Screening Version.* Toronto: Multi-Health Systems.

Harter, S. (2006). The self. In W. Damon, R.M. Lerner and N. Eisenberg (eds.). *Handbook of child psychology* (6th edn., vol. 3, pp. 505–70). New York: Wiley.

Hassall, J., Boduszek, D. and Dhingra, K. (2015). Psychopathic traits of business and psychology students and their relationship to academic success. *Personality and Individual Differences*, 82, 227–31.

Heath, A.C. and Martin, N.G. (1990). Psychoticism as a dimension of personality: A multivariate genetic test of Eysenck and Eysenck's psychoticism construct (p.111). *Journal of Personality and Social Psychology*, 58, 111–21.

Hecht, L.K., Latzman, R.D. and Lilienfeld, S.O. (2018). The psychological treatment of psychopathy. In D. David, S.J. Lynn and G.H. Monegomery (eds.). *Evidence-based psychotherapy: The state of the science and practice* (pp. 271–98). Hoboken, NJ: Wiley.

Hemphälä, M., Kosson, D., Westerman, J. and Hodgins, S. (2015). Stability and predictors of psychopathic traits from mid-adolescence through early adulthood. *Scandinavian Journal of Psychology*, 56(6), 649–58.

Henderson, D.K. (1939). *Psychopathic states*. New York: W.W. Norton and Company.

Hennigan, K.M., Kolnck, K.A., Vindel, F. and Maxson, C.L. (2015). Targeting youth at risk for gang involvement: Validation of a gang risk assessment to support individualized secondary prevention. *Children and Youth Services Review*, 56, 86–96.

Hickey, E.W. (2002). *Serial murderers and their victims* (3rd edn.). Belmont: Wadsworth.

Hicks, B.M. and Patrick, C.J. (2006). Psychopathy and negative emotionality: Analyses of suppressor effects reveal distinct relations with emotional distress, fearfulness, and anger hostility. *Journal of Abnormal Psychology*, 115(2), 276–87.

Hicks, B.M., Vaidyanathan, U. and Patrick, C.J. (2010). Validating female psychopathy subtypes: Differences in personality, antisocial and violent behavior, substance abuse, trauma and mental health. *Personality Disorders: Theory, Research, and Treatment*, 1, 38–57.

Hildebrand, M. and de Ruiter, C. (2004). PCL-R psychopathy and its relation to DSM-IV Axis I and Axis II disorders in a sample of male forensic psychiatric patients in the Netherlands. *International Journal of Law and Psychiatry*, 27, 233–48.

Hill, C.D., Rogers, R. and Bickford, M.E. (1996). Predicting aggressive and socially disruptive behaviour in a maximum security forensic psychiatric hospital. *Journal of Forensic Sciences*, 41, 56–59.

Hillege, S., Das, J. and de Ruiter, C. (2010). The youth psychopathic traits inventory: Psychometric properties and its relation to substance use and interpersonal style in a Dutch sample of non-referred adolescents. *Journal of Adolescence*, 33, 83–91.

Hirsh, J.B., DeYoung, C.B., Xu, X. and Peterson, J.B. (2010). Compassionate liberals and polite conservatives: Associations of agreeableness with political ideology and moral values. *Personality and Social Psychology Bulletin*, 36(5): 655–64.

Hirschi, T. (1969). *Causes of delinquency*. Berkeley: University of California Press.

Hobson, C.W., Scott, S. and Rubia, K. (2011). Investigation of cool and hot executive function in ODD/CD independently of ADHD. *Journal of Child Psychology and Psychiatry*, 52(10), 1035–43.

Hodson, G., Hogg, S.M. and MacInnis, C.C. (2009). The role of 'dark personalities' (narcissism, machiavellianism, psychopathy), big five personality factors, and ideology in explaining prejudice. *Journal of Research in Personality*, 43(4), 686–90.

Holmberg, K. and Hjern, A. (2008). Bullying and attention-deficit-hyperactivity disorder in 10-year-olds in a Swedish community. *Developmental Medicine and Child Neurology*, 50(2), 134–38.

Holmes, R.M. and Holmes, S.T. (2001). *Serial Murder* (3rd edn.). Thousand Oaks, CA: SAGE.

Honourable Sir Thomas, R.J.L. and Turner, R.T. (1992). Mirror Group News-papers plc. Investigation under Sections 432(2) and 442 of the Companies Act 1985. The National Archives. http://webarchive.nationalarchives.gov. uk/+/http:/www.dti.gov.uk/cld/mirrorgroup/summary.htm

Huang, J., Fan, L., Lin, K. and Wang, Y. (2020). Variants of children with psychopathic tendencies in a community sample. *Child Psychiatry and Human Development*, 51, 563–71.

Hughes, G., Hogue, T., Hollin, C. and Champion, H. (1997). First-stage evaluation of a treatment programme for personality disordered offenders. *Journal of Forensic Psychiatry*, 8(3), 515–27.

Hyde, L.W., Waller, R., Trentacosta, C.J., Shaw, D.S., Neiderhiser, J.M., Ganiban, J.M. and Leve, L.D. (2016). Heritable and nonheritable pathways to early callous-unemotional behaviors. *American Journal of Psychiatry*, 173(9), 903–10.

Inchley, J., Currie, D., Budisavljevic, S., Torsheim, T., Jastad, A., Cosma, A., Kelly, C. and Arnarsson, A.M. (2020). *Spotlight on adolescent health and wellbeing: Findings from the 2017/018 health behaviour in school-aged children (HBSC) survey in Europe and Canada. International Report* (vol. 1). WHO Regional Office for Europe. Key findings.

Ishikawa, S.S., Raine, A., Lencz, T., Bihrle, S. and Lacasse, L. (2001). Auto-nomic stress reactivity and executive functions in successful and unsuccessful criminal psychopaths from the community. *Journal of Abnormal Psychology*, 110(3), 423–32.

Jackson, R.L., Rogers, R., Neumann, C.S. and Lambert, P.L. (2002). Psychopa-thy in female offenders: An investigation of its underlying dimensions. *Criminal Justice and Behavior*, 29, 692–704.

Jaffee, S.R., Moffitt, T.E., Caspi, A. and Taylor, A. (2003). Life with (or without) father: The benefits of living with two biological parents depend on the father's antisocial behaviour. *Child Development*, 74, 109–26.

Jang, K.L, Livesley, W.J. and Vernon, P.A. (1996). Heritability of the big five personality dimensions and their facets: A twin study. *Journal of Personality*, 64(3), 577–91.

Jankowski, M.S. (1991). *Islands in the street: Gangs and American Urban Society*. Berkeley: University of California Press.

Jimenez, M., Aguilar, R. and Alvero-Cruz, J.R. (2012). Effects of victory and defeat on testosterone and cortisol response to competition: evidence for same response patterns in men and women. *Psychoneuroendocrinology*, 37, 1577–81.

John, O.P., Naumann, L.P. and Soto, C.J. (2008). Paradigm shift to the integra-tive big five trait taxonomy: History, measurement, and conceptual issues. In O.P. John, R.W. Robins and L.A. Pervin (eds.). *Handbook of personality* (3rd edn., p. 120). New York: Guilford Press.

Johnson, L.K., Plouffe, R.A. and Saklofske, D.H. (2019). Subclinical sadism and the dark triad. *Journal of Individual Differences*, 40(3), 127–33.

Johnson, M.M., Dismukes, A.R., Vitacco, M.J., Breiman, C., Fleury, D. and Shirtcliff, E.A. (2014). Psychopathy's influence on the coupling between hypothalamic-pituitary-adrenal and –gonadal axes among incarcerated adolescents. *Developmental Psychobiology*, 47, 20–27.

Joly, J., Soroka, S. and P. Loewen, P. (2018). Nice guys finish last: Personality and political success. *Acta Politica*. https://doi.org/10.1057/s41269-018-0095-z

Jonason, P.K. (2014). Personality and politics. *Personality and Individual Differences*, 71, 181–84.

Jonason, P.K., Li, N.P. and Buss, D.M. (2010). The costs and benefits of the Dark Triad: Implications for mate poaching and mate retention tactics. *Personality and Individual Differences*, 48, 373–78.

Jones, D.N. and Figueredo, A.J. (2013). The core of darkness: Uncovering the heart of the dark triad. *European Journal of Personality*, 27, 521–31.

Junger, M., Greene, J., Schipper, R., Hesper, F. and Estourgie, V. (2013). Parental criminality, family violence and intergenerational transmission of crime within a Birth Cohort. *European Journal on Criminal Policy and Research,* 19, 117–33.

Kamin, H.S. and Kertes, D.A. (2017). Cortisol and DHEA in development and psychopathology. *Hormones and Behavior*, 89, 69–85.

Karpman, B. (1941). On the need of separating psychopathy into two distinct clinical types: The symptomatic and the idiopathic. *Journal of Criminal Psychopathology*, 3, 112–37.

Karpman, B. (1948). The myth of the psychopathic personality. *American Journal of Psychiatry*, 104(9), 523–34.

Kaufman, S.B., Yaden, D.B., Hyde, E. and Tsukayama, E. (2019). The light vs. dark triad of personality: Contrasting two very different profiles of human nature. *Frontiers in Psychology*, 10, Article 467.

Keenan, K. and Shaw, D.S. (2003). Starting at the beginning: Exploring the etiology of antisocial behavior in the first years of life. In B.B. Lahey, T.E. Moffitt and A. Caspi (eds.). *Causes of conduct disorder and juvenile delinquency* (pp. 153–81). New York: The Guilford Press.

Kets de Vries, M. (2012). The psychopath in the C Suite: Redefining the SOB. INSEAD – Entrepreneurship and Family Enterprise. Working Paper No. 2012/119/EFE.

Kiehl, K.A. (2006). A cognitive neuroscience perspective on psychopathy: Evidence for a paralimbic system dysfunction. *Psychiatry Research*, 142, 107–28.

Kiehl, K.A. and Buckholtz J.W. (2010). Inside the mind of a psychopath. *Scientific American Mind*, 21(4), 22–29.

Klein, M.W. and Maxson, C.L. (2006). *Street gang patterns and policies*. New York: Oxford Academic.

Kobak, R., Cassidy, J. and Ziv, Y. (2004). *Attachment-related trauma and post-traumatic stress disorder: Implications for adult adaptation*. New York: Guilford Publications.

Koenigs, M., Kruepke, M., Zeier, J. and Newman, J.P. (2012). Utilitarian moral judgement in psychopathy. *Social Cognitive and Affective Neuroscience*, 7(6), 708–14.

Konikkou, K., Kostantinou, N. and Fanti, K.A. (2020). Transcranial magnetic stimulation over the dorsolateral prefrontal cortex affects emotional processing: Accounting for individual differences in antisocial behavior. *Journal of Experimental Criminology*, 16, 349–66.

Kraepelin, E. (1915). *Psychiatrie: Eine Lehrbuch für Studierende und Artze* (8th edn.). Leipzig: Barth.

Krain, A.L. and Castellanos, F.X. (2006). Brain development and ADHD. *Clinical Psychology Review*, 26(4), 433–44.

Kyranides, M.N., Kokkinou, A., Imran, S. and Cetin, M. (2021). Adult attachment and psychopathic traits: Investigating the role of gender, maternal and paternal factors. *Current Psychology*. https://doi.org/10.1007/s12144-021-01827-z

Lakatos, K., Nemoda, Z., Birkas, E., Ronai, Z., Kovacs, E., Ney, K., Toth, I., Sasvari-Szekely, M. and Gervai, J. (2003). Association of D4 dopamine receptor gene and serotonin transporter promoter polymorphism with infants' response to novelty. *Molecular Psychiatry*, 8, 90–97.

Lakatos, K., Toth, I., Nemoda, Z., Ney, K., Sasvari-Szekely, M. and Gervai, J. (2000). Dopamine D4 receptor (DRD4) gene polymorphism is associated with attachment disorganization in infants. *Molecular Psychiatry*, 5(6), 633–37.

Lalumière, M.L., Harris, G.T., Quinsey, V.L. and Rice, M.E. (2005). *The causes of rape: Understanding individual differences in male propensity for sexual aggression.* Washington, DC: American Psychological Association.

Latzman, R.D., Megraya, A.M., Hecht, L.K., Miller, J.D., Winiarski, D.A. and Lillienfeld, S.O. (2015). Self-reported psychopathy in the Middle East: A cross-national comparison across Egypt, Saudi Arabia, and the United States. *BMC Psychology*, 3(37), https://doi.org/10.1186/s40359-015-0095-y

Lavery, C. (2012). *The black widower: The life and crimes of a sociopathic killer.* Edinburgh: Mainstream Publishing.

Leake, J. (2008). *The Vienna woods killer: A writer's double life* (pp. 9, 39). London: Granta Books.

Lee, Z. and Salekin, R.T. (2010). Psychopathy in a noninstitutional sample: Differences in primary and secondary subtypes. *Personality Disorders: Theory, Research, and Treatment*, 1(3), 153–69.

Lehmann, A. and Ittel, A. (2012). Aggressive behavior and measurement of psychopathy in female inmates of German prisons – A preliminary study. *International Journal of Law and Psychiatry*, 35, 190–97.

Lenzi, M., Sharkey, J., Vieno, A., Mayworm, A., Dougherty, D. and Nylund-Gibson, K. (2015). Adolescent gang involvement: The role of individual, family, peer, and school factors in a multilevel perspective. *Aggressive Behavior*, 41(4), 386–97.

Levenson, M., Kiehl, K. and Fitzpatrick, C. (1995). Assessing psychopathic attributes in a noninstitutionalized population. *Journal of Personality and Social Psychology*, 68, 151–58.

Levy, N. (2007). Norms, conventions, and psychopaths. *Philosophy, Psychiatry and Psychology*, 14(2), 163–70.

Leyton, E. (1986). *Hunting humans: The rise of the modern multiple murderer* (p.18). Toronto: McClelland and Stewart.

Lilienfeld, S.O. (1998). Methodological advances and developments in the assessment of psychopathy. *Behaviour Research and Therapy*, 36(1), 99–125.

Lilienfeld, S.O. and Andrews, B.P. (1996). Development and preliminary validation of a self-report measure of psychopathic personality traits in noncriminal populations. *Journal of Personality Assessment,* 66, 488–524.

Lilienfeld, S.O. and Fowler, K.A. (2006). The self-report assessment of psychopathy: Problems, pitfalls, and promises. In C.J. Patrick (ed.). *Handbook of psychopathy.* (pp. 107–32). New York: Guilford Press.

Lilienfeld, S.O. and Watts, A. (2021). Not all psychopaths are criminals – some psychopathic traits are actually linked to success. *The Conversation.* https://news. yahoo.com/not-psychopaths-criminals-psychopathic-traits-161421719.html

Lilienfeld, S.O., Watts, A.L. and Smith, S.F. (2015). Successful psychopathy: A scientific status report. *Current Directions in Psychological Science*, 24(4), 298–303.

Losel, F. (1998). Treatment and management of psychopaths. In D.J. Cooke, A.E. Forth and R.D. Hare (eds.). *Psychopathy: Theory, research and implications for society* (pp. 303–54). Dordrecht, Netherlands: Kluwer.

Lykken, D.T. (2019). Psychopathy, sociopathy, and antisocial personality disorder. In C.J. Patrick (ed.). *Handbook of psychopathy* (2nd edn.). New York: Guilford Press.

Lynam, D.R. (2002). Psychopathy from the perspective of the five-factor model of personality. In P.T. Costa and T.A. Widiger (eds.). *Personality disorders and the five-factor model of personality.* Washington, DC: American Psychological Association.

Maccoby, E.E. and Martin, J.A. (1983). Socialism in the context of the family: Parent-child interaction. In E.M. Hetherington (ed.). *Handbook of child psychology* (vol. 4). New York: Wiley.

Main, M. (1985). *Attachment: A move to the level of representation.* Symposium presented at the meeting of the Society for Research in Child Development, Toronto, Canada.

Mallion, J.S. and Wood, J.L. (2018). Emotional process and gang membership: A narrative review. *Aggression and Violent Behavior*, 43(1), 56–63.

Marcus, D.K., Fulton, J.J. and Edens, J.F. (2013). The two-factor model of psychopathic personality: Evidence from the Psychopathic Personality Inventory. *Personality Disorders: Theory, Research, and Treatment*, 4, 67–76. https://doi.org/10.1037/ a0025282

Marsh, A.A. and Blair, R.J.R (2008). Deficits in facial affect recognition among antisocial populations: A meta-analysis. *Neuroscience & Biobehavioral Reviews*, 32, 454–65.

Martens, W. (2014). The hidden suffering of the psychopath. *Psychiatric Times*, 31(10), 1.

Matza, D. (1964). *Delinquency and drift*. New York: Wiley.

Matza, D. (1969). *Becoming deviant*. Hoboken, NJ: Prentice Hall.

Maynard Smith, J. (1982). *Evolution and the theory of games*. Cambridge: Cambridge University Press.

McCrae, R.R. and Costa, P.T. (1987). Validation of the five-factor model of personality across instruments and observers. *Journal of Personality and Social Psychology*, 52(1), 81–90.

McCuish, E.C. and Lussier, P. (2018). A developmental perspective on the stability and change of psychopathic personality traits across the adolescence-adulthood transition. *Criminal Justice and Behavior*, 45, 666–92.

McDonald, R., Dodson, M.C., Rosenfield, D. and Jouriles, E.N. (2011). Effects of a parenting intervention on features of psychopathy in children. *Journal of Abnormal Child Psychology*, 39(7), 1013–23.

Mealey, L. (1995). The sociobiology of sociopathy: An integrated evolutionary model. *Behavioral and Brain Sciences*, 18, 523–41.

Mealey, L. (2005). Evolutionary psychopathology and abnormal development. In R.L. Burgess and K. MacDonald (eds.). *Evolutionary perspectives on human development* (2nd edn., pp. 381–406). Thousand Oaks, CA: Sage.

Mededović, J. and Petrović, B. (2015). The dark tetrad: Structural properties and location in the personality space. *Journal of Individual Differences*, 36, 228–36.

Mendez, M.F. (2010). The unique predisposition to criminal violations in frontotemporal dementia. *Journal of the American Academy of Psychiatry Law*, 38, 318–23.

Merriam-Webster (2022). 'Psychopathy'. *Merriam-Webster.com Dictionary*. https://www.merriam-webster.com/dictionary/psychopathy. Accessed 2 January 2022.

Metcalf, S., Dickerson, K.L., Milojevich, H.M. and Quas, J.A. (2021). Primary and secondary variants of psychopathic traits in at-risk youth: Links with maltreatment, aggression and empathy. *Child Psychiatry and Human Development*, 52, 1060–70.

Miller, J.D., Lynam, D.R., Widiger, T.A. and Leukefeld, C. (2001). Personality disorders as extreme variants of common personality dimensions. Can the five-factor model of personality adequately represent psychopathy? *Journal of Personality*, 69, 253–76.

Miller, J.D., Pilkonis, P.A. and Morse, J.Q. (2004). Five-factor model prototypes for personality disorders: The utility of self-reports and observer ratings. *Assessment*, 11, 127–38.

Miller, J.D., Watts, A. and Jones, S.E. (2011). Does psychopathy manifest divergent relations with components of its nomological network depending on gender? *Personality and Individual Differences*, 50, 564–69.

Miller, R. (1987). *Bare-faced Messiah: The true story of L. Ron Hubbard.* London, UK: Silvertail Books.

Millon, T. and Davis, R.D. (1998). Ten subtypes of psychopathy. In T. Millon, E. Simonsen, M. Birket-Smith and R.D. Davis (eds.). *Psychopathy: Antisocial, criminal, and violent behavior* (p.112). New York: The Guilford Press.

Mischel, W. (1968). *Personality and assessment.* New York: Wiley.

Moffit, T.E. (1993). The neuropsychology of conduct disorder. *Developmental Psychopathy*, 5, 135–51.

Moffitt, T.E. (2005). Genetic and environmental influences on antisocial behaviors: Evidence from behavioral-genetic research. *Advance in Genetics*, 55, 41–104.

Mokros, A., Hare, R.D., Neumann, C.S., Santtila, P., Habermeyer, E. and Nitschke, J. (2015). Variants of psychopathy in adult male offenders: A latent profile analysis. *Journal of Abnormal Psychology*, 124(2), 372.

Molinuevo, B., Pardo, Y., González, L. and Torrubia, R. (2014). Memories of parenting practices are associated with psychopathy in juvenile male offenders. *The Journal of Forensic Psychiatry and Psychology*, 25(4), 495–500.

Morris, S. (2022). Hampshire Tinder fraudster jailed after conning woman out of £150,000. *The Guardian.* https://www.theguardian.com/technology/2022/feb/10/hampshire-tinder-fraudster-richard-dexter-jailed

Morrison, D. and Gilbert, P. (2001). Social rank, shame and anger in primary and secondary psychopaths. *Journal of Forensic Psychiatry*, 12(2), 330–56.

Muñoz, L.C., Qualter, P. and Padgett, G. (2011). Empathy and bullying: Exploring the influence of callous-unemotional traits. *Child Psychiatry Human Development*, 42(2), 183–96.

Muris, P., Merckelbach, H., Otgaar, H. and Meijer, E. (2017). The malevolent side of human nature: A meta-analysis and critical review of the literature on the Dark Triad (narcissism, Machavellianism, and psychopathy). *Perspectives on Psychological Science*, 12, 183–204.

Nai, A. (2019). The electoral success of angels and demons. Big Five, Dark Triad, and performance at the Ballot Box. *Journal of Social and Political Psychology*, 7(2), 830–62.

Nai, A. and Maier, J. (2018). Perceived Personality and Campaign Style of Hillary Clinton and Donald Trump. *Personality and Individual Differences*, 121, 80–83.

Nai, A. and Toros, E. (2020). The peculiar personality of strongmen: Comparing the Big Five and Dark Triad traits of autocrats and non-autocrats. *Political Research Exchange*, 2(1), 1–24.

National Institute for Health and Care Excellence (NICE). (2021). Attention deficit hyperactivity disorder: How common is it? https://cks.nice.org.uk/

topics/attention-deficit-hyperactivity-disorder/background-information/prevalence/

Nesse, R.M. (2019). *Good reasons for feeling bad: Insights from the frontier of evolutionary psychiatry*. London: Allen Lane.

Nickisch, A., Palazova, M. and Ziegler, M. (2020). Dark personalities – dark relationships? An investigation of the relation between the Dark Tetrad and attachment styles. *Personality and Individual Differences*, 167, 110227.

Nielsen, M.W., Stefanick, M.L., Peragine, D., Neilands, T.B., Ioannidis, J.P.A., Pilote, L., Prochaska, J.J., Cullen, M.R., Einstein, G., Klinge, I., LeBlanc, H., Paik, H.Y. and Schiebinger, L. (2021a). Gender-related variables for health research. *Biology of Sex Differences,* 12(23), 1–16.

Nielsen, M.W., Stefanick, M.L., Peragine, D., Neilands, T.B., John, P.A., Ioannidis, J.P.A., Pilote, L., Prochaska, J.J., Cullen, M.R., Einstein, G., Klinge, I., LeBlanc, H., Paik, H.Y. and Schiebinger, L. (2021b). Gender-related variables for health research. *Biology of Sex Differences*, 12(1), 23.

Nikitopoulos, J., Zohsel, K., Blomeyer, D., Buchmann, A.F., Schmid, B., Jennen-Steinmetz, C. and Laucht, M. (2014). Are infants differentially sensitive to parenting? Early maternal care, drd4 genotype and externalizing behavior during adolescence. *Journal of Psychiatric Research*, 59, 53–59.

Nikolidis, A. and Gray, J. (2010). ADHD and the DRD4 exon III 7-repeat polymorphism: An international meta-analysis. *SCAN*, 5, 188–93.

O'Donnell, B.F. and Hetrick, W.P. (2016). Psychophysiology of mental health. In H.S Friedman (ed.). *Encyclopaedia of mental health* (2nd edn., pp. 372–76). Oxford: Academic Press.

Oshukova, S., Kaltiala-Heino, R., Hillege, S., de Ruiter, C., Joff, G., Miettunen, J., Marttila, R., Marttunen, M., Kaivosoja, M. and Lindberg, N. (2016). Short report: Self-reported psychopathic traits in Finnish and Dutch samples of non-referred adolescents: Exploration of cultural differences. *Child and Adolesc Psychiatry and Ment Health,* 10(3). https://doi.org/10.1186/s13034-015-0090-3

Palmer, E.J. and Hollin, C.R. (2000). The inter-relations of sociomoral reasoning perceptions of own parenting, and attribution of intent with self-reported delinquency. *Legal and Criminological Psychology*, 5, 201–18.

Papagathonikou, T. (2020). *Developmental antecedents of psychopathy and sexual sadism amongst forensic mental health patients and prisoners: A psychoanalytic perspective*. Thesis submitted for PhD. Queen Mary University of London, Centre for Psychiatry.

Patrick, C.J. (2019). *Handbook of psychopathy* (2nd edn.). New York: The Guilford Press.

Patterson, G.R. (2002). The early development of coercive family processes. In J.B. Reid, G.R. Patterson and J. Snyder (eds.). *Antisocial behaviour in children and adolescents* (pp. 25–44). Washington, DC: American Psychological Association.

Paulhus, D.L (2014). Toward a taxonomy of dark personalities (p.421). *Current Directions in Psychological Science*, 23, 421–26.

Paulhus, D.L., Buckels, E.E., Trapnell, P.D. and Jones, D.N. (2021). Screening for dark personalities: The Short Dark Tetrad (SD4). *European Journal of Psychological Assessment*, 37(3), 208–22.

Paulhus, D.L. and Williams, K.M. (2002). The dark triad of personality: Narcissism, machiavellianism, and psychopathy. *Journal of Research in Personality*, 36, 556–63.

Pervin, L.A. (2003). *The science of personality* (2nd edn., p.451). Oxford: Oxford University Press.

Pinel, P. (1806). *A treatise on insanity*. London: W. Todd.

Plomin, R. (2018). *Blueprint: How DNA makes us who we are*. London: Allen Lane/Penguin Books.

Plomin, R.J., DeFries, J.C., Knopik, V.S. and Neiderhiser, J.M. (2016). *Behavioral genetics* (7th edn.). New York: Worth Publishers.

Plomin, R., DeFries, J.C., McClearn, G.E. and McGuffin, P. (2001). *Behavioral genetics* (4th edn.). New York: Worth Publishers/W. H. Freeman.

Polaschek, D.L.L. and Skeem, J.L. (2019). Treatment of adults and juveniles with psychopathy. In C.J. Patrick (ed.). *Handbook of psychopathy* (pp. 710–31). New York: Guilford Press.

Porteus, S.D. (1959). *The maze test and clinical psychology*. Palo Alto, CA: Pacific Books.

Power, R.A., Pluess, M. (2015). Heritability estimates of the Big Five personality traits based on common genetic variants. *Transl Psychiatry*, 5(7), e604.

Poythress, N.G. and Skeem, J.L. (2006). Disaggregating psychopathy: Where and how to look for subtypes. In C.J. Patrick (ed.). *Handbook of psychopathy* (pp. 172–92). New York: Guilford Press.

Psychological Scales. Accessed 15/10/2022. https://scales.arabpsychology.com/s/levenson-self-report-psychopathy-scale-lsrp/

Quillan, L. (2018). The isolating life of parenting a potential psychopath: They say it takes a village to raise a child, but what do you do when the village shuns you? *The Atlantic*. https://www.theatlantic.com/family/archive/2018/08/conduct-disorder-parent-support-group/567946/

Raine, A. (1993). *The psychopathology of crime: Criminal behavior as a clinical disorder*. San Diego, CA: Academic Press.

Raine, A., Laufer, W., Yang, Y., Narr, K.L., Thompson, P. and Toga, A.W. (2012). Increased executive functioning, attention, and cortical thickness in white-collar criminals. *Human Brain Mapping*, 33(12), 2932–40.

Rappoport, R. (1960). *Community as doctor: New perspectives on a therapeutic community*. London: Tavistock.

Raschle, N.M., Fehlbaum, L.V., Menks, W.M., Martinelli, A., Prätzlich, M., Bernhand, A., Ackermann, K., Freitag, C., De Brito, S., Fairchild, G. and Stadler, C. (2019). Atypical dorsolateral prefrontal activity in female adolescents with conduct disorder during effortful emotion regulation. *Biological Psychiatry: Cognitive Neuroscience and Neuroimaging*, 4(11), 984–94.

Ray, W.J. (2018). *Abnormal psychology* (2nd edn.). Thousand Oaks, CA: SAGE.

Reader, W. and Workman, L. (2023). *Evolutionary psychology: The basics*. Abingdon: Routledge.

Resler, R.K., Burgess, A.W., Douglas, J.E., Hartman, C.R. and D'Agostino, R.B. (1986). Sexual killers and their victims: Identifying patterns through crime scene analysis. *Journal of Interpersonal Violence*, 1, 288–308.

Rey, R.D., Espino, E., Ojeda, M. and Mora-Merchán, J.A. (2022). Bullying. In P.K. Smith and C.H. Hart (eds.). *The Wiley-Blackwell handbook of childhood social development* (3rd edn., p.591).

Ribeiro da Silva, D.R., Rijo, D. and Salekin, R.T. (2015). The evolutionary roots of psychopathy. *Aggression and Violent Behavior*, 21, 85–96.

Rice, M.E., Harris, G.T. and Cormier, C.A. (1992). An evaluation of a maximum security therapeutic community for psychopaths and other mentally disordered offenders. *Law and Human Behavior*, 16(4), 399–412.

Ridley, J. (2022). How to tell if you child is a future psychopath. *New York Post*. https://nypost.com/2018/03/07/how-to-tell-if-your-child-is-a-future-psychopath/

Rigby, K. and Slee, P.T. (1987). Eysenck's personality factors and orientation toward authority among schoolchildren. *Australian Journal of Psychology*, 39(2), 151–61.

Rijnders, R.J.P., Dykstra, A.H., Terburg, D. Kempes, M.M. and van Honk, J. (2021). Sniffing submissiveness? Oxytocin administration in severe psychopathy. *Psychoneuroendocrinology*, 131, 105330.

Rokita, K.I., Dauverman, M.R. and Donohoe, G. (2018). Early life experiences and social cognition in major psychiatric disorders: A systematic review. *European Psychiatry*, 53, 123–33.

Romero, E., Luengo, M.A. and Sobral, J. (2001). Personality and antisocial behaviour: Study of temperamental dimensions. *Personality and Individual Differences*, 31(3), 329–48.

Ross, S.R., Lutz, C.J. and Bailley, S.E. (2004). Psychopathy and the Five Factor Model in a noninstitutionalized sample: A domain and facet level analysis. *Journal of Psychopathology and Behavioral Assessment*, 26, 213–23.

Rowe, D.C. (1995). Evolution, mating effort, and crime. *Behavioral and Brain Sciences*, 18, 573–74.

Rowell, C.H. and Cannis, T.L. (1972). Environmental factors affecting the green/brown polymorphism in the Cyrtacanthacridine grasshopper. *Schistocerca vaga. Acrida*. 1, 69–77.

Ruble, T.L. (1983). Sex stereotypes: Issues of change in the 1970s. *Sex Roles*, 9(3), 397–402.

Ruble, T.L., Martin, C. and Berenbaum, S. (2006). Gender development. In W. Damon, R.M. Lerner and N. Eisenberg (eds.). *Handbook of child psychology* (vol. 3. Social, Emotional, and Personality Development (6th edn., pp. 858–932). New York: Wiley.

Rush, B. (1812). Medical inquiries and observation upon the diseases of the mind. In T. Millon, E. Simonsen, M. Birket-Smith and R.D. Davis (1998, eds.). *Psychopathy: Antisocial, criminal, and violent behavior* (p.112). New York: The Guilford Press.

Rutter, M. and Giller, H. (1983). *Juvenile delinquency: Trends and perspective*. Harmondsworth: Penguin.

Salekin, R.T. (2002). Psychopathy and therapeutic pessimism: Clinical lore or clinical reality? *Clinical Psychology Review*, 22(1), 79–112.

Sanz-Garcia, A., Gesteira, C., Sanz, J. and Garcia-Vera, M.P. (2021). Prevalence of psychopathy in the general adult population: A systematic review and meta-analysis. *Frontiers in Psychology*, 12, 1–14.

Schimmenti, A. (2012). Unveiling the hidden self: Developmental trauma and pathological shame. *Psychodynamic Practice*, 18, 181–94.

Schimmenti, A. (2020). The developmental roots of psychopathy: An attachment perspective. In S. Itzkowitz and E.F. Howell (eds.). *Psychoanalysts, psychologists and psychiatrists discuss psychopathy and human evil* (pp. 219–34). Abingdon: Routledge/Taylor & Francis Group.

Schimmenti, A., Passanisi, A., Pace, U., Manzella, S., Di Cario, G. and Caretti, V. (2014). The relationship between attachment and psychopathy: A study with a sample of violent offenders. *Current Psychology*, 33(3), 256–70.

Schoeman, R. (2019). In Zakiyah Ebrahim, 5 common types of psychopaths you might find in the workplace – and how you can avoid becoming a victim of their mind games. *News24*. https://www.news24.com/health24/lifestyle/healthy-workplace/employee-wellbeing/5-common-types-of-psychopaths-you-might-find-in-the-workplace-and-how-you-can-avoid-becoming-a-victim-of-their-mind-games-20190708

Scott, C. and Medeiros, M. (2020). Personality and political careers: What personality types are likely to run for office and get elected? *Personality and Individual Differences*, 152, 109600.

Seara-Cardosa, A. and Viding, E. (2015). Functional neuroscience of psychopathic personality in adults. *Journal of Personality*, 83(6), 723–37.

Sellbom, M. and Drislane, L.E. (2021). The classification of psychopathy. *Aggression and Violent Behavior*, 59, 101473.

Sevecke, K., Franke, S., Kosson, D. and Krischer, M. (2016). Emotional dysregulation and trauma predicting psychopathy dimensions in female and male juvenile offenders. *Child and Adolescent Psychiatry and Mental Health*, 10(43). https://doi.org/10.1186/s13034-016-0130-7

Shoda, Y., Mischel, W. and Wright, J.C. (1994). Intra-individual stability in the organization and patterning of behavior: Incorporating psychological situations into the idiographic analysis of personality. *Journal of Personality and Social Psychology*, 67, 674–87.

Sigfusdottir, I.D. and Silver, E. (2009). Emotional reactions to stress among adolescent boys and girls: An examination of the mediating mechanisms proposed by general strain theory. *Youth and Society*, 40, 573–90.

Sijtsema, J.J. and Lindenberg, S.M. (2018). Peer influence in the development of adolescent antisocial behavior: Advances from dynamic social network studies. *Developmental Review*, 50(Part B), 140–54.

Skeem, J., Johansson, P., Andershed, H., Kerr, M. and Louden, J.E. (2007). Two subtypes of psychopathic violent offenders that parallel primary and secondary variants. *Journal of Abnormal Psychology*, 116(2), 395–409.

Slee, P.T. and Rigby, K. (1993). The relationship of Eysenck's personality factors and self esteem to bully-victim behaviour in Australian school boys. *Journal of Personality and Individual Differences*, 14, 371–73.

Smith, P.K. (2016). Bullying: Definition, types, causes, consequences and intervention. *Social and Personality Psychology Compass*, 10(9), 519–32.

Smith, S.F. and Lilienfeld, S.O. (2013). Psychopathy in the workplace: The knowns and unknowns. *Aggression and Violent Behavior*, 18, 204–18.

Soloman, J. and George, C. (1999). The measurement of attachment security in infancy and childhood. In J. Cassidy and P. Shaver (eds.). *Handbook of attachment* (pp. 287–318). New York: Guilford Press.

Standiford, L. (2006). *Meet you in hell: Andrew Carnegie, Henry Clay Frick and the bitter partnership that transformed America.* New York: Crown Publication.

Sutherland, E.H. (1939). *Principles of criminology.* Philadelphia, PA: J. Lipinicott.

Sutherland, E. (1983). *White collar crime: The uncut version* (p.7). New Haven, CT: Yale University Press.

Sutton, J. and Keogh, E. (2000). Social competition in school: Relationships with bullying, Machiavellianism and personality. *British Journal of Educational Psychology*, 70, 443–56.

Sykes, G.M. and Matza, D. (1957). Techniques of neutralisation: A theory of delinquency. *American Sociological Review*, 22, 664–70.

Takamatsu, R. and Takai, J. (2019). With or without empathy: Primary psychopathy and difficulty in identifying feelings predict utilitarian judgment in sacrificial dilemmas. *Ethics and Behavior*, 29(1), 71–85.

Tassy, S., Oullier, O., Duclos, Y., Coulon, O., Mancini, J., Deruelle, C., et al. (2012). Disrupting the right pre- frontal cortex alters moral judgment. *Social Cognitive and Affective Neuroscience*, 7, 282–88.

Taylor, S. (2016). *Crime and Criminality: A Multidisciplinary Approach.* Abingdon: Routledge.

Taylor, S.R., Lambeth, D., Green, G., Bone, R. and Cahillane, M. (2012). Cluster analysis examination of serial killer profiling categories: A bottom-up approach. *Journal of Investigative Psychology and Offender Profiling*, 9, 30–51.

Taylor, S. and Workman, L. (2018). *The psychology of human social development.* Abingdon: Routledge.

Terburg, D., Morgan, B., van Honk, J. (2009). The testosterone–cortisol ratio: a hormonal marker for proneness to social aggression. *International Journal of Law and Psychiatry*, 32, 216–23.

Theophrastus (371-287 BCE, 1714). *The moral characters of Theophrastus*. London: Montgomery.

Thomas, A. and Chess, S. (1986). The New York Longitudinal Study: From infancy to early adulthood. In R. Plomin and J. Dunn (eds.). *The study of temperament: Changes, continuities and challenges*. Mahwah, NJ: Lawrence Erlbaum Associates.

Thomason-Darch, N. (2021). The Dark Tetrad of personality and the tendency to engage in revenge porn. *The Plymouth Student Scientist*, 14(2), 651–68.

Thomson, N.D. (2019). *Understanding psychopathy: The biosocial approach*. Abingdon: Routledge.

Thornberry, T.P., Freeman-Gallant, A., Lizotte, A.J., Krohn, M.D. and Smith, C.A. (2003). Linked lives: The intergenerational transmission of antisocial behavior. *Journal of Abnormal Child Psychology*, 31, 171–84.

Thornton, L.C., Frick, P.J., Shulman, E.P., Ray, J.V., Steinberg, L. and Cauffman, E. (2015). Callous-unemotional traits and adolescents' role in group crime. *Law and Human Behavior*, 39(4), 368–77.

Tither, J.M. and Ellis, B.J. (2008). Impact of fathers on daughters' age at menarche: A genetically- and environmentally-controlled sibling study. *Developmental Psychology*, 44, 1409–20.

Toates, F. and Coschug-Toates, O. (2022). *Understanding sexual serial killing*. Cambridge: Cambridge University Press.

Toof, J., Wong, J. and Devlin, J. (2020). Childhood trauma and attachment. *The Family Journal: Counselling and Therapy for Couples and Families*, 28(2), 194–98.

Tsaousis, J. (2016). The relationship of self-esteem to bullying perpetation and peer victimization among schoolchildren and adolescents: A meta-analytic review. *Aggression and Violent Behavior*, 31, 186–99.

Tzoumakis, S., Dean, K., Green, M.J., Zheng, C., Kariuki, M., Harris, F., Carr, V.J. and Laurens, K.R. (2017). The impact of parental offending on offspring aggression in early childhood: A population-based record linkage study. *Social Psychiatry and Psychiatric Epidemiology*, 52, 445–55.

Ullrich, S., Farrington, D. and Coid, J.W. (2008). Psychopathic personality traits and life-success. *Personality and Individual Differences*, 44(5), 1162–71.

van Geel, M., Toprak, F., Goemans, A., Zwaanswijk, W. and Vedder, P. (2017). Are youth Psychopathic traits related to bullying? Meta-analyses on callous-unemotional traits, narcissism, and impulsivity. *Child Psychiatry Human Development*, 48(5), 768–77.

van Goozen, S.H.M., Matthys, W., Cohen-Kettenis, P.T., Gispen-de Wied, C., Wiegant, V.M. and van Engeland, H. (1998). Salivary cortisol and cardiovascular activity during stress in oppositional defiant disorder boys and normal controls. *Biological Psychiatry*, 43, 531–39.

van Goozen, S.H.M., Snoek, H., Matthys, W., van Rossum, I. and van Engeland, H. (2004). Evidence of fearlessness in behaviourally disordered children: A study on startle reflex modulation. *Journal of Child Psychology and Psychiatry*, 45(4), 884–92.

Venables, N.C., Hall, J.R. and Patrick, C.J. (2014). Differentiating psychopathy from antisocial personality disorder: A triarchic model perspective. *Psychological Medicine*, 44(5), 1–9.

Verona, E. and Vitale, J. (2018). Psychopathy in women: Assessment, manifestations, and etiology. In C.J. Patrick (ed.). *Handbook of psychopathy*. 2nd ed. (pp. 509–28). New York: Guildford Press.

Verschuere, B., van Ghesel Grothe, S., Waldorp, L., Watts, A.L., Lilienfeld, S.O., Edens, J.F., Skeem, J.L. and Noordhof, A. (2018). What features of psychopathy might be central? A network analysis of the Psychopathy Checklist-Revised (PCL-R) in three large samples. *Journal of Abnormal Psychology*, 127(1), 51–65.

Viding, E. (2019). *Psychopathy: A very short introduction*. Oxford: Oxford University Press.

Viding, E., Blair, R.J.R., Moffitt, T. and Plomin, R. (2005). Evidence for substantial genetic risk for psychopathy in 7-year-olds. *Journal of Child Psychology and Psychiatry*, 46, 592–97.

Viding, E., Hanscombe, K.B., Curtis, C.J., Davis, O.S., Meaburn, E.L. and Plomin, R. (2010). In search of genes associated with risk for psychopathic tendencies in children: A two-stage genome-wide association study of pooled DNA. *Journal of Child Psychology and Psychiatry*, 51, 780–88.

Viding, E., Jones, A.P., Paul, J.F., Moffitt, T.E. and Plomin, R. (2008). Heritability of antisocial behaviour at 9: Do callous-unemotional traits matter? *Developmental Science*, 11, 17–22.

Viding, E. and Kimonis, E.R. (2018). Callous-unemotional traits. In C.J. Patrick (ed.). *Handbook of psychopathy*. 2nd ed. (pp. 144–64). New York: Guildford Press.

Viding, E. and McCrory, E.J. (2018). Understanding the development of psychopathy: Progress and challenges. *Psychological Medicine*, 48, 566–77.

Viding, E., Price, T.S., Jaffee, S.R., Trzaskowski, M., Davis, O.S., Meaburn, E.L., Haworth, C.M. and Plomin, R. (2013). Genetics of callous-unemotional behavior in children. *PLoS ONE* 8, e65789.

Wagner, N.J., Mills-Koonce, W.R., Willoughby, M.T. and Cox, M.J. (2019). Parenting and cortisol in infancy interactively predict conduct problems and callous-unemotional behaviors in childhood. *Child Development*, 90(1), 279–97.

Wagner, N.J., Mills-Koonce, W.R., Willoughby, M.T., Zvara, B. and Cox, M.J. (2015). Parenting and children's representations of family predict disruptive and callous-unemotional behaviors. *Developmental Psychology*, 51(7), 935–48.

Waller, R., Dishion, T.J., Shaw, D.S., Gardner, F., Wilson, M.N. and Hyde, L.W. (2016). Does early childhood callous-unemotional behavior uniquely predict behavior problems or callous-unemotional behavior in late childhood? *Developmental Psychology*, 52(11), 1805–19.

Warren, J.I. and South, S.C. (2006). Comparing the constructs of antisocial personality disorder and psychopathy in a sample of incarcerated women. *Behavioral Sciences and the Law*, 24(1), 1–20.

Watts, A.L., Lillienfeld, S.O., Smith, S.F., Miller, J.D., Campbell, W.K., Waldman, I.D., Rubenzer, S.J. and Faschingbauer, T.J. (2013). The double-edged sword of grandiose narcissism implications for successful and unsuccessful leadership among US Presidents. *Psychological Science*, 24(12), 2379–89.

Weiss, B., Dodge, K.A., Bates, J.E. and Pettit, G.S. (1992). Some consequences of early harsh discipline: Child aggression and a maladaptive social information processing system. *Child Development*, 63, 1321–35.

Weiss, G. and Hechtman, L.T. (1993). *Hyperactive children grown-up: ADHD in children, adolescents, and adults* (2nd edn.). New York: Guilford Press.

Weizmann-Henelius, G., Grönroos, M., Putkonen, H., Eronen, M., Lindberg, N. and Häkkänen- Nyholm, H. (2010). Psychopathy and gender differences in childhood psychosocial characteristics in homicide offenders – a nationwide register-based study. *The Journal of Forensic Psychiatry and Psychology*, 21, 801–14.

Wennberg, T. (2012). *There are differences between men and women with psychopathic personality traits regarding sub-types of psychopathy, criminality, aggression and victimization.* Dissertation submission at Örebro University.

Werner, K.B., Few, L.R. and Bucholz, K.K. (2015). Epidemiology, comorbidity, and behavioral genetics of antisocial personality disorder and psychopathy. *Psychiatric Annals*, 45(4), 195–99.

West, D.J. and Farrington, D.P. (1973). *Who becomes delinquent?* London: Heinemann.

West, D.J. and Farrington, D.P. (1977). *The delinquent way of life.* London: Heinemann.

West, H. (2021). What is intrusive parenting and how to stop it. http://www.harperwest.co/what-is-intrusive-parenting-and-how-to-stop-it/

Widiger, T.A. and Lynam, D.R. (1998). Psychopathy and the five-factor model of personality. In T. Millon, E. Simonsen, M. Birket-Smith, and R.D. Davis (eds.). *Psychopathy: Antisocial, criminal, and violent behaviors* (pp. 171–87). New York: Guilford.

Widom, C.S. (1977). A methodology for studying noninstitutionalized psychopaths. *Journal of Consulting and Clinical Psychology,* 45(4), 674–83.

Widström, A-M., Brimdyr, K., Svensson, K., Cadwel, K.L and Nissen, E. (2019). Skin-to-skin contact the first hour after birth, underlying implications and clinical practice. *Acta Paediatrica*, 108(7), 1192–204.

Wilkinson, S., Waller, R. and Viding, E. (2015). Practitioner review: involving young people with callous unemotional traits in treatment–does it work? A systematic review. *Journal of Child Psychology and Psychiatry*, 57, 552–65.

Williams, H.E. (1997). *Investigating white-collar crime: Embezzlement and financial fraud*. Springfield, IL: Charles C Thomas Publisher.

Willoughby, M.T., Mills-Koonce, R., Propper, C.B. and Waschbusch, D.A. (2013). Observed parenting behaviors interact with a polymorphism of the brain-derived neurotrophic factor gene to predict the emergence of oppositional defiant and callous-unemotional behaviors at age 3 years. *Development and Psychopathology*, 25(4), 903–17.

Willoughby, M.T., Waschbusch, D.A., Moore, G.A. and Propper, C.B. (2011). Using the ASEBA to screen for callous unemotional traits in early childhood: Factor structure, temporal stability, and utility. *Journal of Psychopathology and Behavioral Assessment*, 33(1), 19–30.

Wolff, K.T., Baglivio, M.T. Limoncelli, K.E. and Delisi, M. (2020). Pathways to recidivism: Do behavioral disorders explain the gang-recidivism relationship during reentry? *Criminal Justice and Behavior*, 47(7), 867–85.

Workman L. and Reader W. (2021). *Evolutionary psychology*. Cambridge: Cambridge University Press.

Workman, L. and Taylor, S. (2021). Nature loads the gun, the environment pulls the trigger: The interactive nature of evolutionary psychology. *Open Access Journal of Behavioural Science Psychology*, 4(3), 180062.

Workman, L., Taylor, S. and Barkow, J. (2022). Evolutionary perspectives of social development. In P.K. Smith and C.H. Hart (eds). *Wiley-Blackwell handbook of childhood social development* (pp. 88–100). Hoboken, NJ: John Wiley & Sons.

Yang, J., McCuish, E.C. and Corrado, R.R. (2020). Is the foster care - crime relationship a consequence of exposure? Examining potential moderating factors. *Youth Violence and Juvenile Justice*, 19(1), 94–112.

Yang, Y. and Raine, A. (2009). Prefrontal structural and functional brain imaging findings in antisocial, violent and psychopathic individuals: A meta-analysis. *Psychiatry Research – Neuroimaging*, 174(2), 81–88.

Yang, Y. and Raine, A. (2018). The neuroanatomical bases of psychopathy: A review of brain imaging findings. In C.J. Patrick (ed.). *Handbook of psychopathy*. 2nd ed. (pp. 380–400). New York: Guildford Press.

Yildirim, B.O. and Derksen, J.J.L. (2013). Systematic review, structural analysis, and new theoretical perspectives on the role of serotonin and associated genes in the etiology of psychopathy and sociopathy. *Neuroscience and Biobehavioral Reviews*, 37(7), 1254–96.

Yochelson, S. and Samenow, S.E. (1976). *The criminal personality: A profile for change* (vol. 1). New York: Jason Aronson.

Zeigler-Hill, V., Besser, A., Morag, J. and Campbell, W.K. (2016). The Dark Triad and sexual harassment proclivity. *Personality and Individual Differences*, 89, 47–54.

Zych, I., Farrington, D. and Trofi, M. (2019). Protective factors against bullying and cyberbullying: A systematic review of meta-analyses. *Aggression and Violent Behavior*, 45, 4–19.

INDEX

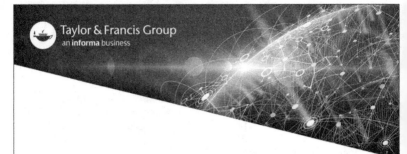

Printed in the United States
by Baker & Taylor Publisher Services